Praise for *And Then...* ...

"This is the best kind of memoir, re... enough to make readers turn many of the questions on themselves. A delightful trip down the road less traveled."

—BOOKLIST

"(Jane Christmas) is a wonderful writer, entertaining, self-deprecating and yet not cynical or worried about stating her spiritual affinities... It's a fresh eye on a kind of spirituality that is often mocked or treated superficially. It was a quick, absorbing read and I truly enjoyed it."

—THE INDEXTRIOUS READER

"(Jane Christmas) is an accomplished writer, careful researcher and deep thinker. And she has the heart of a lion. I'm glad she was courageous enough to share her story."

—THE ANGLICAN JOURNAL

Praise for *Incontinent on the Continent:*

"Christmas is a fine travel writer, and the personal journey she shares is one with which more and more of us are dealing as all our lives move, with welcome and enriching detours, down their one-way streets."

—GLOBE AND MAIL

"(Jane) Christmas recounts her travel adventures so vividly and with such down-to-earth experience that you feel connected to her and her mother from page one. It is truly a pleasure to read."

—BELLA ONLINE

Praise for *What the Psychic Told the Pilgrim:*

"The title, subtitle and first line of Jane Christmas's memoir tell you almost everything you need to know about the book: who, what, where, when and why are laid out neatly, and the first sentence, 'Impulse is intuition on crack,' sets both the hook and the tone... It's a great first line, and its price is back, which is relentlessly smarter,

"Jane Christmas is, in a word, hilarious. She is definitely up there with Bill Bryson in the genre of funny travel writers. The Hamilton woman also exhibits wonderful candour as she recounts her one-month pilgrimage... Christmas writes with an edge and she is painfully (and hilariously) candid about her own foibles... It makes your feet ache and your lungs gasp for air just reading it."

—KINGSTON-WATERLOO RECORD

"Former newspaper editor and author Jane Christmas gives the gears to the midlife crisis travelogue with this... Forget Elizabeth George and her Oprah field memoir about a pilgrimage of rediscovery in middle age. This is the real deal... Fortunately, Christmas avoids reducing her experience to a pat epiphany or platitude about how the trail changed her life (though it did). Her style is equal parts Nora Ephron and Bill Bryson, balancing pithy observation with the history of the trail and her own experiences upon it... The warts and grottiness of Christmas's journey... are recognizable and relatable, much more so than a glossy religious experience or steamy love affair, and much more enjoyable for its accessibility."

—QUILL & QUIRE

"It's a good, funny read with descriptions so lucid and real it almost felt like the author was holding my hand and guiding me through this brutal walk. The 800-kilometer walk with its mountainous, muddy, rocky terrain, its cranky and competitive pilgrims and the crowded and mostly full pilgrim lodges sound(ed) quite daunting to me, but it's not without its good moments and of course, the wonderful humor of our host... *What the Psychic Told the Pilgrim* is however so much more than just the walk... it is a conversation on women's friendships, motherhood, a reflection of one's faith, of pushing oneself to the limit, the celebration of a milestone and a journal of self-discovery."

—LOTUS READS

Jane Christmas

ADVENTURES
in a
CLOISTERED
LIFE

And Then There Were Nuns

LION

Published by Lion Books
an imprint of
Lion Hudson plc
Wilkinson House, Jordan Hill Road,
Oxford OX2 8DR, England
www.lionhudson.com/lion

ISBN 978 0 7459 5644 2
e-ISBN 978 0 7459 5795 5

First published by Greystone Books Ltd, 343 Railway Street,
Suite 201, Vancouver, BC, VA6 1A4
This edition 2014

A catalogue record for this book is available from the
British Library

Printed and bound in the UK, January 2014, LH26

255.9

I will lead her out into the desert

and speak tenderly to her there.

HOSEA 2:14

Contents

. . . .

In the Beginning, There Was a Proposal

. . . .

Essex, England

HE TIMING WAS so unbelievably awkward, it was hard to know whether to laugh or cry. In the end, I did neither. I just said, "Yes."

I had dreamed of this moment for six long years (very patiently, I might add, because six years in female terms is like, what, fifty years?). A marriage proposal. Who doesn't love that? Despite having two failed marriages under my Spanx, I remain intractably optimistic about wedlock.

I was visiting my beau, Colin, over Christmas. Our six-year transatlantic relationship had evolved into a contented pattern of visiting each other every three months in our respective countries: England (him) and Canada (me). The subject of marriage had been broached several times in the intervening years (by me), but it had hit a sticking point—specifically, a complete lack of interest (by him).

So here we were in a guest room of a seventeenth-century village pub in rural Essex. It was a bright Boxing Day morning, and a thin crust of frost shimmered on the surrounding fields. I was absorbed in a near-commando-type mission to find a missing earring. *How does an earring so easily disappear? It was on this table a minute ago.*

Colin was gathering up our bits and bags in preparation for check-out. From the corner of my eye I saw his lean, lanky frame methodically checking drawers and closets to ensure nothing was left behind. He is a quiet man by nature, but he was more so this day, and I assumed he was perturbed that I was taking so long to get organized.

Ah, there it is!

"Found it!" I said triumphantly, as I plucked the earring from its hiding spot beneath the corner of a clock radio. I whispered a prayer of thanks and hooked it into my lobe.

Suddenly, Colin grabbed one of my hands.

"I'm ready now; sorry to have taken so long," I said, trying to wrench my hand from his so that I could get my coat. But he wouldn't let go. When I turned to face him, he was on the floor. On bended knee.

Oh dear, has he stumbled? I yanked his arm to help him up, but he resisted, pulling me toward him instead. This tug-of-war went on for a few seconds until I noticed his smiling blue eyes gazing up at me through a fringe of gray-flecked ginger hair.

Uh-oh! My heart raced, my face flushed. I saw a small velvet box bloom from his unfurling hand as Colin said softly, "Will you marry me?"

I stood in a state of ecstatic disbelief, one hand holding his hand (more for balance now), the other covering my mouth as I blubbered like a schoolgirl, "Yes!"

And this is where the awkward-timing aspect came into play, because moments earlier I had been rehearsing in my mind how to tell Colin that I had decided to become a nun.

(1:ii)

I DON'T want to give the impression that I am one of those nut jobs who listens to the voices in her head, but in all honesty I *am* someone who listens to the voices in her head.

Like most people, I hear the voices of my children, my parents, past and present partners, friends and acquaintances who babble away and bounce off the walls of my head.

But there is another voice—the Voice Within—that originates not from my head but from my heart. A kind, soulful, authoritative voice, a sort of Dumbledore-meets-Peggy-Wood-when-she-played-the-mother-superior-in–*The Sound of Music*. The voice of God. And for a big chunk of my life the Voice Within has been steering me toward a religious vocation: the Voice Within has been calling me to be a nun.

At least, I am pretty certain He said "nun." God is a bit of a low talker and from time to time He gets drowned out by some of the louder, more excitable voices.

Did He absolutely say "nun"? Or did He say "run"? If it was "run," then wouldn't I be gravitating toward spandex and marathons rather than habits and convents? Bun? Done? Fun? Gun? Pun? Sun? Oh, sun. I could so get behind "sun."

But no, there were no sibilants in what He had said. It was definitely "nun."

If that was the case, then what sort of nun-to-be accepts an engagement ring? It was like two-timing God.

During our courtship, Colin's laconic attitude toward marriage had always pulled me up short, and in the long stretches of solitude I alternately nursed my bruised ego and reassessed my future. If he didn't love me enough to marry me, who would? If marriage wasn't in the cards, what was? Did I need to be married again? What would I do with the rest of my life? Subconsciously, I was writing a new chapter for myself.

What I was absolutely certain about was that I was done with what Isak Dinesen referred to as the business of being a woman; in this case, the type of mature woman that society was funneling me toward: a tepid, somewhat infantilized character obsessed with appearance, dithering about whether to consign every wrinkle to a syringe or a surgeon's scalpel, mulling over dubious fashion advice, and sprinkling in light amusements such as gardening and cooking. The world seems in an awful hurry to scoot midlife women into a pre-retirement stupor.

By contrast, I had an urge to explore, question, prod; to belong and yet to set myself apart and take up the challenge Carolyn Heilbrun passionately declared: "We should make use of our security, our seniority, to take risks, to make noise, to be courageous, to become unpopular."

Oh, it is easy to be unpopular these days. You just have to mention that you're in your fifties to feel the slap from the media, society, and governments for not looking or being twenty, for not responding to their coos to retire early and hustle into the cocoon of a retirement home, for not making way for the stampeding generations behind you. You can hear Western society's toe tap with impatience as it waits for us to shuffle into the shadows. It used to be the churches that railed at us from the pulpit about our unworthiness; now it is the media that preach and tell us we are too fat, too old, not attractive enough, not rich enough, not smart enough.

After two decades of juggling single-parenthood and deadline-driven jobs, I didn't need any preaching, not that kind anyway.

There's a natural inclination as you age to draw toward the spiritual, but the restless energy and the itch in my soul that needed to be scratched had nothing to do with joining a church group or attending religious conferences. It was a stronger and deeper tug that had a note of urgency to it. So when the Voice Within piped up for the umpteenth time with the suggestion *Become a nun,* it was a perfectly logical and sensible proposition.

Of course, I did not heed the call at first. I said yes to marriage.

Then, a few days after Colin and I became engaged, as the plane returning me to Canada sliced through the atmosphere dividing Heaven and Earth, I had a change of heart.

I loved Colin, and I did not want to hurt him, but by agreeing to marriage, I would be firmly closing the door on the nun option and tossing away the key forever. The idea of ending my days without ever responding to this persistent call to religious life broadsided me. I saw the opportunities of life, rarer as you get older, trickle away; saw myself on my deathbed, encircled by a Greek chorus of wailing ex-husbands and ex-boyfriends and being asked about "regrets," and my response would be, *I had the chance to see if I was nun material, and I regret not testing that vocation.* That's how I knew I had to do it.

As soon as I got home, I phoned Colin and poured it out to him.

"I'm thrilled that we're engaged, really I am. But there's this... thing. I had been thinking of looking into religious life."

"You want to be a priest?" he ventured.

"Um, no. A nun."

There was a sharp intake of breath on the other end of the phone line.

"Look, it's probably a silly idea," I said quickly. "Maybe just something I need to get out of my system. But it has been on my mind for ages. Like, since I was fifteen."

In the ensuing long, awkward pause in the conversation, I scrambled together some reassuring words, something that would prevent him from thinking *What kind of a lunatic is she?* But bless him, he said, "Well, it's not like we have a biological clock ticking. If this is something you feel strongly about, then you have to go off and see if this is what you want."

He didn't even ask for the ring back.

He did ask if he could come and visit me in the convent, but I told him that visits from boyfriends were almost certainly frowned upon.

We quietly disengaged our engagement, and I set about searching for a place where I could find out whether I was meant to be the bride of Colin or the bride of Christ.

(1:iii)

LIKE MOST families in the fifties and much of the sixties, ours went to church on Sundays. Mine was not an overly religious upbringing but it was certainly unconventional. I was raised an Anglican, but because I was the product of a mixed marriage (as it was called in those days)—having an Anglican father and a Roman Catholic mother—I learned to move comfortably between both faiths. I attended an Anglican Sunday school and learned hymns, Bible stories, and the

Lord's Prayer, and I sometimes attended Catholic Mass with my mother. My parents ensured that I said grace before meals and prayers before bed. I figured everyone did this.

My father augmented my religious education by taking me to churches of other denominations. This was pretty forward thinking for the times, but my father was a gentle and sensitive man. He had served in the war as a gunner, an experience that had horrified him and left a lasting impression about what happens when people are locked into narrow mindsets about religion and politics.

As a youngster, I enjoyed church—the Bible stories, the Sunday-school crafts, and the anthem-like hymns belted out by the congregation, but when I reached my teens, Sunday mornings became a battleground in our household. I was bored and impatient with church. God felt flimsy, and besides I wanted to sleep in. This latter reason was more inflammatory than telling my parents that church was boring or God seemed flimsy. We were not a family that slept in. Ever. We were expected to be up, dressed, and at the breakfast table by 7:30 a.m. regardless of the day of the week.

Like every other teenager caught in the crosshairs of rebellion, I questioned God's existence. My arguments were half-hearted; I don't know whether I entirely convinced myself of it or whether I simply enjoyed the adolescent thrill of contradicting my parents. Regardless, I was always left with the distinct feeling that God was rolling his eyes at the whole business, much like a parent does when a biological child insists that she was adopted.

Oddly enough, it was during this rebellious phase that the call to be a nun began to flicker. It did not happen suddenly. There was no dramatic religious conversion or stunning epiphany. It grew slowly but steadily, as if the possibility was placed on my tongue, and I was being given a chance to swish it around in my mouth, to get a sense of its taste, its texture, its heat, its sharpness, its sweetness. To digest it or spit it out. I never spit it out. Instead, I began to relax about religion. I treated it more like G.K. Chesterton's characterization: "Let your religion be less of a theory and more of a love affair." I liked that. And the more relaxed I was about religion, the more intrigued I became. I saw the beauty and the fluidity of it. Faith in God was not about sermonizing and rigidity. It was a complement to life, not an adversarial stance. I could never understand those who insisted on a line of demarcation between science and religion as if it were the Great Wall. Why couldn't people be more like Augustine of Hippo, who said that Genesis should not be read literally, or like Albert Einstein, who said that "science without religion is lame, and religion without science is blind"? Frankly, everyone needed to chill out a bit more when it came to the Bible.

I began to pay less attention to religion's glittery ceremonial aspects and more to its outer edges—the attitudes, the politics, the people who toiled in its shadows. That's when I first noticed nuns.

My first real connection with nuns was not entirely positive. It occurred during a hellish year at a Catholic girls' school where the nuns were more intent on converting me than on educating me. When my classmates taunted me about my religion, the nuns did not come to my rescue but rather subtly fanned the flames.

"Now class, take out your rosaries, and we'll say the Hail Mary," Sister would say. "Of course, Jane doesn't have a rosary, do you Jane? What religion are you again?"

All heads would pivot toward me, my classmates scandalized by how anyone on the planet could be anything but Roman Catholic.

"Um, I'm Angli..."

"Never mind, dear. Just go to the back of the class and you can do some homework."

From that standpoint, no one could ever accuse me of having a case of the warm fuzzies for nuns, and yet they were mesmerizing creatures. They had an air of secret-agent cool as they glided along the stone corridors of Loretto Abbey. Their floor-length black habits swooshed and billowed like approaching storm clouds, while the edges of their white veils fluttered like angel wings. The black and white, the dark and light, the good and the not-so good—it was this duality that drew me toward nuns. While their heads were bowed in serene surrender, their faces bore smirks of feminist defiance. They operated beyond the boundaries of conventional society, and I felt an affinity, which never went away, with that sort of life.

I cannot explain why the fire of faith burned so steadily and intently in me; it's not like I was the angelic type. Nor can I explain my aspirations to be a nun, except that whenever I thought about being a nun, the idea passed through me like an electric current, as if my heart's desire had made contact with a rogue cell residing in my DNA. Like a Geiger counter, the signal intensified whenever I approached a church or spotted a nun, a monk, or a cross or heard someone mention Jesus or God.

My tableau of a nun's life was pieced together with literary and historical remnants and richly embroidered with imagination (rather a lot of imagination, in fact), and it became my teenage template for religious life. I wove myself into a fantasy as a way of trying on a virtual habit. In my mind I could hear the Angelus echo through a green, undulating valley and see myself dashing into a medieval chapel and falling to my knees on the cold, worn stone floors, head bent and hands clasped in prayer. I would be dedicated to Christ, to God, and to all His saints. I would do His will. I would be a model of simplicity and goodness. I would never swear or complain. (How far off the track I have fallen from those teenage aspirations!) If I were put on floor-washing or toilet-cleaning duty, I would carry out my chores with industrious humility. I would till the gardens, peel potatoes for dinner, and polish the altar chalice until it shone like the star over Bethlehem. The trade-off would be the provision of plenty of time for lazy contemplation. It would be a dreamy, calm existence, offering the luxury of time to count the petals on a flower or compose poetry. The idea of being silent, unbothered by the drama of life or of trying to fit in with my peers, appealed to the misfit in me.

Frequently inserted into this sunny scenario was a monk from a neighboring monastery who was tall and gentle, with a soft mop of hair and a witty sense of humor. We would arrange secret meetings in the woods and flirt, maybe fall in love. I would be Héloïse to his Abelard.

OK, so my attraction to convent life back then was neither realistic nor pure, but at its heart was the understanding that monastic life offered a stable, God-centered ethos. I wanted to be part of it, so I waited for a sign.

When I was seventeen, one arrived in the form of those highly unscientific punch-card career tests that were popular in high schools in the 1970s. Frankly, the Sorting Hat in *Harry Potter* does a better job. A week after I wrote the test, the results arrived. I tore open the envelope and stared at the verdict: rabbi.

Rabbi? Rabbi! I shook my head slowly and heaved a quiet sigh of resignation: like I needed further proof that I was weird. Besides, even I knew that female rabbis were not yet a kosher concept. I scanned the rows of classmates and overheard them discussing their results, the more sensible occupations: doctor, lawyer, engineer, nurse, teacher.

"What did you get, Jane?" a pal whispered across the classroom aisle.

"Teacher," I replied with a who-knew shrug, and stashed the results in the back of a textbook.

I never mentioned my attraction to religious life to anyone. Who would understand? How could I explain my feelings without sounding like a Jesus freak? Some would have laughed or thought my desire was eccentric—positively medieval. Others might have been happy for me, but I worried that even the approving comments might jinx my convictions. I wanted to do things under my own steam without anyone's approval or disapproval.

Another reason for playing my cards close to my vest was that religion wasn't having an easy time in the seventies. What was once a cornerstone of society, even a grudgingly admitted one, was now openly mocked and scorned. This cataclysmic cultural shift occurred right before my eyes: one moment you were regarded with suspicion if you did not attend church or synagogue; the next, you were regarded with suspicion if you did. Religion had lost all authority and almost all respectability. People did not even bother to pretend to tolerate it anymore. When they turned their eyes toward heaven, it was for moon walks and space missions.

This downgrading stung, for even during my nihilistic God-is-flimsy periods, I had felt protective of God or at least the idea of God. Now, expressing an affinity for anything religious left you open to mockery.

One Christmas Eve, a friend and I joined the happy throngs of fans leaving Maple Leaf Gardens after a hockey game. I think the Toronto Maple Leafs actually won the game but I'm not sure. (The Maple Leafs have always been better as a theory than they were on the ice.) Not that it mattered: my friend and I were excitedly reliving the moment a few hours earlier when we had found ourselves walking alongside our heartthrob, the Leaf defenseman Jim McKenny, as he strode into Maple Leaf Gardens for the night's game. (There was a time, boys and girls, when professional sports players arrived at a venue under their own steam and not in a chauffeured limousine with tinted windows.) My friend and I were swooning about this thrill as we climbed into the car of the boyfriend of my friend's sister, who had arrived to pick us up and drive us home. As we neared my home, I asked the boyfriend to drop me off at church because I was meeting my parents at the midnight service.

"Church? Church?" he exclaimed loudly, as if it were a ridiculous concept.

When he stopped the car in front of St. Timothy's Anglican Church, he turned his head and stared at me with a smirk that dripped contempt. My hand was already groping for the door handle.

"Hey, make sure you say hi to God for me," he sneered, putting sarcastic emphasis on "God." He might as well have said "the Lucky Charms guy."

My face burned with shame. I would have told him to go screw himself, but it would be another decade before I developed that kind of courage. Instead, I offered a cheerful "Merry Christmas," got out of the car, and watched it squeal off into the night.

I had pretended not to care what he had said, but in truth the remark cut deeply. Beneath the beam of a streetlight dappled with falling snow I walked slowly toward the church and let the frigid night air shock my tears into submission.

(1:iv)

I MANAGED to hang on to my faith through the vicissitudes of religious attitudes and societal upheavals, but I never did become a nun: I finished high school, graduated from university, and merged into a journalism career, along with marriage, home ownership, motherhood, divorce, remarriage, divorce, and single parenthood.

I was blessed with mostly exhilarating jobs, and I loved the caffeinated rush of working to heart-stopping deadlines amid a cacophony of shouts across the newsrooms, phones ringing, computer keys clacking, and underlying it all the seismic rumble of a printing press from the basement. Nowadays, of course, newsrooms are preternaturally quiet. Like convents. I left journalism just before it got uninteresting, and moved into the gulag to where all ex-journalists migrate—communications and public relations.

By my mid-fifties, the daily grind had turned into a murky decaf slop of office politics that was sucking out my soul and turning me into the worst version of myself. My boss had taken a sudden dislike to me, and lacking the courage to fire me, embarked on a silent campaign of humiliation and bullying. I could no longer smell the coffee; I could only smell change.

That's when the Voice Within perked up: *You could be a nun now.*
The very idea made me gasp in a thrilling sort of way.

One cold January night, as wreaths of snow swirled outside
my window, I tapped a few words into a search engine and
was brought to the website for the Sisterhood of St. John the
Divine (SSJD), an order of Anglican nuns in Canada. I hadn't
expected to find Anglican nuns in Canada, but, well, there is
no end to the surprises found on the Internet.

The sisters were running a month-long program that
summer with the tantalizing title of Women at a Crossroads,
"for women who are seeking direction in their lives."

That's me! I practically yelled out.

I scrambled together the required documents and called
on a couple of friends to provide character references; I filled
out the necessary forms, wrote a letter begging to be accepted,
and mailed everything off to the reverend mother. I had four
weeks remaining of vacation time at work, and I promptly
booked it off. (Unaware of my disengagement, my colleagues
assumed I was getting married.) Then I prayed like I had
never prayed before and anxiously waited out the next two
months for a reply from the convent.

In the meantime, I told my minister what I had done.

"Good Lord," he said. "You're the third woman in two weeks
to ask me about entering the sisterhood. What's going on?"

(1:v)

IN 2010, there were 2,154 celibate religious in more than 80
Anglican communities around the world and another 3,500
in acknowledged religious communities (as opposed to holy

orders). Of the celibates, 1,231 were women and 923 were men, with the majority residing in the Australian and Pacific regions (865), followed by Europe (566) and Africa (343). It was a paltry cohort when juxtaposed with the nearly 60,000 Roman Catholic nuns in the U.S. alone.

Although media reports would have us believe that these are grim times for nuns—what with convents being shuttered and aging nuns being decanted into nursing homes—there are shoots of regeneration. The biggest growth is in Roman Catholic ranks—an order of Dominican nuns in Tennessee had 90 sisters join between 2007 and 2012—but new monastic orders, both Anglican and Catholic, have cropped up in Britain and North America. Some are dispersed communities; others are cloistered. Some are single sex; others are mixed. Some are urban; some are rural.

Interestingly, a religious vocation is not an uncommon second career for women. There are two stages in life when women are drawn to spiritual change—in their teens and twenties, and again in their late forties and fifties.

You do not hear much about nuns these days unless they are being parodied, singled out for their cruelty, or scolded by the Vatican for espousing feminist ideals. For too long, a veil has been drawn over their remarkable contributions.

Eons ago, convents were Christian hubs of classical culture and education, the places where the clever gals could be found writing theological treatises and historical tomes, composing hymns and prayers, painstakingly illuminating manuscripts, and devising new applications for everything from health care to education. Nuns cut their hair short and dressed like men to infiltrate the realms of medicine and law. Their natural acumen earned them high praise from Jerome, the avuncular theologian and historian, who wrote in his commentaries on St. Paul's epistles that the nuns "were more capable of forming a judgment [on the epistles] than most men."

Nuns were envied by their secular sisters. They were well read, often spoke at least two languages, and had unparalleled freedom; their living conditions were usually better and safer than those of women who lived outside the convent.

Throughout history, a few nuns have risen to prominence: Hildegard von Bingen for polyphonic music and chant and for her *Liber simplicis medicinae (Simple Book of Medicine),* written in 1160 and considered a seminal book on herbal remedies; Teresa of Avila and Thérèse of Lisieux for their visions; Mother Teresa for her orphanages and homes for the dying; Sister Helen Prejean for her crusade against capital punishment; Sister Wendy Beckett for her fresh interpretation of art history; and Sister Joan Chittister for her vision and courage in standing up to the Vatican. One of my favorites is Ani Pachen, a Tibetan nun who, in 1959, led six hundred guerrillas on horseback against the Chinese Communists. She was captured and imprisoned, and upon her release in 1981, she walked for nearly a month to Nepal to meet the Dalai Lama. I also admired Princess Alice, the profoundly deaf mother of the Duke of Edinburgh, who established a small and short-lived nursing order of Greek Orthodox nuns.

More prevalent and less known is the heroic legion of nuns who run urban drop-in centers, clinics, food banks, soup kitchens, orphanages, and schools, and whose contribution to the poor, the elderly, and the marginalized goes unacknowledged by governments and churches.

Monks, on the other hand, are seen as the nice guys. You always hear about how they invented accounting and developed aqueducts and other marvels of engineering during medieval times. It was a Benedictine monk, Dom Pérignon, who made advancements in viniculture in the Champagne region of France. Francis of Assisi sang in the hills with his friar buddies, and today the Dalai Lama enjoys global influence and respect. In return, Hollywood has given us cool, somewhat goofy, kid-friendly monks (Jackie Chan in *The Karate Kid,* Jack Black in *Nacho Libre,* and the *Teenage Mutant Ninja Turtles*).

When it comes to nuns, however, you'll find them in popular culture's cliché pile. It's either spring-loaded Streep in *Doubt* or Whoopi in a wimple or the aforementioned Sister Wendy, a bona fide nun in the socially awkward vein. At the far end of the scale is the nun as temptress or rubber-clad bondage dominatrix.

Nuns are also singled out in the scandals—the atrocities involving nuns and priests against many First Nations children in Canadian residential schools, at the Magdalene laundries in Ireland, in an abundant succession of pedophilia cases in the United States. All these reveal religious life's evil, cancerous side and deserve the strongest punishment possible.

And while the scandals reinforce the myth of nun as ruler-wielding crone, they completely discount the huge contribution made by many whose self-discipline, kindness, and unsung good works have been eclipsed by the despicable deeds of a very small percentage. Some former residential school students, for example, have insisted that without the care and encouragement of the many good nuns, they might never have escaped the cycle of poverty and alcohol abuse that pervaded their home communities.

As I continued my own preliminary research into religious life, I sought out nuns and former nuns. I did not gain much practical advice. The opposite, in fact. Most were still spilling their pent-up rage against both the church and cloistered life despite having left religious life forty years earlier. They spoke angrily about the stuffiness of the convent, how the surrender of self had shorn away their confidence, how the lockstep, muzzled routine had felt like prison. One admitted that she had only joined a religious order to escape her domineering mother.

Another former nun, a friend of mine, was more measured. Mary Lou, who readers may recall from my book about Pelee Island, had been kicked out of the convent in her late twenties by a mother superior who felt she was too spirited for religious life. Although Mary Lou has gone on to have a full and creative life as a wife, mother, and grandmother, she admitted to still feeling a tinge of sadness about the experience. "I still consider myself a nun," she said. "A nun of the world." I liked that sentiment.

Sister Eileen Schuller seemed to embody that paradigm. A member of the Ursulines, she had more freedom than most nuns I had met. She was a university professor and traveled extensively as an expert in Dead Sea Scrolls research. The Ursulines are a radical bunch in this regard. The order was founded in Italy in 1535 by St. Angela Merici, who believed that women could live holy lives without living in convents and could stay connected to their sisterly community through regular gatherings. This approach was revolutionary and practical, and it blended the spiritual with the secular while fashioning a countercultural lifestyle within a conventional framework.

The few people in whom I confided my monastic intentions sputtered alarm that I would waste my time with an entity as corrupt and murderous as the church. Even a few of the former nuns were repelled by the idea that I would consider religious life when I should be working instead to eradicate a "repressive" system. They obviously had not inhabited my convent fantasy.

Truth be told, I had a lot of issues with organized religion myself. I had to keep reminding myself that churches, like any institution and human construct, are prone to moral failings and dysfunction. Just as the prettiest vineyard doesn't produce the best wine, neither does the grandest cathedral or the most respected theology think-tank produce the holiest specimens.

And yes, the church itself has a cathedral-sized closet's worth of skeletons, but convents and monasteries have often been the antidote to organized religion's seedier side. Indeed, many men and women have fled the oppressive hierarchical structure of organized religion for the relatively less politically charged atmosphere of religious communities.

Yet, the reality can be crushing. We heap considerable trust on religious institutions and clergy, and feel utterly betrayed when they fail to deliver on their promise of caring for our spiritual health.

A few years ago, I put my own church to the test. I had been a relatively active member for about twenty years; gave of my purse regularly and of my time in the Sunday school and in the day-care center, provided baked goods and professional advice—whatever was asked. One day I stopped going to church to see how long it would take before my absence was noticed. Two years went by, and there was not a peep from them, not a phone call or an email, though I did receive a letter asking if I would please increase my weekly donation. That stung.

It should have been my cue to change churches, but I returned to the same one for sentimental reasons until I eventually moved to another city. It says a lot when you can keep your faith in spite of the unholy thoughts you harbor about your church.

That's what faith is to me, a grand adventure of the soul, at times exhilarating, at times disappointing. Sort of what Chesterton was saying. Faith is not the surrender of the mind, as some have characterized it, but the expansion of it, and of the heart and spirit as well. It is head-scratching, yes, weird at times, nonsensical, but also brilliant and moving in its simplicity and in the good it succeeds in doing.

Maybe part of my journey into religious life was subconsciously about seeking a new spiritual home. Or maybe it really was about simply wanting to be a nun. I had to find out.

And if I believed that God indeed inhabits each of us, then perhaps those "calls" were invitations to grow and to live a more purposeful life. It is more socially acceptable to put on our secular hats and call it "wanderlust" or "itchy feet" or "midlife/later midlife crisis," but at the heart of these intuitive prompts is the pulsating desire to enter the soul, the God zone.

A call to be a nun. *Really?* Even though I had gone over this a million times, the idea had a frisson of lunacy to it; at other times it seemed like the most logical of actions. *Yes, be a nun. Why not?* And then the other side of my brain would kick in with *Oh, c'mon! Are you really going to trade a condo for a convent? Colin for Christ?*

(2)

At a Crossroads

. . . .

The Sisterhood of St. John the Divine
Toronto, Canada

WHEN I STOOD at the door of the Sisterhood of St. John the Divine, a tremulous finger poised at the doorbell, I got a sudden case of the willies. *What the hell am I doing here?*

During the previous months I had been a veritable religion sponge. When I wasn't attending church and reading the Bible, I was gobbling up stories in the media about faith and religion, poring over research and studies of a religious or quasi-religious nature, googling religious communities, dipping into religious blogs, scouring the religion section of bookstores, and joining discussions about religion at every opportunity. I visited churches that were experimenting with new forms of worship, such as Contemplative Fire, and that were trying to steer religion back to its monastic roots. It was terrifically exciting. I could not have been more enthusiastic had I stumbled upon a new series of cave drawings.

But if you nose around something long enough, you may discover that what appears on the surface to be decent has pale squirmy stuff writhing just beneath.

And what I realized was this: organized religion was bitchy territory. Never have I encountered more malcontents in a sector that was meant to uplift people while they searched for answers about the existence of God.

There were complaints about leadership, hypocrisy, the pomposity of the priests, the masonic-like cliques that ran the church, the incessant rearrangement of the pews being done in the name of pulling in more (and younger) worshippers. And this was just from the churchgoers. Internally, the church was in trouble, too. Priests were overworked and stressed out. Two priests separately confided that they doubted the existence of God; another had been practically run out of town under suspicions that he was gay; and still another was forced to step down over allegations that he had seduced a female parishioner.

All that was only the tip of the iceberg. Christianity was in a state of rope-a-dope as it careened from one smackdown to another by a brigade of New Atheists. These wise guys had the easy charm, glib wit, and condescending smirks of stand-up comedians, mocking the faithful as being delusional and possessed of infantilized minds. Persecution dressed up as intellectual snobbery.

I've never understood why atheists waste their time debating the existence of God. People who get foamy mouthed over something they insist doesn't exist in the first place strike me as being rather shaky about their convictions. If you don't believe in something, why give it a second thought?

God-bashing is nothing new, but in this latest incarnation, the voices for the defense were weaker. No one courageously spoke up and told the New Atheists to push off and pick on a deity their own size. The churches just sucked it up and shrugged.

Now, some argue that to fight back is un-Jesus-like, but to that I say, "Phooey." Sure, Jesus refused to engage his enemies, as when he appeared before Pontius Pilate or when people taunted him and asked him to prove he was the Son of God. But he could also open a can of whoop-ass, as he demonstrated in the temple when he screamed blue murder at those who had turned a house of God into a marketplace, and another time when he called the Pharisees hypocrites after they tried to trap him with a trick question.

Defending your turf shows that you stand for something, right? Other faiths have the guts to speak up when their faith is slammed: Why can't the Christians?

It was the sort of stuff that stirred my militant side. If no one was going to defend God, then I would. *Screw those New Atheists. I'm going to fight for my faith. I'll be Jane the Warrior Nun!* A vision materialized in my mind of me standing bravely on a hilltop, the wind fluttering the veil of my wimple while I brandished a crucifix at the approaching horde of faith bashers.

Which is precisely when I began to panic. As I stood on the doorstep of my newly embraced vocation, part of me was afraid of not being deemed nun material; the other part was afraid that I might be exactly the sort of candidate that a religious order would want.

I pressed the bell. Seconds later, the door clicked open.

For some reason I had expected to be met by an oversized and overworked matron thrusting a balled-up smock at me and barking orders to get changed and report to the kitchen on the double to peel carrots for dinner. The reality was alarmingly different. I stepped into a tranquil reception area of modern sofas and plump chairs upholstered in cheerful chintz and arranged convivially around a polished mahogany coffee table. The walls were white and decorated with a few watercolors depicting pleasant landscapes. The air smelled fresh and lacked the odor of sanctimony.

An impish woman with a bouncy walk and a broad smile approached me. She was dressed in civvies—a beige tunic over a white t-shirt—but her nametag identified her as Sister Anne. She handed me a thick folder with my name on it and began telling me something important, but my senses were still taking in this strange environment. *This doesn't look or feel like a convent. Is this the right place?*

Another sister wandered by. Beneath her warm smile sprouted a considerable growth of chin hair. I smiled back while my brain shouted: *What? No waxing or threading here?*

"ok? Got it?" Sister Anne asked.

"Pardon?"

"St. Elizabeth. That's the cell—the room—you've been assigned. Here, let me show you again."

Without a smidgen of irritation, she ran her finger along a poster-sized schematic layout of the convent's guest wing and then slowly—she must have thought I either was deaf or had arrived from Stupidville—repeated the instructions.

"Up the stairs and turn to your left," she said. "Got it?"

"Um, yes. Thanks." I started to walk away, still bewildered, and then asked, "What about a key, you know, to the room?"

Sister Anne let out a high-pitched giggle, as if that was the most insane thing anyone had ever said to her. "We don't use keys. Your things are safe here."

I lugged my suitcase up a stairwell, turned left at the top, and followed a narrow white corridor carpeted in dark gray to the door marked "St. Elizabeth."

My cell didn't look like what you would refer to as a "cell." Sun was streaming in through a large window, and like the reception area, the room was bright, airy, and modern. Measuring about ten feet by twelve feet, it easily accommodated the essentials: a tall chest of drawers, a desk and chair, and a bedside table all made from the same blond wood. An Eames-style chair, a footstool, and a pole lamp tucked to one side filled the area in front of the window. To the right of the window, a single bed was stacked with crisp white linens. There was a note instructing me to make up the bed. The bedside table held a small lamp, a digital clock, and a Bible. On the other side of the room, near the door, white towels hung from a chrome rod next to a small wall-mounted sink. The walls were white and bare except for a small mirrored-front medicine cabinet above the sink, a watercolor of a Muskoka landscape above the desk, and a small, slim crucifix that faced the bed. The large closet contained a clothing rail with a motley assortment of hangers—wire, wood, plastic, and crocheted.

I parked my suitcase at the end of the bed, then picked up a black binder from the desk. Its cover displayed an icon of St. Elizabeth of Hungary.

Coincidentally, my grandmother was Hungarian and was also named Elizabeth; in fact, we nicknamed her St. Elizabeth because she was such a devout and saintly creature, constantly baking or sewing something for her church and for a variety of charitable organizations.

I flipped to the short biography of St. Elizabeth inserted into the binder.

She was born in 1207, a princess, the daughter of Andrew II of Hungary. At the age of fourteen she married Ludwig IV, who had just been crowned king of Thuringia, a region of modern-day Germany. By all accounts it was a happy marriage, and with her husband's encouragement and support, Elizabeth not only cared for their own growing brood but also established homes for the elderly, the orphaned, and the abused. The marriage was only into its sixth year when Ludwig, en route to join the Sixth Crusade, died of the plague. Elizabeth joined the Franciscans as a lay associate and adopted a life of poverty while she continued to work in the hospices she founded. At the incredibly young age of twenty-four, she died from a combination of overwork and a virus. Four years later, in 1235, the church declared her a saint.

St. Elizabeth's feast day, I noted from the bio, was the same as my grandmother's birth and death dates.

Coincidence? Is this a sign that I'm on the right path? I wondered what my Roman Catholic grandmother would have made of her argumentative Anglican granddaughter coming to a nunnery. Maybe she was smiling benignly down at me, pleased that I had embraced my faith so seriously. Or maybe she was appalled that I had breached sacred territory: I could hear her admonishing me in her broken English, "You shame yourself!"

(2:ii)

FOR SOMEONE with the title Reverend Mother, Sister Elizabeth Ann did not fit my image of a convent's mother superior. She was a few years younger than I, with short, wiry ginger hair and a freckled face that displayed a warm, mischievous smile. Nor was she dressed in a habit, unless the sisterhood's habit happened to be a beige khaki A-line skirt with matching jacket worn over a sage T-shirt. She had Birkenstocks on her feet and a pager on her hip. She greeted each of us with a happy nod as we entered the room.

Nine of us, ranging in age from early thirties to mid-sixties, had been admitted to the Women at a Crossroads program. We entered the room weighted down with trepidation and hugging to our bosoms the thick navy blue folders that each of us had been given upon arrival. Perhaps we were all wondering whether by month's end we would be wearing habits and clutching signed ironclad pledges to the sisterhood. Months earlier, everything had seemed so clear, and I had been suffused with a sense of purpose about this new life. Now, my so-called purpose seemed more like recklessness, as if I was about to unlock Pandora's box and unleash something resembling that freaky scene in *Raiders of the Lost Ark*.

"Good morning," Sister Elizabeth Ann purred. "We're delighted to have you with us. Before we go any further, let's begin with a prayer, shall we?"

Heads bowed and eyes closed on cue.

"Heavenly Father..."

Sister Elizabeth Ann's calm voice flowed over my pummeled psyche like warm caramel. The tension from my secular job that had made me rigid and paranoid began to ease as Sister Elizabeth Ann's prayer massaged my stress: joints unclenched, the Gordian knot of anxiety and fear that had resided in my stomach the last few years began to loosen, my muscles awakened, my spine straightened, and my ears began to detach themselves from my shoulders. There was a time, years earlier, when I had been able to cavalierly deflect the slings and arrows of the daily grind and clamber over the walls of my self-doubt. But the projectiles in the form of daily humiliations at the office had become harder lately; the arrow piercings to my self-confidence, deeper. The emotional armor I had forged was supposed to be temporary, but over time it had welded itself so tightly to my being that it was what now held me together. With every syllable that Sister Elizabeth Ann uttered, the armor started to loosen, and it felt so good that I had to restrain myself from emitting a loud "Ahhhhhhh!"

With head still bowed, I cracked open my eyes to check out the others in the group. We had all been sent instructions about what not to wear at the convent: no sleeveless tops, no shorts, no jeans, no skirts above the knee, all of which deep-sixed about 80 percent of my summer wardrobe. Some of the women had their own interpretation of the dress code, deciding that "no sleeveless tops" did not mean no sleeveless dresses. Shawls or light sweaters were layered over these or brought along in case objections were voiced.

Sandals had been given the all-clear, thank goodness, but as I scanned everyone's footwear, I inwardly gasped: I was the only one with nail polish on her toes, or rather the only one wearing a shade that was the color of hellfire. Sparks might just as well have been shooting from the tips of my toes and devils doing the can-can with their pitchforks.

My face flushed. I tucked my feet under my chair and hoped no one had noticed. A few weeks later, when I upended the bottle of nail polish, I noticed the name of the shade: Friar, Friar, Pants on Fire. Not the best choice for someone hoping to embrace the life of a contemplative nun.

I returned to Sister Elizabeth Ann's prayer, but my mind had the attention span of a three-year-old.

The morning sunlight from another torridly hot summer day slashed through the vertical blinds and splayed itself in long, straight fingers of gold on the beige Berber carpet. My mind bubbled with a gazillion questions: *How hot is it outside? Will we have any of our sessions outside? Did I pack sunscreen? How old is this convent? Do nuns miss sex? What was I thinking when I put on this garish nail polish?*

Then, with the inconsequential questions out of the way, the Big Question stormed to the front of my thoughts, hands on hips, and blared, *Excuse me, but what in hell's name are you doing in a convent anyway?* My brain erupted into a vision of flashing red sirens, shrieking alarms, and urgent "Mayday!" commands as it scrambled for an answer. My heart rate sped up; a cold sweat beaded my forehead. I was ready to flee the room, but then the Voice Within floated serenely into the scene, silencing the sirens and the brain babble, firmly reassuring all assembled that my entire life had been leading me here. *This is exactly where she should be.*

I relaxed and returned once more to Sister Elizabeth Ann.

She was talking about orientation now, an appropriate subject for her, given that before entering religious life, she had worked as a forester. She loved the outdoors, particularly the wild regions of Northern Ontario, and she told us she was happiest and at her most peaceful when she was camping.

"Camping" is not a word to which I respond positively, but Sister Elizabeth Ann's description suddenly sent my thoughts back to the pilgrimage I had taken in Spain several years earlier on the Camino de Santiago de Compostela—I had met Colin there, in fact—where I had experienced the delicious freedom that comes from being without possessions, responsibility, and conformity, and where I came to understand that the more I tried to fit in with society, the more distant I became from my true self. And yet nothing says conformity more than a nunnery. What *was* I doing here?

Orientation, Sister Elizabeth Ann continued, has both spiritual and practical connotations. As a noun, "orient" means "east"; as a verb, it means "face east." She asked us to consider our presence in the program within that context: Were we here to root ourselves and prepare for a new journey, or were we here to focus on a faith that took root in the East?

"As you continue through this period of discernment, this challenge—because it is a challenge—keep in mind that silence is key so you can listen to God," said Sister Elizabeth Ann. "We have a tendency to fill up God with our prayers, but we don't give God time to speak back to us."

By listening deeply and earnestly, she said, we would be able to discern whether we were choosing God or whether God was choosing us. In the monastic life, you do not enter a monastery or convent on your own instruction but on God's.

"Listening can instruct us, but it's often hard out there," she bowed her head toward the window where the light was streaming in, "to hear yourself think, let alone hear what God is saying."

We all nodded agreement.

"Pay attention to yourself. Life is about our willingness to change and take risks, and we get those cues from our hearts and our intuition. Likewise, and this is just as important, pay attention to your overreactions: when someone gets under your skin, ask yourself why that is. What have they stirred up? That can provide clues about who you are. To be true to yourself, you need to listen. As St. Augustine said, 'Behold what you are; become what you see.'"

Wow. A place that understood and practiced intuition, that spoke unabashedly about God, and that quoted the saints rather than a politician or a departmental head was exactly where I wanted to be. My enthusiasm and confidence surged again. I did not necessarily have to be Jane the Warrior Nun, but I could find a place among like-minded people and live out the rest of my days focusing on my faith and on concentrated prayer.

I glanced around the circle at my fellow discerners. I got the sense that they were a lot like me: high achievers, hard on themselves, eager to mine the trenches of our nature to discover what it was that was missing in our lives; the wherefore and the why of this desperate longing within us. To get there, we would need to defrost that part of ourselves that had become frozen under an icy layer of distraction and disappointment.

"At the heart of discernment is the unmasking of your ego," Sister Elizabeth Ann continued.

We shifted uncomfortably in our seats. We knew we had flaws, but we weren't about to expose our jagged edges and trauma-filled journeys to one another. Not yet, anyway. So we spent the next two hours doing the female thing of sniffing the air for kindred spirits and dropping threads of vulnerability into the conversation to see if they would be picked up and spooled by a sympathetic soul.

It became quickly apparent that a few of the women— two were priests, two were theology scholars—were more knowledgeable than the rest of us in quoting passages from the Bible or summoning a quote from a theologian. When someone mentioned, say, John's gospel or the book of Isaiah, the clever ones deftly flipped to the correct part of the Bible, while the biblically challenged (like me) had to first consult the table of contents to see if it was in the Old Testament or the New Testament and then locate the proper page. By then, the conversation had usually moved on.

It was also clear that we were at different stages in our faith and had different ways of approaching God. One older woman with short brown hair and glasses perched on the end of her nose quoted heavily from modern writers such as Jean Vanier and Philip Yancey; a youngish, skinny woman with long red hair referred to her "personal relationship with Jesus Christ," a phrase that makes me cringe and want to blurt out, "Really? That's not what He told me." (There is a smug, evangelical ring to that phrase. The other phrase that rankled was "the Good News," as in "Let's pray for the Good News of Christ on Earth." Wasn't it all "good news"? What was the "bad news"?) I pegged her for a relative newbie to the faith scene. Like former smokers, they are quick to proselytize in order to expiate their sins, which can be endearing as well as pain-in-the-ass annoying. I dug my fingers into my thigh to stop my cynicism, and to remind myself that I was at least in a place where the words "God" and "Jesus" could be said without the room erupting into scoffs or someone huffing that her human rights were being violated.

The talk that first day wasn't all religion: there were practicalities to go over.

Sister Elizabeth Ann asked us to take out the grid-format schedules that had been tucked into our thick folders.

When Benedict of Nursia was setting up his monastery at Monte Cassino at the turn of the sixth century, he recognized that even religious folks could be consummate lazybones. It was one thing to chat all day with God, but someone had to run the place, and Benedict had no intention of getting stuck with all the cooking and cleaning. He came up with a brilliant and sensible schedule that has been adopted by almost every Christian monastic community since. The days were organized around eight periods of communal worship, called offices, during which prayers would be recited, psalms chanted, hymns sung, and the Bible read. The offices—vigils, lauds, prime, terce, sext, none, vespers, compline—were the pillars of the monastic day, while the periods in between were for work, study, meals, and recreation.

The Sisters of St. John the Divine had scaled back Benedict's version to four daily offices: morning prayer or matins, Eucharist at noon, evening prayer, and compline. I was not familiar with compline, but as I was to find out, the term comes from the Latin *completorium,* or completion, which is rather apropos for the final office of the day.

I stared at the schedule in my hand. Oh dear. Convent life was more regimented than I expected. There were no blocks marked "free time" unless sleeping was considered free time; no segments marked "Swan around cloister." And what were these bits marked "chores" and "work"? A rest period was indicated, but it was only one hour and fifteen minutes. Classes were in the morning, but the timetable did not specify what they were about.

Our day looked like this:

6:00 a.m.	Rising and quiet time
7:45 a.m.	Breakfast
8:30 a.m.	Morning prayer
9:30 a.m.	Classes
12:00 p.m.	Eucharist
12:45 p.m.	Dinner
1:15 p.m.	Rest period
2:30 p.m.	Work
5:00 p.m.	Evening prayer
5:30 p.m.	Supper
6:10 p.m.	Chores
7:00 p.m.	Recreation
8:10 p.m.	Compline
9:00 p.m.	Greater Silence

I hadn't had a schedule that rigid since I gave birth to my first child. However, I chalked it up as all part of the obedience vow. Besides, after half a lifetime of single parenting and being in the driver's seat, I was happy to let someone else make decisions.

(2:iii)

AT FIRST the silence felt extreme. I had forgotten how much chatter filled my day, and if it wasn't the chatter of my own making, it was the voices of others on the street, on the bus, on the radio, on TV, in hallways, in shops. Noise is the aural wallpaper that decorates modern life. Silence, on the other hand, is the interloper, the disturbing element that can be as torturous in its sensory deprivation as noise can be at its most ear-shattering. I began to appreciate why so many people plug into their headphones or mobile phones to avoid it.

In the corridors of the convent, silence was expected; indoor conversations were conducted *sotto voce* in designated areas. You did not chat in the library, and you most certainly did not chat in chapel. This ensured that everyone's peace was respected and that idle gossip was discouraged (though I was under no illusions that gossip never occurred).

Where silence was particularly unnatural was at meals. After all, long communal tables filled with forty women and food just beg for conversation.

"In monastic practice the refectory is an extension of chapel," explained Sister Elizabeth Ann. "In chapel, your spirit and soul have been fed by God through prayer; in the refectory, it is the body's turn for nourishment."

It didn't help. The silence made me feel self-conscious and exposed. Without the distraction that talking creates, I didn't know where to look except in my plate or at others going up for food and returning to their seats. Under so many watchful eyes, I took extra care with how much food I took so that no one would think I was a pig, and with how I handled the serving implements so that they didn't scrape loudly against a dish or drop and clang on the table. I became hyperaware of my posture, my table manners, how I chewed my food, slurped my water, the speed at which I ate (always too fast), and even the way I held the cutlery. It was unnerving.

As I acclimatized to the routine and the social nuances, the self-consciousness gradually fell away. We were all awkward beings; get over it. Besides, I wasn't supposed to be thinking about my discomfort; I was supposed to be thinking about God. But all I could think of was how different this was from the workaday world and from everything I had ever known.

In my secular life, if something pinged, rang, chimed, buzzed, or vibrated, I was all over it. In the convent, however, no one rushed to answer the phone or the doorbell. It was like living in "whatever" world or being on Mexican time.

While it was a nice change not to worry about grocery shopping and housekeeping, that brought on its own anxiety: I kept thinking that I was forgetting something or that I needed to make a list. I worried how my local grocery store would cope with my absence. *Gosh, if I become a nun, I might never have to make another list again.* The thought was as delicious as it was panic inducing.

The toughest challenge was trying to exchange my competitive nature for a contemplative one. A brain accustomed to being in overdrive can't help fueling itself with critical observations and superior thinking. I was in chapel one day waiting for the Eucharist to begin when I began to scan the rows of sisters, heads bowed submissively in prayer behind their little prie-dieux, their sweet faces aglow with gentle smiles. *Passive? For sure. Naïve? Perhaps. Feeble? Many of them.* My arrogance shot to the surface like a jackal sensing weak prey in the vicinity: *Yeah, I could do this, I could become a nun. And I'll bet in five years' time I could make reverend mother. Easy.*

Well, that sort of attitude wasn't going to go unnoticed by God. And when God knows, He either lets you off easy or He turns off your dog-poo radar and allows you to step right into it.

The next morning, having lingered too long over email, I raced down the hall toward chapel, my sandals clattering on the bare floor and echoing disturbingly through the cloister corridor. I practically skidded into my prie-dieu. At least I got there on time. As soon as I sat down, I realized I had forgotten to pick up the numerous handouts needed for the service. I got up, shuffled along the row of sisters who were deep in prayer—"Excuse me, excuse me," I whispered—and went to the back of the chapel, retrieved the necessary handouts, and returned to my seat, disturbing the still-praying sisters with a second round of "Excuse me, excuse me." All the sisters were gracious and did not appear the least bit annoyed, but I knew what they were thinking behind those forgiving smiles: "Bimbo."

Our Crossroads group was assigned specific seats in the choir stalls among the sisters. Mine was next to Sister Helen Claire, a petite and poised woman who always sat erect with a dignified, graceful bearing. She was immaculately groomed and was always dressed in a pretty skirt and blouse. Beside her, I was a yeti. She bristled at this invasion of her spiritual privacy.

That morning in my prie-dieu, as my clumsy paws scrunched the haphazard mass of handouts printed on colored sheets of paper, a few fluttered to the ground and landed on Sister Helen Claire's feet. I glanced at her, embarrassed, but her eyes were closed in prayer. Phew. I edged my foot toward hers to see if I could snag the errant sheets and retrieve them without disturbing her, pivoting my foot so that the toe of my sandal would catch the paper. One sheet was stubbornly caught on the edge of Sister Helen Claire's sandal, so I shifted out of my seat and surreptitiously lowered myself to the floor in order to grab the paper with my fingers. As I tugged gently on the piece of paper, I glanced up. Her eyes were wide open now, staring down at me with a look of perturbed alarm that could only be interpreted as "What in the name of all that is sacred are you doing with my feet?"

I smiled sheepishly. Without moving a muscle or changing her expression she closed her eyes, and resumed praying. She was likely praying that this clown beside her would be moved to another part of the chapel.

(2:iv)

FORGET ABOUT making reverend mother in five years; I wasn't sure I could make nun in five years. We were only several days into the program, and my unsuitability was glaringly apparent. As streaks of sunlight snuck between the vertical blinds in the classroom, I mentally calculated my sins, large and small, certain I had been grossly deluded about my religious ambitions. *What was I thinking?* I slumped dejectedly in my seat.

And then in walked Sister Jessica.

Toronto had just issued one of its numerous heat advisories—it had to be 140 degrees Fahrenheit outside—but Sister Jessica clearly did not monitor the Weather Network. She was dressed in a long-sleeved turtleneck sweater, a long wool tartan skirt, and black tights. Gray-peppered cropped hair framed a careworn face.

She sat down with a notebook jammed full of loose papers. A few slipped from her clutches and slid over her tartan skirt to the floor. She cursed softly. We loved her immediately.

"Dears," she began in a Scottish brogue that was somewhere between Maggie Smith and Mrs. Doubtfire, "we're going to talk today about *lectio divina,* a marvelous form of contemplative prayer. *Lectio divina* means 'divine reading'—I'm sure some of you already knew that—and it's as old as the hills but oh-so effective. Society bombards us with so much information that we speed-read everything and retain nothing. *Lectio* is the opposite: it is the slow, reflective reading of Scripture."

Lectio divina, she said, was practiced by the early monks and nuns not so that they could gain knowledge but so that they could directly encounter Christ. They memorized the psalms and read the Bible in small bites, meditating on the passage and whispering it to themselves throughout their day like a mantra so that their bodies were engaged in a continual conversation with God.

"Prayer," said Sister Jessica, "deepens your relationship with God, and the only way to get the most out of it is to show up and do it. In time, your life becomes a continuous prayer."

Teresa of Avila once said of prayer that it wasn't merely about spending time with God; it was an opportunity to take off your mask. When you are engaged in deep prayer, you expose to God and to yourself your deepest fears and concerns.

There are a gazillion prayers out there: some prayers leave you dry, others leave you yawning, but certain prayers resonate so strongly that you can almost feel your chemistry change as you say them. You might not even understand why they resonate; they just do.

As Sister Jessica spoke, my mind latched onto those prayers that spoke to me. One was the Anglican Collect for Purity:

Almighty God, unto whom all hearts be open, all desires known, and from whom no secrets are hid; cleanse the thoughts of our hearts by the inspiration of thy Holy Spirit, that we may perfectly love thee, and worthily magnify thy holy Name; through Christ our Lord.

THE WORDS *cleanse* and *secrets* seemed to speak directly to me.

Sister Jessica closed her notebook. "Can I give you some advice? Don't go out and buy a bunch of books about prayer. There are as many ways to pray as there are people, but no one can teach you to pray, dears. It has to come from here." She knocked softly on her heart. "Find a quiet place, close your eyes, and listen for God. That's it. Some people will rave about a new book about prayer like it's a bestseller, but you don't need that."

She paused, looked at the semicircle of women staring at her, and smiled broadly. "Are you having a good time here? We do keep you awfully busy; I'm sorry about that. But life is busy, even here. Let me tell you a few things about what it's really like in a convent."

All nine of us leaned forward in our chairs. You could have heard a pin drop three rooms away.

"Sometimes the pace of life here is a bit more hectic than people think. We nuns get stressed out—oh yes!—and we need to take retreats. Oh, don't be surprised. We're not all floating around in a state of serenity with shimmering halos—you might have already figured that out. Life in a convent is much the same as life outside a convent. We drift off during chapel, just like you drift off in meetings; we get bummed out about not concentrating on prayer, just like you might have difficulty concentrating on writing a report or not paying attention to the sermon or the liturgy. We're human. And we have to be reminded to go easy on ourselves and try not to be super-whatevers. Nuns have the same crises of mind and soul as you workaday dears."

Sister Jessica was born and raised in Glasgow, she told us, and had trained as a nurse. She never planned on becoming a nun, but when she reached her early forties, she found herself edging closer toward the sisterhood. "Me, called to religious life? I thought it was a joke!"

She was now in her mid-seventies, plucky and fun, with a deep rolling laugh. The way she humanized religious life captivated us. Convent life was not the romantic bubble some of us had envisioned, but neither was it austere or humorless. Not with people like Sister Jessica around. What's more, nuns were not the saintly, virginal beings we assumed they were. Any one of us could be nun material. Even me.

(2:v)

"AT LEAST we're getting a cardio and strength-training workout," said Lorraine, our feet shuffling along a dusty concrete floor as we lugged a six-foot wooden altar from one end of the basement to the other.

As part of our daily labor—*Laborare est orare* (to work is to pray) was St. Benedict's ethos—Lorraine and I had been assigned the job of sorting through a jumble of old furniture and knickknacks discarded by the sisters and then cleaning and pricing it for a garage sale that was to take place in two weeks. It was the first garage sale the sisters had held.

I was glad to be paired with Lorraine. She was a strong, good-humored woman with wavy shoulder-length hair, and like me, she was divorced and in her fifties. She was working toward a theology degree: her thesis argued that Western churches had misinterpreted the gospel when it claimed that justice was central to Jesus' teaching, and she was comparing the Greek and Hebrew texts of the Bible to support her theory.

"But the Anglican Church in Canada is all about peace and justice at the moment," I said slightly puzzled.

"Don't get me started on that," Lorraine said, gritting her teeth. But usually she *would* get started on it and rant a little to explain her point.

"The church has hijacked Jesus' call to righteousness and created an assumption that it's a call to social justice. I don't believe that it is. Did you know that in the King James Version of the Bible—*the* Bible of the English-speaking Protestant world for several hundred years—the word 'justice' doesn't appear once—not once—in the New Testament? And it appears only twenty-eight times in the Old Testament. And the word 'justice' is almost never defined by the people who use it: What does it mean? Fairness? Equity? Equality? And what's the relationship between justice and the law? The whole social justice thing is a great deflector, a patronizing finger-pointer that says 'The problem is with systems and not within us.' It's easier for the church to talk about social justice than to talk about the inner journey or the inner work that individuals need to do."

In the early hours of morning, Lorraine and I would often bump into each other in the small library down the hall from our cells. When the sisters and some of the more devout among our Crossroads group were tuned to private prayer, Lorraine and I would be in the library checking our email. (The convent had Wi-Fi.)

Lorraine loved books, and she was forever recommending titles for me to read. Occasionally, while sitting across from one another in the library, my laptop would ping with the arrival in my inbox of yet another book recommendation from her. By the time I left St. John's, the list had grown to about twenty-five books. (The sheer number of books about faith that are published each year is staggering. The moment you express an interest in a religious vocation, everyone has a dozen books that "you absolutely have to read." They are rarely loaned and seldom stocked in public libraries; you can find them only in religious book centers. It required a self-imposed vow of poverty to save me from the tyranny of book recommendations.)

I looked forward to Lorraine's suggestions because she would often throw in a title that had nothing to do with religion, and once in a while she would email me a joke, which sent us into uncontrollable giggles during what was supposed to be the Greater Silence.

In the basement, as we sorted, cleaned, and hauled furniture, we chatted and joked some more.

The other thing that made our basement work enjoyable was our supervisor, Sister Sue.

Like Sister Jessica, Sister Sue was a character. In her pre-nun life, she had been a professor of ancient history in the United States—and an atheist. It was while dealing with an addiction via a twelve-step program that she forged a bond with God, likening the experience to being wrapped in a big electric blanket of comfort and warmth. She gradually began yearning to be part of a community that was rooted in a common faith, and ended up baptized, much to her surprise. After becoming Christian, she realized that she wanted "more God" in her life, and that got her thinking about the religious life. She visited the Canadian convent hoping she wouldn't like it, "but as soon as I got here, I felt at home." She entered religious life at age fifty.

A side-parted chin-length blunt cut, which she hooked behind an ear, gave her a girlish look, but it was her inscrutable expression with its Mona Lisa smile that hinted at a feisty side.

It came as no surprise when we discovered that Sister Sue had a "colorful" past, as they like to say in hagiographic accounts. A few of the nuns had alluded obliquely to their past relationships, but Sister Sue was entirely upfront about hers— she had lived with a few men.

We adored her candidness, and during our tea break, the other members of our Crossroads group would come in from dusting the library shelves or cleaning the guest house— Lorraine and I had obviously drawn the short straw when it came to manual labor—and migrate to our table to hear Sister Sue dish the goods about a nun's life.

Was convent life really just high school in a habit?

"If you mean, 'Do the others get bitchy and are there bruised egos from time to time?' the answer is yes," said Sister Sue. "What do you expect from people who live and work together day in and day out?"

Do you feel oppressed?

"Ha! Are you kidding? There is a great sense of freedom here. I don't feel I'm missing anything from the outside world. I've been liberated from consumerism and all that other crap."

No one had the nerve to ask, "Do you miss sex?" Well, not yet.

She did not sugarcoat convent life, nor did she castigate it. She seemed proud, defiant even, that she had taken the brave and unconventional path, though she was quick to admit that the call to religious life had taken her by surprise, as it had Sister Jessica. "This is the last place I thought I'd end up."

(2:vi)

IN NO time, I was as embedded with the nuns as I could hope to be. I loved every minute of it.

The place bubbled with optimism and activity, and it had a collegial, noncompetitive vibe.

Being a bit of an architecture freak, I was initially disappointed that the convent wasn't a dark Gothic cliché. It had been built in the past five years and was airy, with an abundance of windows. Glass lined the corridors and the entire wall in the refectory, which faced out to a beautiful courtyard of swaying wildflowers and young trees; the nuns' cloister featured a glass-enclosed porch on all four sides; and the chapel had a glass clerestory that allowed you to watch the clouds pass as you listened to a sermon or a Bible reading.

The light and airiness had a great impact on my well-being. I felt as if every care in the world had fallen away from me. I began to regard myself more as one who could be useful to others than as one with something to prove. My ambition was subsiding nicely, thanks to regular ministrations of kindness, and I glowed with the radiance and earnestness of a new recruit. At times I had to pinch myself to believe that I was really there.

The more I saw of Sister Elizabeth Ann scurrying around the place, listening to everyone's two cents—always with a genuine smile, not a patronizing one—the more I appreciated what a mammoth job it must be to lead thirty or so women *and* run a convent. My thoughts returned to the Camino pilgrimage where I had been the de facto leader of fourteen women. I had lost the group a week into the hike, which says something about my leadership abilities, but was a blessing for the others in that group because by then I had used up a small reserve of patience. A reverend mother supports, counsels, consoles, works with, lives with, and eats with her sisters 24/7. I couldn't do that.

Far from feeling detached from the secular world, I actually felt more connected to it. The sisters monitored national and international events and brought these into the daily corporate intercessions during the offices. That summer, one or two professional sports teams and those competing in the Tour de France were included. We prayed also for people known to the sisterhood, and the prayers became very personal petitions for those who were in hospital or who were bereaved, depressed, or unemployed. Some of the sisters had specific areas of interest: Sister Helena always prayed for Bible societies, Sister Helen Claire prayed for the community's associates and oblates, and Sister Beryl prayed for First Nations dioceses. Frequently, one of the sisters would pray for "those in our Women at a Crossroads program, that they may be guided toward a vocation with our community."

I took to the routine and the arrangements so easily that I began to wonder whether the attraction was for the wrong reasons. I had a tendency to latch on to an idea and burrow into it, nose around for information and sniff out the truffle of truth, at which point my interest usually waned. I didn't want that to happen to my ardor for monastic life.

...ny objective-thinking cap, tamped my zeal,
... "the life" with more practicality than passion.
... pen and a pad of paper, and made a list—*Finally.*
... make a list!—of pros and cons.

F... a practical standpoint, religious life was the perfect all-inclusive lifestyle: an excellent balance of prayer, work, and leisure; three squares a day; small but comfortable rooms; a chapel; a couple of libraries; Wi-Fi; and an infirmary. I privately wondered whether the nuns would consider installing an outdoor pool in the courtyard garden. You know, just for exercise. A large barbeque was already set up against a wall in the courtyard, and when I allowed my imagination off the rein, I could conjure up a scene of white umbrellas and teak patio tables and perhaps a covered bar along the wall manned by a couple of cabana boys—cabana monks, perhaps?—who would serve gin-and-tonics and nibblers while I sat on a chaise longue in my tankini habit and pondered God.

In all seriousness, the convent was sublime, a masterpiece of serenity and order. No divas or drama queens that I could see. And the pace was good: I liked being on convent time.

With my pen, I drew a vertical line down the middle of the page and made a secondary list of the emotional and material sacrifices:

- *Limited family contact.* **Difficult one.** The kids were older and independent, and I was probably just a nuisance to them now, but I would miss being involved in their lives, and if they ever had children of their own, I would miss the grandparent stage.
- *No more boozy, giddy lunches with the girls.* I loved hanging out with my friends, but the opportunities for getting together were not as frequent anymore:

everyone was glued to their job. As for eating out, it was becoming less satisfying and more expensive: alcohol was the new smoking; food, the new sloth.

· *No more luxury shoes or nice clothes.* Give up my only pair of Blahniks? And how would I handle seeing a great pair of boots or kitten-heeled shoes that I could not buy? Then again, amazing age-appropriate fashion for middle-aged women just doesn't exist, so it would be a blessing to no longer have to worry about any of it.

· *No more travel.* Yeah, that would be tough. I get a thrill from seeing the world and immersing myself in different cultures, and I revel in the freedom to go where I want.

· *No more Colin.* Very tough; ending our relationship would be close to traumatic. I thought of some of the highlights of our time together: a year earlier, we had been in Spain, exploring Andalusia's whitewashed villages, spending hours cavorting on clothing-optional beaches and diving into sapphire waters. Was I really willing to trade that for a habit?

LOTS TO think about. There was no rush to make a decision; I hadn't been in the convent that long. Still, at the back of my mind the idea had lodged: *Yes, I could definitely live here.*

(2:vii)

"SO? HAVE you come to a decision?"

We were in the courtyard garden, taking a morning tea break from our class. The sun was shining, the birds were chirping, the little pond was burbling like a coffee percolator, and a slight breeze was causing the flowers to sway as if they were listening to a gospel choir.

The question, asked by a member of our group, had not exactly surprised me. I had been asked it half a dozen times since Day One. This was only Day Seven. What was I—the vocational bellwether? Talk about pressure. If I made a move, would the rest fall like dominoes?

"There's a lot that I'm liking about this life," I said cautiously. I didn't want to tip my hand, especially with Sister Elizabeth Ann within earshot—she was weeding among the snow queen hydrangeas and pink spirea. "But it's also not an easy decision. Lots to consider. How about you?"

"Nah. That's not the reason I'm here," said the woman. She was one of the younger ones in our pack. "But it is really nice. I don't know. I thought by this stage in my life I'd be married or at least have a boyfriend. I worry about my future—I don't want to be alone for the rest of my life. If some of you guys join, though, I might be tempted."

Our group—the Crossroads Coven, I dubbed it—had gelled easily. A good bunch. Lots of intense discussion, but lots of laughs, too. Most of us were divorced with grown children; I think I was the only one with a steady partner: steady in my case defined as being romantically attached to someone who lived more than 3,700 miles away.

If our group was so interested in what each of us was thinking in terms of commitment to the sisterhood, I could only wonder what was going on among the sisters themselves. Had they placed bets on the odds-on favorites for the novitiate sweepstakes? Maybe there were some of us the sisters did not want. Ouch.

One evening, after supper and before compline, a few of us gathered in one of the sitting rooms. We made tea and piled a plate with chocolate digestive biscuits and then settled ourselves on the sofas and chairs, our bare legs tucked beneath us.

(For a place that was supposed to eradicate desires and appetites, the convent had done a good job of giving me a new one—chocolate digestive biscuits. Who invented these things? They are beyond yummy. I was scarfing down at least six a day.)

We chatted about our classes and shared new intelligence we had unearthed about convent life from the sisters. It was clear that I wasn't the only one in the group kicking the tires of religious life. It was all very well what Sister Sue and Sister Jessica and some of the other sisters were telling us, but it wasn't enough. Was monastic life just another frustrating autocratic system? A Venus flytrap for the spiritually eager? And what about those three vows of poverty, obedience, and chastity: Was there some wiggle room on that last vow, a sort of Clintonesque definition?

"You know, there is a difference between celibacy and chastity," said Lorraine, once the giggling subsided. "The vow at SSJD specifies chastity, so technically that does not rule out a stable relationship with a man. I mean, you might not be able to have sexual intercourse, but you could at least hold hands. Maybe cuddle."

Would Colin be willing to downgrade our relationship to cuddling and hand-holding status? Would I?

"Maybe we need to start our own convent and establish our own version of Benedict's *Rule*," I quipped.

The remark brought the room to an abrupt silence.

Sonya, one of the young ones in our group, as well as the quietest, looked as if she had gone into shock. Her large brown eyes widened.

"Would we still work in secular jobs outside the convent?" she asked eagerly.

"Yes, it would probably be a good idea. How else would we support ourselves?" I answered, not knowing a thing about what I was proposing but continuing on in my merry fashion. "And maybe we'd only be nuns in our convent for a season or two, a sort of rota: you arrive for, say, two or three months, then return home to your family or whatever, but you would still be connected to the convent and be expected to keep it going in various ways."

"Where would it be?" someone else asked.

"Not Toronto," I said. "It should be somewhere inspiring and remote. And warm. Like Morocco."

"I *love* Morocco," enthused Sonya. Clearly, she was getting into the idea.

"Have you ever been?" I asked. "Because I haven't, but it looks great."

"It's fabulous. You'd love it. There is something holy and mystical about it."

"Great. So that's settled: a convent in Morocco."

"Would we wear habits?" another asked. "I hope they're more attractive than what the sisters wear here."

"At least wearing it is optional," murmured Laurie, who was sketching something on a pad of paper. Maybe she was designing new habits.

Laurie and I had become fast friends. She was an effervescent gal with light brown hair, a big laugh, and a flair for the creative. She was a priest and an artist who lived along the Nova Scotian coastline. On the first day of the Crossroads program, we realized that we had met several years earlier—at her brother's funeral. Fred had been a spirited man whose demons had carried him away much too soon. Laurie and

Fred could have been twins: when I looked at Laurie, I saw Fred; when she cracked a joke, I heard Fred; when she spoke about her art, it reminded me of Fred, and I would miss him all over again.

Like me, Laurie was checking out convent life. We both agreed: as shallow as it seemed, the habits would be an issue.

Now, I do not for one minute suggest that a habit should be body-hugging, lacking in modesty, or—God forbid—concocted by a committee of designers, but SSJD's were shapeless and bulky, and their floor-grazing length was impractical. The design appeared to be taken from a traditional monk's habit, with a scapular worn over a floor-length cassock, and tied at the hip by a thick black cord. (The cord is a mark of a professed religious. For those who have taken life vows, the cord has three knots tied into it, each signifying a vow.)

Habits are uniforms, as well as symbols of devotion and sacrifice, but I wanted a habit I could run in, one that was somewhat attractive and that would prompt a passerby to comment, "Now there goes a nun with God-given purpose and style. Gee, I'd like to join up."

Then there was the color: SSJD's habits were royal blue. They looked like something an order of flamboyant gay monks might wear. Royal blue is certainly distinctive if you happen to be on an expedition and need to keep the community within your sightlines, but as a general daily color? I don't think so. A color like that just screams to be dressed up with chunky silver jewelry or a bold Mondrian-style scarf.

"We could grow our own vegetables," interjected Sonya, who was more interested in nutrition and didn't want the entire evening deteriorating into a blather about habits.

Sonya was a bohemian-scholar type: tall, slim, with long, straight brown hair and brown, square-framed glasses. She had done a lot of traveling and was now back at university finishing her master's degree in theology with a focus on urban and international development. Quiet and observant, she seemed to be furthering her education as a way to buy time until she figured out what she really wanted to do. Maybe she knew exactly what she wanted to do but was held back by the same thing that holds back so many of us—what we *want* to do doesn't fit the prescribed pattern of what we're *supposed* to do at various stages of life. For thirtysomething women like her, that meant career, marriage, family, and home ownership. But really, who sets these rules?

Talking about setting up our own convent, however, animated Sonya, and she dove into the conversation.

As I padded back to my cell that evening, I thought about how all age groups are saddled by the expectations of society and how those limits intimidate many women (and men, for that matter) and keep them from pushing the boundaries.

Granted, not everyone has the freedom to seize the life they want: some are housebound because of disability or illness or are caregivers to their spouses, disabled children, or elderly parents. But there are many others who do have energy and freedom and who squander their time and their money on trivial things like obsessively managing their appearance. If you choose to ignore modern guidelines for the fiftysomething woman, you are considered irresponsible. If you don't pursue your lost youth or figure with life-or-death zeal, you are deemed slothful and neglectful; if you don't hit the nail bar every other week, people question your grooming standards; if you stop coloring your hair, people think you've "given up."

In the convent, the sisters did not seem to give a toss about any of that, and they were as happy as a litter of Labrador puppies. They lived life on their own terms without anxiously measuring their appearance against the standards of a fashion magazine or going into debt in a desperate attempt to plump up their sagging jowls. Imagine the freedom.

(2:viii)

I WAS struggling to keep pace with Lorraine. What was supposed to be an evening stroll around the leafy neighborhood beyond the convent grounds had turned into a power walk: Lorraine was exercised about the Lord's Prayer. At evening prayer, the sisters had used a new version that went like this:

Abba, Amma, Beloved,
your name be hallowed,
your reign spread among us,
your will be done well, at all times, in all places,
on earth as in heaven.
Give us the bread we need for today.
forgive us our sins
as we forgive those who sin against us.
Let us not fail in the time of our testing.
Spare us from trials too sharp to endure.
Free us from the grip of all evil powers.
For yours is the reign, the power, and the glory,
the victory of love, for now and eternity,
world without end. Amen and amen.

IT HAD not bothered me too much, but it had sent Lorraine into a near-apoplectic state. Her stride and speed increased as she got more worked up about it.

"You know, it's one thing to bring in new versions from time to time, but what drives me up the wall is when they bring in prayers with that gender-neutral crap," she fumed. "It completely eliminates God-as-Father, and turns Him into a eunuch."

"Is this about erasing the paternal aspect of God?" I asked. I didn't always grasp the reasons why the church made such changes.

She sighed heavily.

"It is part of an effort to be sensitive to people who were abused by their fathers. And while I get that "father" can be a loaded term for some people, it's absolutely insane to neutralize God just so you can make Him more palatable to everyone. Really. It's like the nanny-state has invaded church life. It drives me crazy!"

The argument is also made that non-gender–specific language for God prevents us from putting God in a box. "God is so much more than 'Him,' than 'Father,'" Sister Sue told me later on. "God transcends all, and that includes masculine, feminine, neutral language. God never self-identified as male or female; we assigned God's gender."

Lorraine and I shared a strong affection for *The Book of Common Prayer*, the four-hundred-year-old Anglican prayer book, and often our rants about the tinkering and politically correct fastidiousness going on in the present-day church would invariably cycle back to the BCP, as it is known colloquially.

Much more than a collection of liturgies for morning prayer, evening prayer, Holy Communion, funerals, weddings, and baptisms, the BCP contains some of the most soulful and intimate language you could find. There is not a pedestrian prayer in the entire book, and its elegant wording makes you strive to be something better than you are.

Some thirty years ago, *The Book of Common Prayer* was relegated to the sidelines when *The Book of Alternative Services* was introduced in Canada. (Revised versions also appeared in the United States as *The New American Prayer Book* and in Great Britain as *The Alternative Service Book*, later revised as *Common Worship*.) It was done to make the prayer book more accessible, which was ecclesiastical code for "modernizing it so that we can get more bums in pews and by extension more cash in the collection plate." But the tinkerers missed the point of the BCP and of religion itself: dumbing down a prayer book doesn't make it more accessible; it insults the reader by assuming she or he is too stupid to understand the prayers in their Elizabethan form. For who cannot comprehend these lines from the General Confession?

> *Almighty and most merciful father, we have erred and strayed from thy ways like lost sheep; we have followed too much the devices and desires of our own hearts.*

WHILE YOUNGER people may indeed have trouble making sense of some of the ancient wording in the BCP—though, really, they just need someone to read it with them a few times— it is a prayer book of beautiful and comforting language for adults, for people who have lived a bit and are grappling with life's often overwhelming passages.

I never understood why the church was so anxious to bring out a new book. You don't rewrite Shakespeare's sonnets to make them more understandable; you grow in understanding with the words. Prayers are not portals to instant gratification; they are meditations. The prayers I read when I was sixteen have taken on new meaning and relevance as I moved through the decades and through pivotal experiences.

"There was a prayer we said at the Eucharist today," I said. "Did you catch it? I'd never heard it before; it had all sorts of space imagery."

"Oh God," Lorraine groaned. "It's officially known as Eucharistic Prayer number four, but I call it the *Star Wars* prayer. All that language referring to interstellar space and galaxies; you half expect Darth Vader to pop up."

The sisters were firm adopters of *The Book of Alternative Services,* and they frequently added prayers from different Anglican sources to the offices. I had a grudging admiration for their desire to pray outside the book; though some of the language in the new prayers did not evoke the holiest of images. Whenever they said the doxology in its modern, androgynous version—"Glory to God, Source of all Being, eternal Word and Holy Spirit"—I felt as if I had been thrown into a scene from *Children of the Corn.*

(2:ix)

IT HAD to happen, didn't it? A few things about convent life started to niggle, as my Colin-or-the-convent dilemma bore down on me.

Before I arrived at St. John's, someone had mentioned that it would not be the chastity vow I would struggle with but the obedience vow. I had dismissed the remark: How difficult is it to follow orders? But monastic obedience is different from run-of-the-mill obedience. It goes beyond obeying orders: it is about taming appetites and habits and about pulling yourself away willingly from things that distract you from God.

Case in point: The previous night, one of the sisters and I had been playing cribbage during recreation hour. We were halfway through the second game (the aim was for the best two out of three) when Sister Elizabeth Ann announced that recreation hour was up. Just like that. We were not allowed to finish our game, not allowed to determine a winner or a loser. I'm a person who likes to complete what she starts, who derives satisfaction from ticking things off a list. I tried to entice my sisterly partner back to finish the game, but she shook her head and said resolutely, "Oh no, we mustn't. Reverend Mother said recreation is over." Cribbage interruptus.

The following afternoon during tea break, another issue arose. A few of us were sitting with Sister Sue, peppering her as usual about what we would have to give up to become nuns. Makeup was a definite no-no; ditto for jewelry, nail polish, hair-coloring products. I knew this and had long accepted it, but now these strictures rankled my rebellious nature.

"This strips away a person's self-expression, her eccentricities, and identity," I argued. "Eyeliner, hoop earrings, and silver bracelets are as much a part of my identity as the mole above my lip."

"But that's the whole point of becoming a religious," explained Sister Sue. "You have to give up self."

"But does God want us to be colorless versions of what He gave us in the first place?"

"God wants us to love one another," she replied. "That's all. He doesn't care what's on us."

If He doesn't care, why would a community care?

Just when I felt certain that I could relinquish all my attachments and not let it bother me, I returned to my cell and stared longingly at a photo of my children that I take with me whenever I travel. Gazing at their optimistic faces and quiet smiles, I hardly noticed how quickly my tears began to fall. I whispered thanks for the blessing of parenthood—despite its ups and downs, it is a true blessing—and thought of how the easy phone calls and spontaneous visits would effectively end if I became a nun.

My eyes bounced from the photo of my kids to the one of Colin. Our former once-a-day emails had become considerably less frequent, and I wondered whether he had lost interest in me. Who could blame him? It was one thing to maintain a transatlantic relationship and another to maintain it when one partner is cloistered in a convent.

My engagement ring felt loose, and I knew damn well it had nothing to do with weight loss: the sisters were keeping us well fed and watered. Was a loose engagement ring some kind of a sign? And was it a sign that I should let my engagement fall away or a sign to be careful and hold on to it? Why can't God be more explicit?

(2:x)

WEEK THREE. Aspects of institutional living were chafing; in particular, the lack of private time, which I began to hoard like a secret treasure. I would feel a peevish streak asserting itself whenever demands were made on my time. Even a conversation felt like an invasion of privacy. Then again, maybe it was just the heat.

It was murderously hot outside. The sun's harsh, relentless laser rays seemed to be on a scorched-earth mission. I sat limply in the chair in front of my cell window staring at the twelve slender white pines *(One for each apostle?)* that stood like soldiers, the clump of furry nettles at the ends of their outstretched branches like palms pleading for God's mercy.

There were few audible sounds: a papery rustle from a copse of poplar trees; the drone of a distant car blending with the vibrating buzz of the cicadas. An airplane jetted by, and I wished I were on it.

I could feel my faith wilting. The intensity of the Crossroads program had become as heavy as the heat. Compounding it was the headache-like pressure that comes from indecision. The idea of being a nun no longer struck me as borderline lunacy, but what I wanted and needed was someone who had already been on this quest, someone as kooky and mercurial as I was, who was devoted to God, who yearned for monastic life and yet struggled with its restrictions. I truly wanted to be a nun. Indeed, I felt like one. But I wanted to be a different kind of nun, a more active one, and one with fewer limitations placed on my freedom. I loved all the sisters, and I felt extremely comfortable in my surroundings, but there was something... elusive... missing.

I wandered down the empty, silent hall to the library. The drapes had been drawn as a shield against the oppressive afternoon sun and the effect of the humidity, but a few narrow gaps in the curtains made it look as if the fires of Hell were within reach.

I perused the rows of book spines on the shelves wishing, willing, for something to grab my attention. My eyes landed on *The Seven Storey Mountain* by Thomas Merton. Merton's name was vaguely familiar, but I knew next to nothing about him. I pulled the book from the shelf: it was thick and looked as if it might take a while to read. *It's not as if there's a lot competing for my time right now.*

I sat down, opened the book resignedly, and began to read. Within twenty minutes, you could not pry the book from my hands. I was hooked. With every page that I read, my heart expanded and my excitement mounted.

Merton was a sensitive and conflicted figure. Born in France to artist parents, an American and a New Zealander, he had a peripatetic upbringing. I could identify with that. Although my parents did not move across the globe like Merton's parents, they moved frequently within a single city, Toronto, inching gradually to the fringes and then to its outlying rural towns. The constant upheaval engendered in me a sense of transience.

Merton's mother died when he was very young, a loss that was to forever color his relationship with women, and by the time Merton had reached his mid-teens, his father, too, had died.

A brilliant student, young Merton gave in easily to passion and excess, drinking and screwing his way through boarding school and later Cambridge University. After a serious indiscretion (Merton never fessed up to it in his autobiography, but I later learned it was a pregnancy that was hushed up by Merton's wealthy guardian), he slunk back to New York, where remnants of his family lived. Migrating into writing and into Columbia University, he taught by day and continued to lead a desultory life by night. He was searching for his place in life, for something to connect to his wandering soul. He flirted with spiritual matters—he had been raised in both the Quaker and Church of England traditions—and after one of those glorious epiphanies that are the stuff of religious lore, he was baptized in the Roman Catholic Church. He entered the Trappist Gethsemani monastery in Kentucky—"the four walls of my new freedom," as he poetically described it. His abbot insisted that Merton write his life story as an exercise in shedding his ego, and the result was *The Seven Storey Mountain*. Ironically, the book catapulted both the monk and his silent order to loud international fame.

Neither the fame nor the spiritual transformation attracted me as much as did his style of writing and his struggles and ideas. I suppose the choppy journey of his life resonated because my head continuously bobbed in recognition of many of the sentiments and doubts he laid bare.

This was precisely the kind of role model that could help me with my own vocation. The date of his birth—1915—mentioned in the first line of his book hadn't registered. And why would it? His writing and his thoughts were as modern as anything I had read.

I rushed to my laptop and googled Merton's name to see how I could contact him. And then the crushing discovery that he had died. In 1968. Accidentally electrocuted. I checked other sources in case Google had made an error. Nope. 1968.

As my memory spun through the haze of my own history, I saw my fourteen-year-old self in 1968 sitting at the breakfast table one December morning, and my father looking up from his *Globe and Mail* and reporting to my mother with a mix of surprise and sadness, "Thomas Merton died." Both of them had paused to allow the news to sink in, and there was sadness on their faces. So I had been aware, peripherally, of Merton's death, but its impact had not registered back then. It did now.

A maturation took hold and shook me out of my lazy religious thinking. Merton's attitude and philosophy released me from worrying about whether I was thinking about faith correctly and orderly—do any of us get faith perfectly?—and freed me to approach religion more critically, to stop giving religion—the business of faith—unnecessary and sometimes undeserved reverence. God, not the church (any church) is the goal. Or to put it more crudely: if God is the destination, churches are the gas stations along the route. Then again, to some, God is the destination and churches are the bureaucratic city works department that erects roadblocks and sends you on frustrating detours that eventually force you to throw up your hands and say, "Oh, to hell with it; there's got to be a better route." As Dietrich Bonhoeffer once opined, people come to church in a spirit of hope and openness but leave as if they've staggered from a maze of mind-boggling bombast.

Merton was not without his criticisms of the church, and this too was liberating for me. Although I had labored under the impression that being a good Christian meant being faithful to the church, some big issues made me question why I stubbornly kept faith with it.

On the magazine rack outside the refectory, I had picked up a copy of the *New Yorker* that contained an interview with the Archbishop of Canterbury concerning the Church of England's attitude toward female priests, and particularly toward the ordination of female bishops.

The church was trying to "accommodate" (code for "appease") "those whose theology cannot accept female priests." The church was still talking in soft, pillowy language about the need to bring in male bishops to serve Holy Communion to the thousands of conservative Anglicans in Britain who refused to receive it from a female priest, a female bishop, a male bishop who had ordained a female, or a male bishop who had been ordained by a female. I felt the color rise in my face.

There was a time—it no doubt exists in places today—when white Anglicans refused the sacraments (Holy Communion and baptism) along with religious ceremonies such as confirmations, weddings, and funerals, from a black priest. It was called racism, and t e church rightly took a strong stand against it, though the cynic in me occasionally wondered whether the stand was guided by "the right thing to do" or by the fact that Africans were becoming the fastest-growing cohort in the Anglican Church.

Now the church was dragging its feet on the issue of gender discrimination, and from what I could see, was allowing itself to be blackmailed by Pleistocene parishioners who were threatening to withhold their weekly donations from the collection plate if a miter was placed on the head of a woman. Why didn't the C of E have the guts to shame the blackmailers?

I thought Anglicanism was better than that, that it had guts when it came to ethics and human rights, but it struck me now: What's a nice girl like me wasting my time with a bunch of misogynists?

It was fairly clear from the interview that the Archbishop was in favor of full ecclesiastical parity for women, but he could not muster the moral courage to push it through.

The argument is frequently made that the Archbishop of Canterbury is not the Pope and therefore does not have authority to speak for the entire Anglican Communion. But the fact remains that the world's 85 million Anglicans regard the incumbent as head of the faith and are therefore influenced and guided by what he says. It is true that the Queen of England is head of the faith, but when was the last time she addressed the church's members? With two effectively mute leaders in the Anglican Church, who actually speaks and answers to church polity?

That's the difference, the tension, between faith and religion: faith is belief; religion is the institutional arm of faith.

Can one be fundamentally opposed to church policy and still be a cloistered monastic? What would Merton do?

(2:xi)

"TELL SISTER Constance Joanna what you told me about wearing a nun's habit," Sister Elizabeth Ann goaded me as I sat between the current reverend mother and the former one during recreation one evening.

Recreation was a bit of a misnomer; like all of convent life, it was structured. I thought it might entail kicking around a soccer ball on the convent lawns or playing croquet. Instead, the sisters and our Crossroads group were seated in a large polite circle in the conference room. Most of the sisters were engaged in various types of needlework.

Sister Elizabeth Ann was crocheting a rosary while nudging me to dish out my decades-old anecdote from when I had worked in the marketing department of a record company. One of our promotions involved a British novelty rock band called The Monks, who sang such catchy tunes as "Nice Legs Shame About Her Face," "I've Got Drugs in My Pocket (and I Don't Know What to Do with Them)," and "I Ain't Getting Any."

Sister Elizabeth Ann knew of The Monks and even hummed some of their songs when I first regaled her about it. The story went like this: As part of the promotion for The Monks' album (we called them albums or LPs in those days), my colleagues and I decided to make the rounds of radio stations and deliver the LPs dressed as religious—the men as monks, and me, the sole female manager in the entire company, as a nun. It was the early 1980s, and the men I worked with were foul-mouthed, drug-snorting, sexist boors. (Trust me, I am being kind here.) But when I emerged from my office dressed in a traditional nun's habit, they suddenly turned all gentlemanly. Their tone softened; their swearing stopped; they ran ahead to open the door for me. I did not see a line of coke near any of them the entire morning. As we walked out of the office building together, one of them confided to me a bit sheepishly that he had once been an altar boy. I inclined my wimpled head receptively; it looked as though he was working up the courage to ask if I would hear his confession.

Our first stop was a radio station at the busy intersection of Bay and Yonge Streets in downtown Toronto. As I made my way from the black stretch limo (we always traveled in limos in those days) to the office tower where the station was located, several people on the street genuflected before me; two asked for a blessing. Never have I had so many people falling over themselves to assist me. Who knew that a nun's habit was the ultimate power suit and that it was such a guy magnet?

Sisters Constance Joanna and Elizabeth Ann guffawed at this story.

"When I had on that habit, I was overcome with a serenity and goodness that I had never felt," I told them. "Somehow I knew I was meant to wear a habit."

"Well, just remember that vocations come from the heart, not from the head," smiled Sister Elizabeth Ann as she returned to her handiwork. She was working on an Anglican rosary, braiding sapphire blue thread and tying it into thick knots to resemble beads.

My eyes were drawn to her hands, which were strong but delicate.

Nuns have extraordinarily beautiful hands. I first noticed this as we exchanged the Peace during the Eucharist and I felt their soft skin slide against mine. I watched their hands during mealtimes as they deftly and elegantly manipulated their cutlery, their long, slender fingers showing patience even while struggling with a stubborn piece of meat. In chapel, their hands were folded serenely on their lap, or clasped in prayer, fingers wrapped lightly around the cups of their palms. One sister who sat a few seats away from me in chapel had hands like white marble. These were not idle hands: they gardened, cleaned, cut meat, and chopped vegetables and fruit in the convent and washed dishes and worked with the sick and the sad at the nearby hospital. They were busy, productive hands but entirely without blemish. How did they manage that?

I looked down at my own fidgety hands: lines and wrinkles around the wrists, backs showing signs of crepe along with a few faint age spots, cuticles ragged and raw, nails bitten. No, they were not a nun's hands, but they were hands that had baked and assembled birthday cakes, dug trees and planted gardens, painted children's rooms, and even installed ductwork; hands that had at times slapped in anger and other times soothed away the tears on a child's face. My life was written on my hands.

(2:xii)

SISTER SUE walked into the room where we met for class to teach us about the Ignatius method of prayer. Her lips were turned into that little Mona Lisa smile. A few days earlier I had heard her use the F-word in conversation with another sister. Noticing my shocked second-grader expression, she had

said, "Oh, c'mon, we're nuns, not angels." Weirdly, the year
I gave up saying the F-word was the year in which the only
people I heard use it were nuns.

Sister Sue began her lesson by telling us about Ignatius of
Loyola, the founder of the Jesuits.

Ignatius was a Spanish noble and knight. While recuperat-
ing in hospital from wounds received in the Battle of Pamplona
in 1521, he scrounged around for reading material one day and
picked up *Vita Christi*—presumably because another wounded
knight had grabbed the last copy of *Hello!* It changed his life.
Vita Christi was a collection of essays by Ludolph of Saxony,
a German theologian, who believed that to truly understand
Christ's teachings, a person had to imagine himself as part
of the actual scene: for example, standing before the manger
at the nativity, or walking with the disciples on the road to
Emmaus, or being in the crowd when Christ walked toward
his crucifixion. Ignatius was so impressed with the concept that
he hung up his armor, dedicated his life to Christ, and spun
Ludolph's idea into a series of his own *Spiritual Exercises*.

It certainly sounded simple enough.

"It's a good method for discerning where God is calling
you," said Sister Sue. "But sometimes it takes you places you
weren't expecting, so be careful; it can be pretty heavy."

For our introduction to the Ignatian method, she had
chosen the story of Elijah in the desert when he fled from
Jezebel. We all flipped to 1 Kings 19. If you're not familiar with
the story, here's an abridged version:

Elijah was a prophet who lived in ninth-century-BC Israel.
There was a power struggle at the time between northern and
southern Israel: the Kingdom of Israel (located in the north)
was muscling for religious reform and trying to steer religious
attention away from Jerusalem (located in the southern

Kingdom of Judah). One of the reforms was to reintroduce worship of the god Baal (the god of thunder and rain). Israel was in the midst of a severe famine and drought, so Baal was the ideal idol to offer the rabble. But reintroducing Baal was also about keeping things peaceful on the marriage front because the King of Israel, Ahab, was married to Jezebel, who happened to be a Baal priest. Nepotism and politics—they're like death and taxes, aren't they?

Elijah wasn't impressed with Ahab's reforms or with Ahab and Jezebel, for that matter, and he told them so. He also told them that if they did not end their idolatrous ways there would be hell to pay. Ahab and Jezebel challenged Elijah to a contest to determine who was mightier—Baal or God. Two teams were assembled and told to slaughter a bull and prepare it for sacrifice but not set fire to it. The god who responded to the call of his team and lit the fire would be declared the winner. There are some humorous bits in the passage: The Baal team leaps around all morning trying to summon their god, and Elijah—I pictured him behaving like Russell Brand—taunts them from the sidelines, "You'll have to shout louder. Maybe your god is sleeping or going to the bathroom, or he's left on a trip!" But no matter how much Team Baal cried out, their god would not be roused.

When it was Elijah's turn, he asked Team Baal to gather around his altar. He slaughtered his bull, laid it on the altar, and then asked the Baal guys to dump water on the whole thing, not once but three times. They gladly obliged. Then Elijah dropped to his knees and prayed to God. Come on, baby, light my fire. Bingo! Fire lit.

It was a tremendous victory for Team Elijah, but then Elijah did something stupid: he rounded up all the Baal priests (there were 450 of them) and killed them. Well, when Jezzy heard the news (and you've got her number at this point because she had cannily decided not to join her fellow priests for the contest), she went ballistic. "If the gods don't kill me first, I'll kill you!" the Bible quotes her as screaming.

Elijah hightailed it to the desert. Exhausted and scared, he sank to his knees and begged God to kill him because he was done with running and preaching and trying to score points for the Almighty. Then he fell asleep. But God sent angel after angel to keep Elijah fed and awake, and eventually Elijah escaped from the desert and evaded Jezebel.

It is the quintessential story about perseverance but also about our humanness. We tend to regard ourselves as superhuman, but the moment we detect a flaw we crash and lose confidence. We'd rather die than admit failure. Yet God compels us to dust ourselves off and fight another day. Like he does with James Bond.

"Read the passage over," Sister Sue instructed us, "and after you've thought about it, ask yourself: 'How does God minister to me in the desert?'"

This is easy, I thought. *Sit in a chair, close my eyes, and turn a Bible passage into a soaring Spielberg production. Roll camera. Action!*

Which is what I did. I felt the desert heat, the scorching sun, the burning sand. I imagined being in Elijah's sandals, drenched in perspiration and fear, wondering whether this would be my last day. I imagined staring longingly at a clot of shade trees on the far side of a canyon, trying to muster the energy to reach it. I could feel Elijah's dejection, even when the angels showed up. They came with food and drink, but neither angel ever sat down with the poor guy and commiserated with him along the lines of, "Yeah, that Jezebel. What a bitch, eh? Here's an idea on how to escape her." There are times when an actual solution is more useful than food and drink.

My mind lazily circled back to Sister Sue's question: How does God minister to you in the desert? And my surprised and immediate response was *He leaves me alone to solve my problems. He doesn't send a knight on a white horse or drop a gun into my lap so I can protect myself; He leaves me to fend for myself.*

The response shocked me, but not as much as what followed.

Up sprang an intense and frightening episode from my past. I thought I had done an admirable job of suppressing the memory all these years, but now it blew open with the force of a geyser.

The year was 1983. I was still working for the record label, and that April the annual awards ceremony for our industry was being held. Mucky-mucks from head office in LA were flying into Toronto for the glittering festivities. We were all being put up for the night at the hotel where the gala was being held. I didn't particularly want to attend, but my boss, a nasty little Englishman, had ordered everyone in our department to attend.

It turned out to be a rather fun event. I had splurged on a Wayne Clark design, a sort of iridescent pewter gray mid-calf–length taffeta dress with a wide matching sash that tied in a bow. Everyone said I looked stunning, and a compliment like that always helps you raise your game. At the post-awards party in one of the hotel's hospitality suites, I circulated with remarkable poise and ease, chatting to a range of people—some I knew and some I didn't. For the first time in my fledgling career, I felt truly professional, in control, polished, and suffused with a certainty that life would work out for me. The beverage in my glass was water, ice, and a slice of lemon masquerading as a gin and tonic when anyone asked. I specifically did not drink that evening because my colleagues were all doing a smorgasbord of drugs (drugs were never my scene) and I wanted to be stone-cold sober so that I could make a fast getaway before people started getting out of hand. Just before midnight, when the coast was clear, I slipped away unnoticed from the party and made a triumphant dash to my room. I changed out of my party clothes, packed my bag for an early morning departure, and went to bed pleased with myself for having survived the party and gotten away unscathed. It is my last memory of feeling truly and unreservedly confident.

An hour or so later I was awakened by the ringing of the telephone. It was one of the executives I worked with, saying he had to see me right away. He asked for my room number, and in my half-awake state I grabbed the key from the bedside table, peered at the number on it, and repeated it into the phone. I hung up the phone and promptly fell back to sleep.

The next thing I knew the executive was pounding my door, urgently calling my name. Had there been an emergency? I wondered. As the company's publicity manager, I was required to craft news releases and respond to the media or else find an appropriate executive to respond to a crisis. Was this a crisis now? Or maybe I was in trouble because I had left the party early. It always irked my bosses that I wasn't more like one of the guys (they were all guys): stoned, drunk, or in various stages of hangover recovery. Anyway, I flew toward the door, guided by the strip of light seeping in from the hotel corridor. I opened the door a crack, and the executive barged in. He quickly bolted the door, pushed me onto the bed, unzipped his trousers, pushed up my nightgown, and raped me.

It happened so quickly that I didn't even have time to gasp out my shock. He was a large, fleshy man, and when he collapsed on top of me I felt smothered, and could feel my bones crushing. I squirmed slightly as his sweat dripped onto my skin. I did not know if he was under the influence of the *drug de soir,* but I was scared that if I put up a fight he might hurt me more.

I lay still, silent. It felt like I was being murdered. My only act of self-defense occurred when he demanded that I tell him I loved him; instead, I told him I hated him, and I tensed my body so that it would be wooden and unyielding.

As his body continued to rip into me, I immediately disassociated myself from my physical self, drifting into a sort of altered state in which—this sounds bizarre and even strikes me now as an odd reaction—I imagined my hand reaching into my chest and pulling my soul from my body because it was the only part of myself I could rescue. The soul hung in the air, arm's length above my head, and while I was being raped, I did not take my eyes off it for a second. It was a small, golden orb, a little smaller than a tennis ball onto which was superimposed a holographic face whose hands were pressed together in prayer.

When my attacker was finished, he zipped up his trousers, slapped me across the face, and called me "a dead f**k."

I remained where I was, afraid to breathe, until he left the room. When the door shut and the lock clicked, I ran into the bathroom and threw up. Too stunned to cry, I turned on the taps of the bathtub and sat in it, scrubbing myself frantically as if trying to erase a disease.

I waited out the night standing by the window watching for the sun to break the horizon. Then I checked out of the hotel and drove home.

There was no way I could tell my family or friends what had happened. I was too ashamed to reveal my stupid error in judgment, afraid that someone might think, "Maybe she was asking for it." If I went to the police, the case would hit the newspapers. If I reported it to human resources at my place of employment, I would lose my job.

I did, however, confront my attacker privately the next day at the office.

"That was rape," I sputtered angrily.

"Yeah, I know. Sorry." And the big fat brute shrugged it off.

In the days, weeks, years, decades that passed, the shame of the rape would not lift. As I lay in bed at night, the episode would play over and over in my mind; during the day, an innocent comment by a friend or co-worker would send me spiraling backward in time to the event, and I would escape to the nearest washroom before a flood of tears erupted. I never knew when the memory might pounce and for thirty years I remained in a state of constant high alert. It was my awful, little secret, the Achilles' heel that undermined and sabotaged relationships, work, and happiness. I even considered suicide as a way to escape the shame.

Now, in the convent's meeting room, I began to seethe as I focused on Sister Sue's question about how God cared for me in the desert: *Was He in the little orb praying for me while I was being attacked? Well, thanks a bunch. Really helpful. Could You not have given me the strength to fight back, or the presence of mind beforehand to not answer the phone or the door? Or how about giving me the courage to speak up in my own defense after the attack?* Trauma has a way of misdirecting your emotions. In blaming God, I sought to shift the blame from myself.

I glanced around at the other women in the room, all visiting their own private deserts: some were staring out the window; some were journaling madly; one sat with tears leaking from her closed eyes.

I got up from my chair and left the meeting room without making eye contact with Sister Sue. I fled to a small kitchen nearby, closed the door, and quietly wept. I could feel all the rage and humiliation from the assault surging through me. I thought I would explode.

Goddamn God, I muttered as tears streaked my face. *All those years I prayed and pretty much stuck to the straight and narrow, and this is what I get in return? You abandoned me in the desert while the ravens circled and picked at me.*

I stayed in the kitchen for several minutes, splashing cold water on my face, trying to cool my flushed face and my anger. Across from me, hanging on the wall like a picture, was a tea towel—one of those souvenirs sold at tourist sites. This one depicted a castle, and beneath it were the words "Sneaton Castle—Whitby."

As I struggled to pull myself together, I stared at the tea towel, and immediately a clear voice spoke: *You need to go there.*

I looked over my shoulder. No one was there. *Did I imagine that?*

I froze on the spot and listened again.

You need to go there, the Voice repeated. There was no mistaking it this time.

Boiling with anger and rage, I sneered back: *Are you kidding me? Why would I need to go to a castle? To be honest, I think you've become a little punch-drunk with your go-here-go-there missives lately. And when I do follow your direction and find myself in a pile of shit, you're suddenly AWOL. You know what? You go to Whitby. And have a wonderful time, OK? Send me a postcard.*

I was certain I was losing my mind. Yeah, that was it. The

trauma of reliving the rape had disordered my senses. Besides, Whitby was just east of Toronto, and there was no castle there.

Just go, the Voice insisted a third time. *You need to go there.*

I swatted the idea away with a dismissive wave and dried my tears. Not wanting to linger any longer in a small room with a pushy, disembodied voice speaking to me from a tea towel and dispensing dodgy travel advice, I returned to the meeting room.

Sister Sue was winding up the session. I made a mental note to never attempt the Ignatian method again.

(2:xiii)

A FEW days later I sat in a small room off the cloister with Sister Maggie Smith—I mean, Sister Jessica. She had been assigned as my mentor for the program, and although we had had a few casual conversations in the past few weeks this was the first formal one-on-one session.

"How are you getting on, dear? Do you miss your fiancé?"

I paused a long time before answering. It wasn't that I did not miss Colin, but the nature of our six-year transatlantic relationship meant we were more often apart than together. I told her that Colin and I had continued to email, and then I told her I was thinking of becoming a postulant.

It was her turn to pause.

"Tell me a bit of what you've been doing. How's your praying coming along?"

It was a good segue into my meltdown during the class on the Ignatian method. Poor Sister Jessica. I dumped it all on her—my desert, the rape, my silence, the whole shebang.

She gently scolded me for not coming to her sooner—"You should have come to me right after the Ignatian session"—and then she reached out and held my hand and asked me more about the rape. There was sadness on her face. She herself had been emotionally and physically abused during her honeymoon, she said, and understood something about my experience.

"Dear, you must pray about it, pray for strength and for resolution. What that man did was horrible. Oh, you poor wee thing. I'm so sorry."

We sat in silence, holding hands, trapped in memories of abuse and violence.

I summoned the nerve to tell her about my vision in front of the tea towel and about the voice that had instructed me to go to Sneaton Castle. I needn't have been concerned about her reaction. It was one of the things I loved about the nuns: you could talk about visions, dreams, and intuition, and no one would be privately sizing you up for a straitjacket.

"You know, dear, Sneaton Castle is a wonderful place. It's the home of the Order of the Holy Paraclete. They are in Whitby. No, not the one near Toronto, you silly thing. The Whitby in North Yorkshire. England. Our two communities have a long history. I visited them a few years ago; I'll show you the pictures I took. It was marvelous, and I know you would love it. Look, let me talk to Sister Elizabeth Ann. I'll bet she could email the prioress, Dorothy Stella—oh, she's a great gal, you'll adore her—and see about you staying there. If you've been called by God to go there, then, my dear, you must go."

The next day, I was in Sister Elizabeth Ann's office. I wanted to throw myself at her feet and beg her to take me in. I desperately needed to belong to something that gave my ragged soul a measure of goodness, where I could hide from the shame of the rape and feel worthy and clean again.

I can't remember if I told her I wanted to be a postulant, an associate, an oblate, or all three—I was grasping for anything and everything—but she steadied me and asked me to think hard about it for a year.

A year? I could be dead by then!

"In the meantime, why don't I email the prioress of the Order of the Holy Paraclete. If God has called you to go there, then you must go. It's a great community, and you'll love Whitby. Let's see how you feel after that."

(2:xiv)

IT WAS the final day of our Crossroads retreat and the last time I would hear lauds for a long time.

I sat with Sister Sue in an anteroom of the chapel while she rang the Angelus: three successive tolls, a pause, then three more, a pause, and a final three, followed by nine distinct bells. It is the monastic world's Morse code to God that the community is worshipping Him. Silently, the sisters prayed: *Hail Mary full of grace the Lord is with you. Blessed are you among women.* But all I could summon were the lines from Psalm 17 that Sister Elizabeth Ann always said at compline: *Keep me, O God, as the apple of your eye; hide me under the shadow of your wings.*

Calmness washed over me, and for a moment life made sense. God was all of us; God was Sister Sue and Sister Jessica and every sister and every member of my family, every friend, every co-worker, every person I passed on the street. If I could treat every person I encountered as a child of God, I would be transformed. Isn't that what I wanted?

The memory of the rape was riding the surface of my

emotions. I could no longer hide from it. A few nights earlier I had gone out with Lorraine and had told her about it. I needed two glasses of wine before I could broach the subject, but at least it was a start.

The bells of the Angelus now rang steadily and my thoughts turned to *bells, cow bells, dusty path, pilgrimage*—and I remembered that it was July 25, the feast day of St. James the Apostle. I knew all about James: he was the patron saint of Spain's Camino de Santiago de Compostela. I was on another pilgrimage now, one that didn't come with a map.

(2:xv)

I MISSED the convent of St. John the Divine the moment I returned home. Some of the routine there had chafed, but now that I was home it was my freedom that chafed. I would look at my watch and imagine what the sisters were doing: I pictured them in their places in chapel chanting the litany, praying for Bible societies; for peace; for the homeless, the sick, the depressed, the disenfranchised; and for their fellow sisters around the world. I pictured them silently processing from chapel to the refectory and withdrawing into their own zone of silent reflection while eating their meals. I missed my twenty-five new friends.

I molded my newly acquired monastic skills around a full-time job. At work, I stole off to read the psalms (part prayer, part sonnet for my thirsty soul), and sought out prayer meetings and ecumenical services. At home, I said the offices each morning and evening, but it was not the same without a community of chanting cheerleaders.

"Every time you begin something, pray. It marks the start

of a new chapter in your day and your life," Sister Jessica had taught me.

And pray I did. I became a veritable praying machine. Monastic life is about a way of looking at the world, of directing your gaze toward God's creation—the good and the not-so good—of engaging with reality. On my way to work in the morning, I viewed those I passed not as street people or business people or tourists or single moms or up-to-no-good students, but as children of God. On the bus I prayed for the driver, for the old woman struggling with her walker, for the student zoned out on his MP3 player. Instead of being irritated by them, I marveled at them. Good heavens, that person across the aisle is a child of God! I prayed silently before meetings started, for co-workers who were off sick, for those I passed in the hallway. I even prayed for my scheming boss.

I did not let on where I had spent my summer vacation. The reaction would have been predictable. Had I said I was at an ashram, a Buddhist retreat, or a kibbutz, people would have said, "Wow." But if I told them I had been to a Christian convent they would have said "Ew."

The few friends I did tell were surprised that nuns still existed and even more surprised that there were Anglican nuns. George Carey, the former Archbishop of Canterbury, once remarked that nuns were "the best-kept secret of the Anglican Communion." He got that right, but why has the church been reluctant to talk openly about their religious orders?

Three things became clear within a few weeks of being back in the secular world: I could no longer stay in my job; I could no longer worship in a parish church, or rather not the one I had been attending; and I had to find a convent to join and start living a monastic life.

The weekly Sunday church service, a sort of church lite, seemed so watered down compared with the rich monastic version I had come to know. There was no room for prayerful reflection. Hymns were sung at breakneck speed; ditto for the prayers. The intercessions were particularly lazy territory. Instead of praying for the unemployed and the dying, the congregation prayed for the Queen, for the prime minister, for the Anglican primate, and for high-ranking clergy in Canada and around the world. Sure, these people need our prayers, but when your intercessions are loaded up with political and religious luminaries what place do you assign to the common man or woman? I wanted a more creative and more civic-minded approach: to pray for specific environmental problems in the town or city, for the mother who had lost her son in a gang murder the day before, for the children who were battling for their lives in the local cancer wards, for the father who had suddenly found himself out of work, for street people, and for the new immigrants to the city.

The politicization of religion was there, all right; the prayers for peace and justice and other buzz words and feel-good notions. Lorraine would have burst a blood vessel had she been present.

Four months later, I left my job. I teetered in a state of bewilderment; rarely had I been without employment in thirty-five years.

As if called by a siren, I was drawn back to the convent, back to where I knew my equilibrium would be restored. The only place I knew where I fit in. A bus took me from Hamilton into Toronto and then a subway carried me north. Emerging from the subterranean jungle to the blare of street-level traffic, my legs took over, as if on auto pilot, taking me toward the convent.

Sister Jessica was there, and she took me in her arms. So did Sister Helen Claire and Sister Sue. *Yes, I do belong here.*

Sister Elizabeth Ann had contacted the prioress of the Order of the Holy Paraclete in England, and my visit was arranged. I would spend three months immersing myself in cloistered monastic life. All that remained was to book my flight and confirm my arrival date.

From there, things proceeded with lightning speed—always a sign that you are on the right path. Incredibly, everything I prayed for was miraculously answered. I prayed that my former employer would give me three months' severance before my pension kicked in: approved. I prayed that a tenant would be found to sublet my condo: done. I prayed that my children would get jobs and placements that would enable them to be entirely self-sufficient while I was away: granted. I prayed for a few freelance jobs to sustain me until my departure for England: check.

Almost overnight I was emptied of everything I had known and refilled with tough, direct questions: *Are you prepared to give up your life and follow Me? Can you rid yourself of material possessions and the distractions of this world and commit your life to Christ? Can you shed your ego, your vanity, your attachments and desires, and disappear into my world?*

Yikes! *Would you like fries with that?* I wasn't sure whether I had the attitudinal rigor for such a life, but that was apparently immaterial because, with or without my consent, the transformation was underway.

First, my femininity pretty much packed up and walked out the door. I used to be a fairly fashion-conscious woman: I loved intense colors, jewelry, makeup, and shoes—oh, I could not get enough of shoes.

Now I had completely lost the will to shop. On the rare

occasions when I ventured into a shop, I would gravitate to the same color palette: black, gray, brown. (On those days that I felt daring, I'd peruse the rack of navy-colored clothes.) I developed—out of nowhere—a fondness for dull thick shoes with sensible heels. I used to love kitten-heel shoes; now I was lacing up Doc Martens. Docs!

I stopped wearing makeup, cut off my hair, and stopped coloring it. Catching sight of myself in the mirror one day, I wondered, *When did I become a lesbian?*

My personality flatlined. I used to be high-spirited; always game for a bit of fun. Laugh? I'd laugh plenty and tell dirty jokes, to boot. But all that evaporated. Gone. Just like that.

This metamorphosis had all the markings of a midlife crisis, but in the deepest reaches of my being I knew it was not; it was the long beginning of an awkward awakening.

What I did not realize at the time was that my actions were typical of someone wrestling with post-traumatic stress. The desexing, the defiance against the status quo are as much a reaction as they are coping mechanisms for those of us who have sustained physical and emotional abuse.

In advance of my long stay in Whitby, I decided to spend a few weeks at St. Cecilia's Abbey, home to a community of Benedictine nuns on the Isle of Wight. They were renowned for their Gregorian chant, and I longed to bathe in that music so that its crystalline sounds could flow over me and flush away the toxins of cynicism, weariness, pride, shame, hurt, anger, disappointment, fear, stress—oh, it was a long list—and purify me.

However, St. Cecilia's could only accommodate me for a week, so it was suggested that I contact the monks at nearby Quarr Abbey. I had never heard of Quarr Abbey—not that a males-only monastery would have been on the radar of a wannabe nun—but nonetheless, I sent off an email to its guestmaster, who accepted my booking for the week preceding my stay at St. Cecilia's. A week at Quarr would, I reasoned, ease me into the routine of religious life.

St. Benedict was not a fan of religious tire-kickers. He considered these "gyratory monks" to be aimless, "restless servants to their own will and appetites." What choice did I have? Either I risked Benedict's scourge for being a dilettante or I ignored the tug inside me that propelled me on my way.

Both Quarr and St. Cecilia's were Roman Catholic communities, but given my dual religious upbringing and my ease at toggling between the Anglican and Roman Catholic traditions, I did not think it would be a problem.

Meanwhile, Colin, bless his heart, offered to drive me from London to the Isle of Wight and drop me off at Quarr.

As much as I tried to remain upbeat about my upcoming journey, the truth was that I was scared. Now I was working through two issues: finding out whether I was being called to be a nun, and finding resolution to the rape.

God never makes these things easy.

3

Battling Demons

. . . .

Quarr Abbey
Isle of Wight, England

M Y FIANCÉ IS *driving me to a nunnery.*

The words drummed steadily in my mind like a mantra as I tried to make sense of the ludicrous reality of it all. I turned my face toward the passenger window and quietly shook my head. *Why does my life have to be this weird?*

Colin's car clipped along the A36 (or was it the M2?) through the Somerset countryside (or were we in Wiltshire now?) toward Southampton and to the ferry that would take us to the Isle of Wight.

My mind was swirling with enough what-ifs, whys, and what-was-I-thinking admonishments to trigger a breakdown. Perhaps that was where I was headed: toward a breakdown. I invoked some calming strategies—deep slow breaths, imagining a blackboard eraser wiping clean the clutter in my brain, even commanding myself to relax—*Relax!*—but nothing

worked for long. I tried to distract myself by turning my attention to the English countryside that was whizzing past the car
window—*Look how green everything is! Like spring! The leaves on
the holly and azalea bushes are so glossy you can practically see your
reflection in them. You'd never get a January like this in Canada.*
But as soon as I locked onto the lichen-covered tree limbs,
vines, and tree trunks, my thoughts disassembled into word
association: *They look like they've been wrapped in a mossy veil
of chiffon. Veil. Gown. Wedding.* Gulp. The distraction-therapy
tactics came to a screeching halt, and the mantra resumed: *My
fiancé is driving me to a nunnery.*

I alternated between weepiness and excitement. I couldn't
decide whether I was doing the right thing or the wrong thing.
A babble of voices in my head jeered in unison: *Why are you
doing this? Are you mad?* Each time that happened, the Voice
Within would calmly intervene: *Have faith. There's a reason
for this. Keep going.* I was beginning to wish I had never paid
attention to those voices.

We missed the entrance to Quarr Abbey, not once but twice.
On the third attempt we spotted a small sign partially obscured
by dry, desiccated vines at the edge of a narrow roughly paved
driveway and turned in. The car bounced over and around ruts
and potholes as Colin steered it with care. It lent a jaunty air
to the excursion, and combined with the unusually sunny and
warm January weather, it felt like we were going on a picnic.

The road eventually brought us to an uneven parking area
set amid barns and garages.

I got out of the car, stretched my legs, and took a measure
of the place.

Quarr Abbey's rose and yellow brick bell tower loomed
over us. It was a curious style of architecture: a fusion of
Moorish, medieval, and masonic sensibilities that made you

wonder whether the architect had been channeling Fritz Lang. The dome of the bell tower resembled a minaret topped by a squat cross. On the main building, sharp triangular shapes like eyebrows raised in surprise topped the stylized gothic windows; broad gothic arches marked doorways; and the partially crenellated façades and blind arches gave the monastery a severe, almost militaristic look.

By contrast, the landscaping was soft and undulating, from the serpentine contours of the flower beds and hedges to the rise and dips of the terrain. Tall, dark green iron fencing delineated the gardens from the main buildings, and benches and pieces of religious statuary encouraged contemplation. Everything pointed to a property tended with great care and affection, a place where peace and stillness were sacraments.

(3:ii)

"I'M AFRAID, because you're, um, female, you can't eat in the refectory with us. We'll serve you your meals in this dining room instead. I'll make sure the door is left open between the two rooms, though, so you feel part of us. Oh, and you can't enter the church through this door: it leads to our cloister and, well, men only, you know. Your room is on this floor: you can't stay upstairs, because that area is for men only, too."

In the space of thirty seconds, Father Nicholas had uttered three *can't*s. The word caused a jerking reflex in my shoulders.

As Quarr's guestmaster, Father Nicholas had the duty of providing an orientation to guests. His slightly rushed delivery left the impression he would rather be doing something else.

The three of us were standing in a long, narrow dining room where I would take my meals. The dining-room table, which ran almost the length of the room, easily accommodated the dozen chairs that had been neatly arranged around it. A side counter held a toaster, bread, coffee mugs, and kettle; on a far wall stood two massive and somewhat forbidding wardrobes that I guessed served as pantries for cereal boxes and dishes. A pair of doors, now closed, separated the dining room from the monks' refectory. I was hoping Father Nicholas would permit a peek.

"Let me show you your room."

Guess not.

He turned on his heel and headed out of the dining room, his voluminous black habit swishing and fluttering in his wake.

Colin and I scurried after him like children, down a long white corridor on the main floor of the abbey's guest wing. Halfway down the hall, Father Nicholas stopped abruptly at a door on the right-hand side, drew a key from beneath his black scapular, unlocked the door, and flung it open.

The room was adorable, if that isn't too girly a description for a monastic cell. The walls were white; the floors were polished natural pine. The door and window frames, skirting boards, fireplace mantel, and window shutters were painted a pale sage. All the furniture was natural pine: a single bed—which had a neatly folded stack of crisp white linens atop a pale green bedspread—a bedside table with drawers, two chairs, and a desk in the corner. The window faced a courtyard abutting a quaint-looking outbuilding that housed Quarr's book and gift shop. There was an en suite with tiled terracotta floors, a pine tongue-and-groove ceiling inset with pot lights, a small tiled shower, and a large bowl-shaped sink fashioned out of polished concrete or stone that sat on the tiled countertop. It was all very fresh and modern.

"Does this work?" I asked excitedly, pointing to the fireplace and envisioning cozy evenings curled up with my Bible in front of a cheerful fire.

"Ah, no," Father Nicholas said with a tight smile, as in, "Nice try."

"This is quite nice," Colin murmured with surprise as he surveyed the room, his hands clasped behind his back like a police officer conducting an inspection. It was a posture that came naturally to Colin because he was, in fact, a police officer, though a more unlikely member of the London Met you will not find. He had been sure of his vocation, certain that joining the police would enable him to help people and make society better. (We are all eventually disillusioned by our chosen vocations.)

I was pleased that Colin was concentrating on the physical surroundings rather than on the fact that he was dropping off his fiancée at a monastery so that she could decide whether to marry him or be a nun. If he felt any weirdness or discomfort, he never let on. I would like to think that I would have been equally magnanimous if he were the one exploring a religious vocation. I glanced up at him and imagined him in a black cassock and scapular.

I had been unsure how to introduce Colin to Father Nicholas. To call him my fiancé seemed contradictory, given that I had told Father Nicholas I was discerning a religious vocation. "Boyfriend" sounded desperate, and "friend" would have sounded denigrating to Colin. In the end I just stammered over it all until Father Nicholas, rocking on his heels and looking at Colin, jumped in with a jovial, "So, you're the one who brought her, eh?"

I guessed Father Nicholas to be in his mid-fifties. He was of medium height and build—though it is tricky to determine someone's physique when it is hidden beneath a shapeless floor-length habit—and he had short, wispy light brown hair. I could not determine whether the crown of his head bore a tonsure or indicated naturally thinning hair. His dark-framed glasses gave his long, sharp features an engagingly nerdy and punctilious quality; he struck me as the type who, as a young-ster, probably relished reminding the teacher to assign home-work. He was chatty, perhaps more out of nervousness than a desire to be chatty. He didn't appear to favor eye contact. When he became excited or agitated, his arms flapped like a penguin's wings.

"We don't really have anything written down for you, but here's the schedule: vigils at five-thirty—doubt you'll make that; lauds at seven; then breakfast, followed by Mass at nine. Then it's…"

Whoa, buddy! He rhymed it off so quickly I could not keep up. There was a mention of lunch, but when was that again?

"… by which time it's vespers at five, supper at seven, and then it's topped off with compline at eight-thirty. Of course, you don't have to come to any of the offices, you're free to do whatever you like—walk around the gardens, walk into town, read, whatever you fancy. So, shall I leave you to say goodbye to each other?"

And with that Father Nicholas swooshed out of the room. The sound of the door closing echoed loudly.

Silence hung like humidity between Colin and me. We embraced stiffly and lightly at first to avoid the stickiness of the situation, but gradually our bodies melded together in their natural way. *Who knows: this might be the last time I hug a man.* We reconfirmed that he would pick me up in Yorkshire at the end of my convent crawl, in three and a half months.

As we walked to the parking lot, I kept up a light patter to prevent the conversation from veering into the maudlin and to keep my own doubts at bay. "Aren't the grounds beautiful?" "I wonder if there are other guests here." "Not sure this place has Wi-Fi, so don't get worried if I don't email." "How long do you expect it will take you to drive back to London?"

The next thing I knew, I was waving goodbye as his little car vanished into a cloud of gravel dust.

(3:iii)

I WANDERED back to my cell and sat on the edge of the bed in a state of mild shock with only that nagging, recurrent question for company: *What the hell am I doing here?* How much easier and more fun it would be to plan a wedding and a celebratory reception, to mull ideas for a honeymoon, or to shop for furniture and feather our future nest—maybe a quaint stone cottage in Devon for the two of us to grow old in—than go into a sort of self-imposed exile to see whether I was really meant to live a silent and austere life.

I lay down on the bed and stared at the ceiling, trying to connect the dots of reason. Had I been too hasty, too naïve about all this?

Enough with the second-guessing already, the Voice Within cried with exasperation. *Stop beating yourself up and just accept it.* The Voice Within was sounding less like Dumbledore and more like Jackie Mason.

Of course, I thought, stiffening my resolve. *Others climb mountains, run marathons, join the army, or run for political office. I happen to search for God. Nothing weird about that. Is there? My*

time with the Sisters of St. John the Divine had been, well, divine.
Why would this be anything less?

One major difference was that the moment I had walked
through the doors of St. John the Divine, the sisters, bless their
organized little hearts, had handed me a carefully prepared
package of information that included a schedule. At Quarr I
was completely without guidance or reference, save for that
speedy recitation that Father Nicholas gave, and I could not
remember half of it.

I recalled a mantra I had adopted when I was in my early
twenties: *"Be willing to wait, and listen to the Lord."* The words
had jumped out from a speech I was covering as a reporter
in a small town. I had sat in the audience, rueful and antsy
that I was wasting my time listening to this snake-oil salesman
thump at the podium when I could be sending out résumés
to get myself out of this two-bit town. And then he said those
words, and it was as if he was speaking directly to my heart.
As soon as I began repeating the phrase to myself, it was as
if I became unstuck, that opportunities began to open up for
me. Since then, whenever I have found myself burdened by
impatience or worry, the restorative powers of those words
bring resolution. Now I summoned them again: *ok, God, I'm
listening. Start talking.*

I sat for a few moments and waited.

And waited.

No God.

Ah, He was probably busy with someone else. Eventually,
I lost patience with the tension of the silence. I walked to the
door of my bedroom and opened it gingerly: I looked down
the long hall, to the left and to the right, but no one was
around. Not a peep. I closed the door as silently as I could.

As I checked my watch, a distant bell tolled signaling the call to prayer. I convinced myself that it was much too soon after my arrival to go to church, so I pulled a newspaper from my suitcase and proceeded to do two sudoku puzzles.

A little later, the bell tolled again, this time for vespers. It was now five o'clock. Again I demurred, deciding my time was better spent unpacking my luggage.

I unzipped my suitcase and carefully withdrew each piece of clothing from my 2011 Winter Nun Collection. I shook out each item, appraised it for imperfections and creases, then folded it up and reverently placed it in the drawer of the chest that doubled as a bedside table.

It was a pitiful assortment. One big pile of monochromatic dull. More depressing was that most were new purchases. No heart-pumping colors; no red, fuchsia, mustard, sage, emerald, turquoise, amethyst. Just a morose palette of brown, gray, black, and for a jolt of color, navy. It was certainly serviceable: three pairs of trousers (brown, black, navy), two skirts (black, gray), one dress (brown), four tops to mix and match with the aforementioned, and one sweater (the color of porridge). The nail polish I used to wear on my toes had been downgraded from hellfire red to a pearly but boring beige.

But so what, I told myself with a forced jauntiness. *I'm going to be a nun, and clothes no longer matter to me. Right? Right?*

Father Nicholas had said something about seven o'clock and dinner, so at the appointed hour I sauntered down the hall to the dining room. No one was about. The double doors that separated the dining room from the monks' refectory were still closed. I pulled on one of them to sneak a peek. A scratchy creak emanated from the hinges and echoed embarrassingly.

The refectory was cavernous. Broad, low brick arches rippled the length of the room like the way sound waves are depicted in illustrations. Five or six narrow trestlelike tables, each with bottles and jars of condiments clustered in the center, and three or four chairs apiece, were lined up on opposite sides of the room, facing each other. The room could easily handle many more, and still have room for a dance floor. I did a quick calculation based on the number of tables and chairs in the room and figured that twenty-four monks must live here. Aside from Father Nicholas, I hadn't seen any others.

I pricked my ears for a sound or movement. Nothing. The door creaked again as I slowly pushed it shut, and then I scuttled over to the solitary place at the table that had been neatly set for me. I stood patiently at my place, not knowing what the protocol demanded. It was a little like Alice waiting for something to happen in Wonderland.

Suddenly, shuffling sounds came from behind the refectory doors. I held my breath and cocked an ear. A voice murmured something and a group of male voices responded in mumbled unison: "Amen."

ok, they're saying grace, I cleverly deduced. Then more shuffling, followed by the sound of chairs dragging across the floor. Someone—I did not see the face—pushed open one of the refectory doors. I craned my head to the left and saw a monk in profile seated at a table. I took that as my cue to sit down. I waited, almost afraid to breathe in case I missed some dog-whistled direction.

The silence was broken by the clattering sound of a trolley, which was pushed through the doorway by a tall, thin monk who looked a bit like Sting. I wasn't sure whether I was supposed to look at him, so I kept my head bowed and whispered "Thank you" as he ladled out my dinner. From the corner of my eye I saw him bow slightly before taking his leave. I nodded humbly in reply.

Impressive. My own serving monk. It made me feel a bit like visiting royalty. *What if I were visiting royalty? Traveling incognito—which would explain the suitcase of drab clothes—to escape some diabolical court intrigue or workplace shenanigans. Quarr was the safe house.*

I ate my food in undisturbed silence, entertained by my little fantasy. From time to time I checked back into reality and craned my neck to see what was going on in the refectory, but I could not really see anything; nor could I gauge the rhythm of the meal. *Or maybe I was smuggling in some secret Vatican document.*

When I finished eating, I placed my knife and fork on my plate in the customary fashion that royalty does and waited, hands folded serenely on my lap. The way the Queen does.

Father Sting reappeared and removed my dirty dishes. Again, eye contact was avoided. He bowed as he took his leave. I nodded thanks. There was no offer of coffee or tea, an after-dinner liqueur, an invitation to join the monks for cigars or a game of billiards or to watch TV.

I waited in silence for someone to tell me what to do. After several minutes I leaned my head to the left to see why the place had fallen so inexplicably quiet. It was then that I discovered that the room had emptied out! *Well! That was rude! They could have at least told me.*

I hauled my royal self up from my chair, bowed my head, said a brief and silent prayer of thanks for my dinner, and harrumphed back to my cell.

I stood in the middle of the room wondering what to do next. Compline was at eight-thirty, and I decided I had better attend. My belongings had been unpacked; books were lined up like soldiers at the head of my desk; my toiletries neatly arranged on the bathroom countertop. The room looked rather homey.

There was a knock at the door. It was so unusual to hear sound after such a great swath of silence that I hesitated in answering it in case I had imagined it.

But when I cautiously opened the door, there stood a monk who beamed with friendliness.

"Hi. I'm Luke."

Father Luke and I had corresponded briefly by email before my arrival—he was the cousin of a friend of mine—and it was a delight to finally meet him in person. In appearance and manner he reminded me of my friend, and this sense of familiarity erased my doubts and put me at ease. Plus, it was great to have someone to talk to. It had been four hours since I had uttered a word.

Father Luke, however, was not the garrulous sort. He was a thoughtful, intellectual man given to long pauses when a question was posed. He also possessed a deferential manner, and when he spoke his head was bowed, eyes fixed on the ground. It was the posture of humility St. Benedict urged for his monks in the *Rule:* "Whether he is in the oratory, at the work of God, in the monastery or garden, on a trip, in the fields; whether sitting, standing or walking—he must think of his sins, head down, eyes on the ground and imagine he is on trial before God."

Born an Anglican, Father Luke had converted to Roman Catholicism in his thirties. He had been a teacher before he became a monk, as well as a parish priest and a prison chaplain. He was a literary fellow—he had written a few books—and fittingly, he was in charge of Quarr's bookshop. He had been at Quarr for seven years, having left a previous community—he did not elaborate on the circumstances—and he said that his relocation to the Isle of Wight had been a natural homecoming.

"I used to come to the Isle of Wight as a child with my parents on holiday. It was a very happy time for me, a golden time, and to come here was always special because it was a place apart from our ordinary lives. When I came to Quarr it was, in some ways, a return to those memories, a place that I could return as a child—as a child of God. Now, what about you? Tell me about your interest in a religious vocation."

I told him about my time with the sisters at St. John the Divine and about my engagement to Colin. He listened thoughtfully, his hands folded under his black scapular.

"Both—marriage and religious life—are huge commitments," he said before retreating into lengthy silence. He pursed his lips and occasionally nodded his head of silvery curls while staring at the floor intently, as if it held divine knowledge.

When it looked as if the poor man had taken on my quandary as a sort of life's work—or he had zoned out and was thinking of something entirely different—I broke the silence.

"Seems to be a big monastery."

"It is," he nodded solemnly. "A big place for eight monks."

"Only eight?" I thought back to St. John's and how the sisters were freaking out that they were down to about thirty active sisters. "Well, at least you get some sort of subsidy from the church to keep the place running."

A smile broke across his face, and he lifted his gaze, his eyes twinkling at me over his wire-rimmed glasses: "Now, that's funny."

"You mean you don't?"

He chuckled softly, which is the monastic equivalent of a belly laugh.

"No, not at all. We survive solely on donations and earnings."

"How do you earn money?"

"We have a piggery, an apiary—they're closed at this time of year, otherwise I'd show them to you—we have this guest house, and we operate a small bookbinding business. There's also the bookshop and the tearoom. We live very close to the bone."

This was an astonishing revelation. I had assumed, like many others, that churches financially supported their religious orders. When your business solely supports the traditions of a larger operation, you would think that would entitle you to some assistance from head office. Artists get subsidized; why shouldn't monks and nuns?

Before I could probe further, Father Luke jolted, and looked at his watch.

"Almost time for compline. I've got to go. You coming?"

Not wanting to be chalked up as a plastic monastic, I got up, too.

We walked down the hall of the guesthouse and paused in the vestibule.

"You have to go out that way," he said, pointing to the door that led outside. "This door adjoins our cloister, and, you know…"

"Yes, men only," I smiled.

I stumbled out into the dark, cold January night and made my way toward the church door.

(3:iv)

IT WAS the aroma that hit me first, though all my senses tingled to attention the moment I entered the dimly lit interior of the Abbey of Our Lady of Quarr.

The thick, sweetly pungent scent of a century's worth of incense had permeated every inch of the church—its bricks, mortar, and stone floors—and as if recognizing a fresh and available receptacle, it rushed toward me, penetrating my skin and bones. My body welcomed it happily, as if reuniting with some long-lost opposite.

Gradually, my eyes registered the cave-like interior. Being somewhat of a troglodyte, I found it appealing in an aesthetic sense, but also in a monastic sense because it was a reminder of early Christianity's humble roots in faintly lit, secretive settings.

Quarr's church looked nothing like a traditional church. There was a lower nave with several rows of chairs. A set of five broad stone steps brought you to the upper nave. Was this an architectural statement about the separation of the secular and monastic worlds? In the upper nave, about ten rows of chairs were arranged on each side to create a central aisle, followed by two rows of dark-wood choir stalls facing each other on either side of the nave. In front of this was the sanctuary.

A series of broad gothic-style and blind arches spanned the width of the interior, and ran the length of the church to create a tunnel effect, rising to a vaulted and ribbed brick ceiling. It looked a lot like the refectory. The combination of soldiered brick on the inside of the arches and linear coursing on the walls gave a sense of texture and subtle movement.

It was a remarkably simple church; no grand works of art; indeed, no decoration at all, just a powerful sense of being in the presence of something immense and holy.

Dom Paul Bellot was the genius behind this design. Born in France, he had trained as an architect before joining the Solesmes order in 1902 just as it was fleeing into exile on the

Isle of Wight. He never expected to practice his profession once he took holy vows, but he humbly accepted the commission from his fellow brothers to build new Quarr Abbey.

Bellot was perfect for the job because only a monk could best understand the monastic mindset and therefore create according to God, not according to man. It was easy to see why, upon completion in 1911, that it was deemed a revolutionary and controversial design.

Just then, a door opened behind me, and a cluster of monks filed in, cowls pulled over their bent heads. The snap and flutter of their habits sounded like a flock of swans about to lift off.

They took their places—four a side—in the choir stalls, and without ceremony, a single voice began to chant, *"Deus, in adjutorium meum intende."*

Eight deep voices fell into unison, and their chant reverberated through the church. Although the language was Latin, I recognized the melodies of a few chants that the sisters used during compline at St. John the Divine, particularly the Nunc Dimittis with its haunting and plaintive plea: *Salva nos, Domine, vigilantes, custodi nos dormientes, ut vigilemus cum Christo et requiescamus in pace. (Save us, O Lord, as we watch, guard us as we sleep, that we may watch with Christ, and that we may rest in peace.)*

The soothing and pulsing rhythm of the chants softened my earlier doubts about a religious vocation, and I felt pulled back into spiritual alignment. Their hypnotic quality recalibrated my breathing and returned it to a calmer, deeper form.

It is hard to believe that when Vatican II was issued in the 1960s, it marked Gregorian chant's fall from grace. It was not exactly jettisoned from worship, but since Vatican II was all about modernity, it rendered Gregorian chant archaic and opened the floodgates to guitar-strumming cantors who were generally awkward, pathetic, or both. Dodgy interpretations of and assumptions about Vatican II kicked to the curb a thousand years of Gregorian chant. Why would anyone chuck something so universally synonymous with religious faith? Chant is practically the brand of the church.

Gregorian chant grew out of the pre-Christian chants heard in Middle Eastern temples and evolved over an eight-hundred-year period from the sixth to the fourteenth century. It stands as one of the shining legacies of the not-so Dark Ages. "Gregorian" comes from Gregory I (540–604), who did not compose a staff of music but just happened to be on the papal throne when Christianity and chant were exploding across the Roman Empire and into Britain.

Chant's minimalist melodies were created to convert Holy Scripture into song. During early Christian times, singers were considered the bridge between Heaven and Earth, and it was believed that the human voice alone brought audiences into direct contact with the Divine. Musical instruments were considered sacrilegious in worship.

Melodies were developed in the evening when candles were ablaze and the faithful were huddled in secrecy during the frequent periods of persecution. Learned by heart and passed from one generation to the next, chant found its way into daily worship, particularly into the offices of monastic communities, where it remained a central and integral liturgical device.

When the Vatican effectively gave the heave-ho to chant, a curious thing happened to the nuns and monks: they became lethargic, and many got sick. The sense of hearing connects and resonates directly to the heart, but when doctors studied the phenomenon of the fatigued nuns and monks, they discovered something remarkable about brains and ears and Gregorian chant: a well-tuned ear takes the sounds we utter and stimulates the brain by charging the cerebral cortex with electrical charges. In other words, vocal sounds act like antioxidants: the higher the frequency, the greater the impact.

Some cultures have a higher count of electrical charges in their language than others. British English, for example, has an extremely high count—2,000 to 12,000 hertz (or cycles per second); French has 1,000 to 2,000 hertz; North American English has a paltry 800 to 3,000 hertz. Try saying a monotonic phrase such as "Hey, how's it going" and then mimic a chirpy British voice saying, "Jolly good, Major!" You can *hear* the difference, but more importantly, you can *feel* it.

When researchers probed further, they found that Gregorian chant contains all the frequencies of the voice spectrum—7,000 to 9,000 hertz. Without this daily dose of brain zaps, it was little wonder that the monks and nuns were getting sick.

These hits of auditory electrical charges benefit not only the singer but also the listeners of chant who follow the same pattern of deep, peaceful breathing as the chanters. Furthermore, chant's rhythmic pattern mimics the gentle ebbing and flowing of water, the source of life.

Though it might on the surface look easy, it actually takes years of practice to master chant. For starters, a novice has to completely subsume his or her personality—chant is no place for the Céline Dions and Pavarottis of the world. The novice must learn to sing at the same pitch as her fellow chanters, sustaining vowels and articulating final consonants in effort-less unison, breathing in the same places, and controlling that breath through long lines of mostly Latin Scripture. The secret is to develop a resonating cavity not only in the mouth and throat but in the entire body: chant is about producing a gorgeous sound, yes, but it is also about internalizing the Word of God.

I can still remember the hypnotizing effect when I first heard Gregorian chant as a teenager. It was as if the music had communicated something inside me. There was a shudder of primordial recognition, and finally a transcendent sense of reverence, as if the universe suddenly made sense. The experience was calming and made me feel as if I belonged to something big and profound. It made me feel connected to God.

Of course, Gregorian chant wasn't exactly on the Billboard Hot 100 back then, but whenever I took a break from banging my head to Steppenwolf, Cream, Black Sabbath, and Led Zeppelin and tossed my sole chant recording onto the turntable, I would drift off to a land of peaceful misty landscapes and heavenly shafts of sunlight.

Like heavy metal, chant is one of the few types of music that improves with volume. Crank it up, and that ethereal echo-like quality will make it sound as if the chant is coming directly from Heaven.

It is also impossible to entertain a bad or negative thought while listening to chant. It has a cleansing quality, like a sorbet that neutralizes the frenzy of life.

Because of the misinterpretation of Vatican II, papal HQ had to reiterate its support for chant, and the musical form trickled back into its monasteries and convents. Nowadays, those are the only places you hear it sung, and a great shame that is, because no other period in civilization like our present could benefit more from its restorative powers.

(3:v)

AS HAPPENED during my time with the sisters at St. John the Divine, I fell quickly and easily into the monks' routine at Quarr. During the offices, I followed along in Latin as best I could and adopted the monks' custom of bowing low every time the doxology was invoked: *Gloria Patri et Filio et Spiritui Sancto: sicut erat in principio, et nunc, et semper, et in saecula saeculorum. Amen. (Glory to the Father and to the Son and to the Holy Spirit: as it was in the beginning is now and ever shall be, world without end. Amen.)*

Occasionally my mind drifted from the page to the monks themselves. They looked to range in age between forty and ninety-plus. One was big and burly; another had a trim gray beard. I had learned through the monk-vine of their diverse backgrounds—construction worker, electrical engineer, marine biologist, teacher, rare-books expert—and that their vocation as monks required them to take up a host of other duties for which they had little previous training: landscaper, infirmarian, housekeeper, guestmaster, bookkeeper, historian.

I scrutinized their inscrutable faces for signs of boredom or rebelliousness. Did it bug them to repeat the same psalms every Tuesday? Did they regret their vocation or privately wonder about how their lives might have turned out had they married or chosen to serve God in the secular world? Had their natures been truly tamed? How did they manage all the physical work at Quarr and still maintain a worship schedule that could be described as a spiritual Ironman triathlon? Did they just accept their lives and get on with it? I wanted to get into a penetrating discussion with them, but at the same time I was mindful about overstepping the bounds of propriety. In my previous life as a journalist, probing questions were a basic necessity for gathering information; now they struck me as intrusive and nosy.

I arrived the next day for Mass to discover that it was the feast honoring the Presentation of Our Lord in the Temple, the day Jesus was formally introduced by his parents to the temple elders. Also known as Candlemas, the feast marks the official end of Christmas.

There were a half dozen people in the congregation that day, five more than there were most days. We assembled in the lower nave and were handed thin tapers by the abbot and monks, who were dressed in white habits and cowls with white embroidered chasubles draped around their shoulders.

With candles lit, we lined up behind the monks to begin the procession. To my delighted surprise, the procession headed through the cloister door. *Finally, a legitimate peek into the guys-only zone!* I was thrilled to bits.

It was a rainy, gusty day, and as we filed beneath the cloister porch chanting Latin hymns and shielding our candles from the threat of extinguishment, billowing clouds of incense engulfed us as the thurifer swung the gold censer rhythmically from left to right. It was an extraordinary experience, almost otherworldly. I glimpsed snippets of the cloister and its courtyard of manicured shrubs and gardens, and of statuary and benches. It no doubt looked nicer in better weather.

The line processed back into the church, where Mass continued partly in English, partly in Latin. It was all so mysterious and profound, and the incense choked the atmosphere like dense fog. I was so caught up in the pageantry and mysticism that I allowed myself to be drawn toward the altar with the other worshippers for Communion. There the spell was broken. I prepared to receive the host, then suddenly remembered that I was forbidden by Catholic doctrine to do so. Whereas Anglicans extend Holy Communion to anyone who believes in God—theoretically a Jew or a Muslim could receive Communion—the Catholic way is nowhere near as accommodating. Thus I found myself gritting my teeth and glumly crossing my arms across my chest as a signal that I was "other." It was degrading, like attending a party and being told you had to sit at the children's table. A spine of rebellion repositioned itself within me. I tried not to appear like a grumpy communicant as the abbot made the sign of the cross above my head and murmured a blessing in Latin, which for all I knew was *"Shame on you for not being a Catholic."*

(3:vi)

I PADDED down the hall the following morning to the guest lounge, where I found Father Nicholas absentmindedly arranging the coffee mugs and biscuit tins on the countertop.

I had spent the previous few days worshipping, walking, reading—the Bible and Merton, mostly—and sleeping. I felt wonderful; I radiated calmness. How could I not? I was living in a spiritual Eden that expected nothing of me except to love and praise God. During my daily walks, I performed my self-directed duties as an itinerant nun-in-training: I greeted strangers and asked God to watch over them. I blessed the birds and wild animals, the players lining up their shots on the golf course. I prayed for peace, for England, for Canada, and for full tummies and warm shelter for the destitute.

In the evenings, when I walked back to the guest house after compline, I stood unafraid in the cold darkness, my head tilted back, mesmerized by a vivid dome of stars. The cosmos never looked so wondrous, so immense.

But boredom began to creep in. A kind of spiritual stupor had taken hold, and I was sleeping more than was good for me. I had missed three consecutive offices, and if I hoped to be a nun, that sort of slackness would never do. I needed to show a bit more productivity.

Seeing Father Nicholas moving the biscuit tins around gave me my opportunity.

"If there's anything you'd like me to do, please let me know. I don't care how menial it is," I beseeched him.

His response was not what I expected.

"What is it with you people?" he chided, flapping his arms in a show of annoyance. "People come here to escape the chaos of the secular world, and then they go barmy with the silence."

His voice softened when he noticed my chastened look.

"Look, the whole point is that contemplation is meant to make you so quiet that you can hear God speaking to you."

"I'm not sure God intends me to be so idle," I pouted.

"I think He does," said Father Nicholas. "Maybe you should enjoy it while you can."

For so many years I had been frenetically active, busy to the point of wondering how I was able to cram so much into a single day. Busyness had become an addiction. Now that I had my wish for tranquility, my body and mind were bucking the peaceful nonsense and craving the next hit of adrenaline and stimulation.

I moved closer to Father Nicholas and fiddled with the biscuit tins and coffee mugs, too. I asked him how he came to be at Quarr.

He said he had initially trained as an Anglican priest, but after serving in a parish church he decided he was more cut out to be a monk. Once he became a monk, he realized that his sympathies were more closely aligned to Roman Catholicism than Anglicanism, so he converted and changed communities. He became a Catholic monk and then a monk/priest. Like Father Luke, he had bolted from the Anglican fold. Was everyone bailing on the Church of England?

Somehow our conversation wound its way around to the topic of abortion. Spend ten minutes in the company of a Catholic, and "abortion" is guaranteed to flare up.

"I don't know what it's like in Canada, but it's a huge issue here," Father Nicholas insisted. "Under-sixteen pregnancies are epidemic in Britain—the highest in Europe—and young women are aborting in astronomical numbers. Seven hundred baby deaths a day!"

His arms were really flapping now. "I studied Vatican II, and there is nothing in there about contraceptives."

"Then why is this an issue?" I asked. "If the abortion campaign by the church has been so prolonged and vociferous, why hasn't it worked? And if contraception isn't in Vatican II, then how come the church won't promote it as a way to stem abortions?"

"Secular politics," he said, peering at me over his filmy glasses. "That's the problem. Government has put money into abortion counseling, but they haven't put any money into pro-life counseling. Governments are in the business of killing: birth control, abortion, eugenics, euthanasia, war. They're handing out condoms to ten-year-old boys, for heaven's sake. Gosh, when I was ten I wouldn't know what to do with a condom."

Father Nicholas was distrustful of politicians, and he expressed reservations about Tony Blair's conversion to Catholicism. "And Cherie Blair is RC, but she campaigns on the pro-choice side." Among traditional Catholics, the two were pariahs.

Father Nicholas liked his religion and his politics clean, simple, and unwavering.

"That's one of the problems I have with Anglicanism," he said. "You can never get a straight answer on anything. At least with the Catholics you know where you stand. The Anglicans are all over the map. They debate the theology ad nauseam; everything to them is open to interpretation. By doing that you have nothing to hold on to, nothing to firmly stick in the ground."

"Is that why you converted to Catholicism?" I asked.

"The constant back-and-forth debate on things was a big factor. I'm all for debate, but it's become insane. It's like, like..."—Father Nicholas had become exasperated, and he sputtered and swung his arms trying to find the right words—"... like the whole institution is run by a committee of academics! Everyone has an opinion, and no one has the guts to make a firm declaration."

"Exactly!" I blurted, stabbing the air with my finger. "I've felt the same way for ages. What is it with Anglicans that makes them that way?"

Father Nicholas exhaled loudly and shook his head. The Anglican Church/Church of England can drive you so mad with frustration that you want to quit. Debates can and do last decades and generations. When a decision does get made, it is written with spectacular vagueness, leaving the decision open to further debate. Even in name, the church is a glaring indication of an institution-wide inability to reach consensus. The church is variously referred to as the Anglican Church, the Church of England, and the Episcopal Church. They are all autonomous churches linked to the Anglican tradition, but there is only a hazy central, universal authority and leader. Meanwhile, go to England, the States, Australia, Canada, South Africa, China, Poland, and you will find the Roman Catholic Church rendered as the Roman Catholic Church. Everywhere. Woody Allen once quipped, "The Roman Catholic Church is the only true 'The' church."

Evidence of Anglicanism's flimsy foundation was all around. The day before, while out for a walk, I had wandered into the churchyard of the forlorn-looking Church of the Holy Cross in the village of Binstead. There was no information to be found on the history of the place, and the so-called welcome board did not so much as list the name of the priest. All contact information had been redacted except for a line saying that there was a service at eight on Sunday morning. There was no sign indicating that the church even belonged to the Church of England—I learned that later from the Catholics at Quarr. In fact, I would find similarly redacted signs on several Anglican churches throughout Ryde during my stay on the island. Why was this happening?

For a faith that was essentially born out of a tyrant's temper tantrum, Anglicanism has evolved into one of the most flexible of mainstream denominations. Indecisive for sure, but also generally tolerant. Still, the Anglican Church seemed to be afflicted with a self-sabotaging gene, and it was worrying me.

The more I thought about the words of Fathers Nicholas and Luke, the more it raised my doubts about Anglicanism. Was it better to belong to a strict faith in which you quietly bent the rules, or belong to a flexible faith with rubbery rules?

I thought more deeply about my own experience as an Anglican. Many of the Anglican priests of my acquaintance *were* like academics: distracted, unhelpful, and afflicted with a strong sense of nose-in-the-air superiority. Of the twenty-five or so clergy I have personally known, all but three or four had been insufferable snobs, so much so that it was the pompous attitude of its priests, not the fuzzy doctrine itself, that was driving away me and others from the church. I once overheard a priest denigrate another parishioner behind the parishioner's back for the heinous crime of pronouncing Magdalen College as *mag-da-lin* rather than the obtuse pronunciation of *mawd-lin*. Who does that?

Wait a minute: What the hell was going on? My spiritual journey was supposed to be about becoming a nun, and here it was being hijacked by religion and semantics. Was this where I, a cradle Anglican, was being led? To switch teams? Or was my desire to be a nun more about finding Christian authenticity? I wanted religion without the busyness, the bitchiness, and the bullshit, but the only places that seemed to offer pure, unadulterated spiritual nourishment were convents and monasteries.

(3:vii)

QUARR'S MONASTIC day began at five-thirty with vigils, but as Father Nicholas so keenly pointed out when I first arrived, it was doubtful I would be putting in an appearance at that hour.

My own monastic day started with lauds at seven o'clock.

Lauds means praise, and of all the offices, it is the one that most brims with positivity. Lauds and compline were my favorite offices, the bookends of my day. I loved the chants at compline and the psalms at lauds. While compline acted as a lullaby, lauds was my wake-up call, coaxing my senses into consciousness like fragile young plants shaking off the morning dew.

As the monks prayed Psalm 97, which exhorts, "Shout to the Lord all the earth, ring out your joy," the pale winter sun streamed through the amber glass windows of the abbey church, igniting the day.

I often headed out for a walk after breakfast. I was girded with an explorer's enthusiasm, not quite sure where I was heading or for what reason but thrilled nonetheless to be in new and unfamiliar surroundings. It's true: it is easier to see beauty in the world when you don't have to slog for a living each day, when you no longer have to worry about your every output being constantly analyzed and judged. My mind cycled back to the workplace I had recently left, and I thought, *Yup, I'd rather be praying.*

I turned left onto a mud-packed lane, where Shetland ponies munched contentedly in a paddock and a pair of large sheep presided in another, and past the ruined remnants of a previous incarnation of Quarr Abbey.

Quarr took root here in 1132, when a small but plucky band of Benedictine monks from Savigny, Normandy, were dispatched by their abbot to the Isle of Wight to build an abbey. The man with the deep pockets for this endeavor was Baldwin de Redvers, earl of Devon and a lord of the island, who believed that funding an abbey and eventually being buried in it would guarantee the everlasting veneration of his soul.

But there are no guarantees in life. Not for de Redvers, not even for Quarr. After four hundred years of tilling the island's soil, the monks were forced to disperse when Henry VIII's reformation banned religious orders and torched their monasteries and convents. Some of Quarr's monks fled across the Solent to the monasteries of neighboring English shires; some went back to Catholic France; others surrendered their vocations entirely. But France held no enduring stability, either. Nearly four hundred years later the monks were on the move again when France took up the sword of religious intolerance. Oddly enough, it happened at the same time that a tolerance for religious orders was on the upswing in England. The changing social tide prompted Prosper Guéranger, the founder of the Solesmes order in France, to round up his monks and up-sticks back to the Isle of Wight in 1901.

There was not much left of old Quarr Abbey when they returned. In 1891, rough archeological excavations on the site showed a monastery that accommodated many monks, a sizeable church, a guest lodge, and an infirmary that served the island's population. The excavation also unearthed three stone coffins, one thought to contain the remains of de Redvers and his wife.

I strolled among these dilapidated medieval walls and foundations, most of them virtually obscured by dense, tangled mounds of vegetation. In one wall a shoot had taken root in some deep cavity, miraculously persevering through the stone and mortar until it burst into the sunlight and air. *How does a tender shoot get the confidence and strength to penetrate a wall of stone?*

My walk took me far beyond the precincts of the abbey grounds and into an area of almost supernatural beauty: thick ropey vines the size of boa constrictors encircled massive tree trunks; a fine coating of lichen made everything appear somewhat reptilian; vines grew everywhere—up utility poles, through barbed wire, and around tree limbs until the foliage was almost indistinguishable from its host. Everything was linked, attached, connected to something else. Once again, Nature prompted self-interrogation: *Could I ever attach myself to anything that firmly and surrender to its power so that my personality and my very spirit were completely neutralized? Is that what it is like living in a monastic community?*

Back in my teenage days, when the idea of being a nun had first launched itself, the notion of melting into anonymity had not seemed like a big deal. Forty years later, it was. My ego had been toughened by decades of jostling and clawing for supremacy—to get the laugh, to offer the quick idea, to have the smart answer, to gain the upper hand in an argument. It was all competition. Everywhere I turned, my ego was on call. I'd had to thrust and fight for a place in line, for a parking spot, for an appointment, for recognition, for compassion, for love. It was exhausting, but not having to do it anymore, admittedly, was like a descent into nihilism. When the ego dies, what's left?

(3:viii)

MY EGO was showing no signs of wanting to be put out to pasture, at least not yet. I had been at Quarr only a few days, but already I had taken to strolling the grounds with a proprietary air and drawing up a list of suggested improvements to the abbey:

- move the tea room to the space across from the bookshop to boost bookshop traffic and revenue
- improve signage to the bookshop
- develop a proactive recruitment strategy that includes outreach in the schools to make young men (and women) aware of religious vocations
- devise weekend or week-long retreats geared specifically to men
- switch from whole milk to semi-skimmed to improve the monks' waistlines and cholesterol levels.

Before I could present my ideas to Father Nicholas—and I'm sure he would have been delighted to receive them—new guests arrived at the abbey. The flurry of activity had a tendency to throw Father Nicholas into a tizzy as he organized accommodations and hasty orientation, so I wisely set aside the list.

One of the guests was an elderly priest from Scotland on his yearly retreat, and the others were a father and son from England.

The father, who looked to be in his early sixties, had a full head of white hair and bushy, wiry white eyebrows. He had a kind, cheery face with rosy cheeks, and that expressive and educated chatty English voice—heavy on those aural antioxidants—that puts you in good humor. He was attired in the uniform of a country squire: dark green wool sweater, corduroy trousers, and tweed jacket.

He and his wife had seven children, he told me—"blessed with seven children" were his exact words—and he had been to Quarr many times on retreats but this was his first visit with his son. He looked lovingly at his son and draped a fatherly arm around his shoulder. The son, I guessed, was the reason for the visit. He was a sorry sight: late twenties perhaps, disheveled, with greasy fair hair, bad teeth, a jaundiced complexion, tattered clothes, and an almost catatonic expression. Crack cocaine? Depression? Definitely something dire.

I was touched by this pair, especially by the father: there was something courageous—or maybe it was desperate—about the love he had for his son, as well as the wisdom to bring him to a place like Quarr. I hoped the place would work its magic on them both.

The following morning after lauds, I sauntered into the guest refectory to help myself to a bit of breakfast. The Scottish priest was there, as was the father (the son, I gathered, was sleeping in). There was also a new face at the breakfast table—a man, perhaps in his forties, with dark hair, a short beard, and a pleasant open face.

"Good morning, Jane!" he said brightly.

After days of anonymity, it was unusual to hear my name spoken.

"And you are...?" I asked tentatively.

"Benedict. Oblate."

Ah, yes. Father Luke had mentioned that someone named Benedict would be working in the bookshop that day.

We chatted a bit. Benedict lived on the island and had been associated with Quarr for about twenty-five years, but only in the last year had he become an oblate. Oblates are men and women who commit to living a simple life in the spirit of St. Benedict and who support monks and nuns in various ways, such as helping with administrative work, landscaping, or in the bookshop.

I had just poured cereal into my bowl and was reaching for the milk when Benedict leaned toward me and murmured, "So, no sex today? None."

Or was that "Nun"? Whatever he said, it brought all my internal organs, cells, and nerve endings to a screeching halt. I pretended to be unfazed by the remark as I turned to face him and asked, "Pardon?" The register of my voice went up a few octaves, and there was an unfortunate edge to it.

"No sex. None today," he repeated.

Should I lob back something equally risqué such as, "Well, I'm not so sure of that. There are eight monks here after all, so it might be one of my busier days."

Or should I play it straight and just nod? Give a loud huff of indignation and stomp off to my cell?

I glanced across the table at the other two guests to gauge their reaction to Benedict's comment, but both were nodding their heads and pursing their lips in a thoughtful, avuncular way while slurping their cereal.

I looked at Benedict again, then back at my cereal bowl. Was he referring to his sex life or to mine? Was this sort of talk indulged at a monastery or just at this particular one? A wave of panic surfed through me as I ran down a mental checklist of what I could recall from the monastery's website. Had I missed something? Perhaps some fine print? Had I inadvertently handed myself over to a sex cult?

I closed my eyes to make it look as if I was saying grace, hoping to buy time before I had to respond.

I heard Benedict sliding a piece of paper toward me. I gave it a sidelong glance. The message was printed in Father Nicholas's hand: *"No Sext, None today."* Sext and none are brief offices—sext is usually around 9:00 a.m.; none (pronounced no-n) is around noon.

I nodded curtly and set my lips in a serious expression hoping Benedict would interpret it as, "Yup, thanks, got it the first time." Inwardly, however, I was screaming hysterically: *You moron! Can you imagine the fallout had you unbuttoned that great gob of yours and blurted out something inappropriate? And you want to be a nun? Do you think a nun hears the words "sext" and "none"—even when they're not correctly pronounced—and immediately thinks of "not getting any"?*

Sadly, the incident wasn't an isolated one. I adore British accents, but despite having an English beau for several years, my ears were not completely trained.

Later that morning, I had an exchange with the elderly Scottish priest who was visiting. It went something like this:

"So, you're returning to Glasgow tomorrow, Father?" I asked.

"Rover," he replied with a smile.

"Pardon?"

"Rover," he repeated, louder but not any clearer.

"Your name is Rover?"

"Brother," someone finally interjected wearily. "He's telling you that he's a brother."

"Oh, you're not a priest then?" I continued blithely. "You're wearing the collar of a priest, and I just assumed..."

"The line," he said, pointing a shaky finger to what, to my eyes at least, appeared to be a faint pencil smear on his collar.

"The line means I am a brother," he said sweetly.

This is the sort of stuff that drives me crazy about organized religion—obtuse symbols such as these. Who can keep track? Why not give brothers a bright blue collar instead of a white one so that the average person on the street can clearly and immediately identify their role? A white clerical collar with a barely visible line up the middle—and you have to lean in uncomfortably close to a person's face to see it—just looks like the priest had dampened the tip of a pencil on his lip (I know, who does that anymore?), and the pencil slipped, marking the collar. Some religious customs are just not helpful, and they reinforce the impression that religion is more secret society than transparent communion.

(3:ix)

THE DAY had dawned bright and mild; it could almost be called warm. It was only early February, and I added a prayer of thanks for being brought to a place where winter does not mean five feet of snow and icy temperatures in the minus double-digits.

I did not get out for my daily walk until afternoon, and my intention was to push beyond my usual end-point and walk all the way into Ryde, but midway into my journey, ominous clouds the color of steel wool began to gather and the atmosphere seemed charged with a deep and unexplained foreboding. I turned around and walked briskly back to the abbey.

It was just before five o'clock when I left my cell for vespers. I was about to push open the door of the guesthouse when, through the window in the door, I noticed a man on the stoop, his back to me, facing a wall. It appeared that he was urinating, so I rattled the door a bit before opening it to give him time to compose himself. I was halfway through the door and was thinking of berating the guy for peeing against a monastery wall *(Buddy, what kind of an animal are you?)* when it became apparent that he was not peeing but masturbating. I kept my back to him as I closed the door, but when I turned to go down the steps he swung around and stared directly into my face. He had the darkest, hungriest eyes I have ever seen. Stringy dark hair obscured part of his face, and he had a short dark beard. His mouth was curled into a lascivious smirk. But it was the eyes that I will never forget: black and soulless. There was an aura of evil about him. A chill shot into my marrow. I scurried down the steps and briskly headed to the church, pulling determinedly on the heavy wooden doors.

Safely inside, I paused to catch my breath. My heart was hammering. *What a scary guy. And what an awful, ugly feeling he gave off.*

I took my usual seat in the upper nave and slid down onto the kneeler to pray. A slow, loud creak came from the church door. I turned around. Wanker Man had poked his head inside;

and in the dim-lit area of the lower nave it looked like a disembodied head with wide maniacal eyes staring directly at me.

I glanced across the aisle to the only other person in the church, an elderly monk whose job it was to greet visitors. He had nodded off. *Terrific.*

I rolled my eyes, as much in disbelief as in an appeal for divine intervention, and turned to face the altar to continue my prayers.

Another sound from the back of the church—this time the scraping of chairs across the stone floor. Again, I looked behind me. Wanker Man had entered the church and was now sprawled carelessly and defiantly on one of the chairs in the lower nave. He continued to glare at me, still smirking; more challenging than lascivious now.

Panic surfed through me. By this time the monks had processed in and had begun to chant vespers. The old monk across the aisle had stirred to life but was oblivious to anything beyond the chanting monks. I tried to resume praying, but I could feel the heat of the stranger's stare boring into me.

Then I heard footsteps moving slowly toward me. I spun around. Wanker Man was now at the top of the stairs, a mere three rows away, still fixing his dark eyes on me. At this point the old monk got up—Finally!—and approached him, but Wanker Man raised his hand, and the monk virtually froze in his tracks. In a deep, authoritative voice, the man said to the monk, "It's OK," and he kept his hand raised toward the monk while continuing to glare at me. I stared back, hoping my defiance would deter him, but he was stronger than me.

I turned away and faced the altar. My body began to convulse with a fear like nothing I have experienced. I began to cry silently because, strange as it may seem, I was certain that my life was about to end.

Looking back on this episode, I am at a loss to explain such an overreaction. At the same time I can vividly summon the fear of that moment. It was awful. I have never been so scared in my life. Then again, I have never been followed into a church by a man who had just been masturbating.

I considered calling out to the monks, interrupting their chant, but what would I say? *A scary man who I caught masturbating by the guesthouse door is staring at me?*

But this was no ordinary man; I sensed that intuitively. I have encountered plenty of unsavory types in my life—drunks, drug addicts, gang members, back-stabbers, thieves, rapists (and these were just the people I've worked with)—but none had made me reel with fear like this man. I squeezed my eyes shut and prayed harder than I have ever prayed: *Lord Jesus Christ, have mercy on me, a sinner.*

Vespers ended and the monks swooshed by my pew, their voluminous black cloaks whipping the air. When I first arrived they had sounded like swans; now they sounded like ravens. A murder of ravens. I tried to get their attention but their hoods were pulled over their bowed heads. With a thud of the cloister door they were gone, and I was left alone in the church. Well, the old monk was still there, but my faith in him as a protector had pretty much evaporated.

I remained in my seat to compose myself and to think of a way to evade Wanker Man or decide what to say or do if he confronted me. When I stood up and turned around to face the back of the church he was nowhere to be seen. Or rather, nowhere I could see him. I could still feel his presence.

By now, it was pitch black outside. There was no way I was leaving the church alone.

I approached the old monk and asked him to walk me back to the guesthouse.

"Did you see that weird man? He followed me in. I don't feel safe."

"Well, we get a lot of odd people up here," the monk chuckled. He reminded me of Clarence, the kind-hearted but bumbling angel in *It's a Wonderful Life*.

He fumbled around and produced a flashlight. It looked painfully inadequate. I wanted to ask whether he had something more substantial. Like a gun. With a silver bullet. And where was a crucifix when you needed one?

The heavy doors of the church slammed behind Brother Clarence and me, and we shuffled across the gravel driveway toward the guesthouse door. A wild wind was knocking the helpless limbs of the trees together and blowing debris all over the place. The night before, I had paused in this darkness and stared up unafraid at the night sky, marveling at the wonder of the stars and the universe; now it struck me as a reckless thing to do especially on a dark and stormy night.

We reached the guesthouse door, and I thanked Clarence; then I bolted for my room. I flicked on all the lights, closed the shutters tight, and sat down on the edge of my little bed before erupting into a shaking, hyperventilating mess. I cried out of fear for the unknown sinister force that was tightening its grip on me, cried out of shame for my gutlessness in not seeking help for myself. Memories of the rape came rushing back, and I was reminded of my lack of courage back then in summoning help. Every fear I had experienced started populating my thoughts. Even Quarr began to take on a sinister feel. An hour earlier, the place had felt idyllic; now, it felt like a medieval prison.

I found Father Nicholas in the dining room and told him about the incident, though I softened the details by saying that Wanker Man had "been urinating, or something." I also told him that I was not going outside in the dark alone, and therefore I would not be attending compline.

Father Nicholas did his best to reassure me that I was completely safe.

"I happen to have," he whispered cogently, leaning toward me and patting the side pocket of his habit, "a phone number for the police."

Well, I'm sorry: A handgun or a Taser I'd accept, even a mobile phone with the police on speed dial, but a piece of paper containing the phone number of the police? This is all that's standing between me and Satan?

I shook my head resolutely. *Nope, not good enough. Not going to compline; not going outside in the dark.*

"I had an experience once," I started, "and..." The vision of a strip of light beneath a closed hotel room door loomed into mind.

Father Nicholas looked at me, waiting for me to finish, but I didn't. I couldn't.

I returned to my cell after dinner. By now the gusts of wind had magnified into a deafening and frightening force, "like a roaring lion seeking someone to devour." What had St. Peter experienced to prompt that metaphor? The window of my room rattled, as if someone was shaking it from the jambs. A sheaf of newspaper, bunched up and stuffed as insulation into the disused chimney flue of the little fireplace, rustled and pulsed like something breathing. Scratching and pawing sounds came from the other side of it. I could hear someone pacing outside my door.

I was beyond scared. I quickly changed for bed and dived between the sheets, pulling the blankets over my head.

It was a restless sleep—when I managed to sleep at all—punctuated with wild, awful dreams. The main dream starred

Wanker Man, who snuck up and grabbed me from behind in the church. I managed to break free, thwarting him with the quick use of a clever Wonder Woman one-arm flip maneuver, and tackling him to the floor of the sanctuary. Then I tied him up and gave him a swift boot in the head, which produced a response of *Exorcist* proportions, complete with all the gory special effects. The monks were aghast but grateful that I had triumphantly wrestled Satan, and they rewarded me with a special Mass (in which they allowed me to take Communion). But Satan proved a slippery catch, and I constantly had to use more Wonder Woman kicks and chops to subdue him.

When I awoke from this mayhem in the morning, the bedsheets were twisted and damp, one of the blankets was balled up at the head of my bed, and my pillow was on the other side of the room.

Were these dreams a metaphor for my battle with my own demons or about my inability to speak up when I feel threatened? Was it possible that a devil, in the form of Wanker Man, had been sent to dissuade me from pursuing a religious vocation? Ridiculous as that may sound, faith is a realm without boundaries or boxes; it is the province of mystics and miracles, of the unexplained and the seemingly nonsensical, of the supernatural stuff you cannot see or do not want to see.

When I opened the shutters the sky was weighted down by pewter clouds. The wind had not abated, and its fury was wreaking havoc on the island.

"Might have to cancel the ferry if this keeps up," Benedict reported at the breakfast table. "Lots of trees on the island came down overnight, and there are power outages everywhere."

I told him about my encounter with the strange man. Benedict's brow furrowed.

"You don't know whether people like that are sent to this place by God for safety, or whether they're sent by Satan to disrupt things," he said thoughtfully.

"Maybe they're sent by God *and* Satan to shake us out of complacency," I mused.

Because the truth was, I had become complacent and selfish at Quarr Abbey. I had participated in almost all the offices every day of my stay, but had my intentions been completely honorable? Was I more seduced by the atmosphere—the architecture, the grounds, the monks, and the romance of being sequestered in a monastery—than by God?

The following day, an end-of-season commotion further disrupted the tranquility of Quarr as the other guests packed up. The Scottish priest had left the previous day; the father and his troubled son were leaving for home after Mass.

"I hope you had a good few days," I said to the son.

"Oh yes, it's very peaceful here."

If you say so. I had been so patronizing in my assessment of the young man's troubles that I had failed to recognize my own. We were both fighting demons.

(3:x)

FATHER LUKE dropped by my room for a visit that evening.

Seeing a book by Thomas Merton on my desk, he sighed with pleasure: "Ah, Merton."

"I love Merton, too," I said eagerly, picking up the copy of Merton's journals that I had purchased from Quarr's bookshop the day before. "Last summer at the convent in Toronto, I discovered *The Seven Storey Mountain,* and it changed my life."

"*The Seven Storey Mountain* had a huge impact on my decision to become a monk," Father Luke said solemnly.

When *The Seven Storey Mountain* was published in 1948, something like seven hundred men beat a path to the Abbey of Gethsemani in Kentucky, where Merton was a monk. Religious orders today can only dream of being inundated with those sorts of numbers.

"What else inspired you?" I asked Father Luke.

"Schuon. Frithjof Schuon. Heard of him? He wrote a book about Islam that influenced me, too. You must read it."

Our conversation moved on to my convent-or-Colin dilemma.

"It's more than choosing one or the other," I explained. "Every time I think I'm close to resolution, more questions crop up. I feel like one of those Russian matryoshka dolls: every question contains another question, which contains yet another question. All I want are answers and a decision right now."

"Well, marriage is a big decision," said Father Luke. We both withdrew into silence as we pondered the situation.

Eventually he spoke. "The chance or risk of becoming too unselfish or selfish is lower in marriage than it is in religious life. In other words, you give up far more in religious life, but the pay off—eternal life with God—is greater."

"Is this some religious Vegas-style game theory?"

He smiled, and picked up a pen. On a scrap of paper he drew a vertical line down the center with the words "unselfish" and "selfish" on either side. Then he drew two horizontal lines: one line was short, and the distance from the center on either side was equal. This was the marriage option: the risk is equal to the payoff. The second line was longer but also of equal length on either side of the center line. This was the religious life option: the risk is greater; but the payoff is bigger.

"Don't be concerned about the questions," he assured me. "It's part of the process. Take your time. Keep thinking. Keep asking. Keep praying."

(3:xi)

JUST AS I resigned myself to being the sole guest at Quarr for the last few days of my stay, a new one showed up.

Her name was Mita, an artist who lived on the Isle of Wight. We bumped into one another in the guest lounge, and she was so interesting and entertaining—it was as if we had known each other for ages—that we pulled up a couple of chairs and chatted freely until supper, ignoring the bells as they tolled successive offices.

Mita obviously had not received the memo about meals being conducted in silence, or if she had, she ignored it. She did not seem familiar with the term "indoor voice" either. I had to be the killjoy and keep telling her to button it. She paid me no heed. Not even when the monks were saying grace. I felt like the head librarian constantly saying, "Shh!"

When Father Sting brought in our food, Mita pounced on him and flirtatiously tried to engage him in conversation. He responded in a slightly baffled but polite way, smiled and quickly retreated.

"He's *cute!*" said Mita as she dug into her food with gusto. I winced, hoping that Father Sting hadn't heard the comment. "Has he been serving you all week? Makes you wonder why they're monks, doesn't it? I mean, what a waste of a man!" She tore apart a piece of bread.

"Well, they have given themselves to serve Christ, so is that a waste?" I whispered.

Mita's mouth dropped open and she gave me a look of disbelief that said, *Are you shittin' me? Are you even female?*

I tried to keep silence at the table, but Mita would have none of it. I was sure Father Nicholas would be storming in any minute to tell us both off.

The next morning, well past lauds, she staggered into the breakfast room wearing fluffy slippers the size of dusters.

"Did you go out last night?" I asked. She looked as if she had consumed twice her weight in alcohol.

"Bloody bells kept me up all night," she yawned, rubbing her heavy, sleep-deprived eyes. "Surely you heard them."

"Nope, not one."

"You must be a really sound sleeper," she said, pouring a coffee. "Or deaf." With mug in hand, she padded back to bed.

I stayed in my room all day. The wind was still ferocious, and it made reading, praying, and concentrating all but impossible. I was packing my bags in preparation for my departure from Quarr the next day when there was a knock at my door.

It was Mita. She had her coat on. Her suitcase sat on the floor beside her like a loyal pet.

"I'm leaving," she said. "I just wanted to say goodbye."

"But you just arrived!"

"I can't sleep here, and the silence is driving me crazy. My husband's on his way to pick me up."

We hugged goodbye. I was extremely sad to see her go. Despite her incessant yakking, her spirit had given me a boost, and I adored her company.

"I was thinking about what you told me about your journey to explore being a nun," she said. "Read Kings One; it's about Elijah in the wilderness when he was fleeing from Jezebel.

Maybe you're in your own desert right now, fleeing from something. Just know that God is with you, and He'll get you through this. Have faith."

And then she was gone, and it suddenly felt lonely and cold once more.

Elijah and Jezebel. Those two again. They were responsible for my being here in the first place. Yeah, best to leave Eli and Jezzy alone for a while. They're trouble.

I sat down at my desk to write. It was so quiet I could hear my pen scratching its way across the paper. I paused to look at it: *Do they sell silencers for these things?* My ears perked up at the sound of low voices in the corridor and doors opening and closing. Footsteps passed in front of my door.

In many ways Quarr was giving me exactly what I asked for. If I joined a convent, this would be my life: sitting alone in a sparse room, reading Thomas Merton or the Psalms, making notes, resigning myself to the monotony of the routine and the pervasive silence, and deriving excitement from the sound of footsteps or a distant door opening.

More footsteps. Gone now. Maybe not. Someone opened a door. Door closing.

The windowpane in my cell rattled. A door in the hall slammed shut, and it scared the crap out of me.

Yes, it was time to leave Quarr. Silence has a way of preying on you. Preying while you pray. Mita had told me that she had been texting back and forth with her husband. How can you prepare your mind for the voice of God when you're waiting for a text message? Then again, who was I to talk? I had my laptop with me, and at certain points of the day I was able to pick up a signal and send and receive email. I, too, craved connection with others; I simply used a different poison.

More footsteps in the hall. Someone is putting a key in the door of Mita's room, shuts the door and locks it. Footsteps pass my door once again.

Yup, it was definitely time to move on.

(3:xii)

I WAS up early the next morning to attend vigils at five-thirty. I had not attended vigils at all during the week, and I wanted at least one experience of it. The moment it began, I regretted not making the effort to attend more often. It is the longest of all the offices, but it also was the richest in providing food for thought. There were Bible readings and a homily, and I heard, for the first time, the monks actually speak at length. Father Sting had an Irish lilt; one monk sounded like Terence Stamp; another sounded as if he was auditioning for a BBC production.

I loved Quarr, but as much as I was going to miss it, I was also relieved to be leaving. I had become distracted and confused by my own wild fantasies, and that is never a good thing.

Plus, everyone I had met at Quarr had raved about St. Cecilia's, its soul-stirring chanting, and its fantastic guest accommodations. I could not wait to get there. Yes, time to move on.

Father Luke was saying Mass at St. Cecilia's that morning— the priest-monks at Quarr rotate this duty—and he offered to give me a lift. I loaded my bags in the boot, and once I was in the car I turned my head for a final glance at beautiful Quarr.

The incident with Wanker Man had begun to recede from memory, but it wasn't over yet. The Devil was far from finished with me.

4

An Invalid Religion

. . . .

St. Cecilia's Abbey
Isle of Wight, England

WITHIN TEN MINUTES of my arrival at St. Cecilia's, it became clear that God had reviewed my expectations, crumpled them into a ball, and pitched them far across the universe to that quadrant of space where downgraded, discarded entities like Pluto are left to wallow. And then, with a bit of time on His hands and feeling frisky, God had rolled His gigantic God eye across the planet, latched onto the Isle of Wight, zoomed in on St. Cecilia's Abbey, and, zeroing in on a hapless figure ascending the church steps, said to Himself, "Oh, goody. This could be fun."

Father Luke, having gone off to change for Mass, had handed me over to a happy little nun, as small as a hummingbird. She led me into the church, and I took a seat in a hard, dark pew halfway down the short aisle.

Things felt uncomfortably strange. Normally I can walk into almost any church and love it. Not this time. I closed my eyes to summon a spiritual connection with the place. Nada. I tried to focus on something—a friendly face, a work of art— that would generate a degree of comfort and help me bond with my new surroundings. Nothing.

Steady on, I reassured myself. *You'll warm to it all. You always do. Look at how easily you got on at Quarr.* But my confidence-building pep talk felt hollow. Instead, my nose started to tingle, an early-warning sign of a meltdown.

I shifted in my seat, coughed a little, and attempted to reset-tle myself into a fresh perspective. I rescanned the church for a hopeful sign, but absolutely nothing resonated. It was such a bland, characterless place that I almost cried out of pity for it.

Unlike Quarr's church interior, which had been designed for openness and transparency, St. Cecilia's was designed for segregation and separation.

The layout was L-shaped. One end of the long part of the L housed a spacious domed sanctuary with scrawny ribs stretching to form a gothic vault. At the opposite end of the L, out of public view, were the choir stalls for the nuns. As if to reinforce the separation—and in ecclesiastical architecture, it's all about the symbolism—a tall black iron grill stood between the sisters and the sanctuary. The short extending arm of the L was where the congregation was corralled; it held about fifty people, and on this particular Sunday morning it was three-quarters full. A low black iron railing separated the congregation from the sanctuary. With the altar facing the sisters, the secular congregation saw Mass conducted in profile.

A nun dressed in the traditional, familiar-looking black habit entered through the cloister door and approached the iron grill. With a key attached to the cincture she wore beneath her scapular, she unlocked and opened a door within the grill, bowed to the altar, then turned and proceeded, I assumed, to her seat in the stalls. Seconds later, a procession of about thirty nuns filed in. Each bowed to the altar and turned toward their stalls. Many were young with pretty faces. Judging by their habits and veils, they were in various stages of profession: gray veils were for postulants, white veils were for novices, and black veils were for professed sisters. I felt a little envious.

St. Cecilia's is one of the most strictly enclosed monastic orders in the United Kingdom. Nuns only leave the enclosure for dental and medical appointments. They are not permitted to return home under any circumstances, and mail and phone contact with friends and families is rigorously limited.

Like Quarr, it is an industrious community. The sisters bake and produce Communion wafers for much of the U.K. market; illuminate manuscripts; operate a gift shop that sells CDs of their music, religious books, and small crafts; and run a small guesthouse from which they receive donations from guests and from individual benefactors. They also grow and harvest their own fruits and vegetables.

Every sister at St. Cecilia's is taught to sing. Gregorian chant is central to the community's worship, and it is therefore fitting that its namesake is the patron saint of church music.

Not relevant to any of this but fascinating nonetheless is that St. Cecilia, who died in Rome in 177, is the first saint whose body was found incorrupt when it was exhumed in 1599. I read somewhere that her corpse was found curled on its side in a sleeping position, which leaves the impression that she might have been unintentionally buried alive. Creepy.

I closed my eyes and begged God to warm my feelings toward this church. Immediately, two older women—well, I think they were older than me—appeared at my pew.

"Can you read the lesson today?" the one in the soft pink cardigan asked me in a clipped no-nonsense voice. "We're stuck; one of our regulars can't make it."

Wow. God's working fast today.

"Yes, I suppose I could," I sputtered gratefully. In all my churchgoing years no one had ever asked me to read the lesson, so this was both a thrill and an honor. A feeling of goodwill began to percolate inside me along with the thought that perhaps I *should* convert to Catholicism.

"You're staying at the Garth, aren't you?" asked the other woman. She seemed friendly and had an American accent.

I nodded eagerly. The Garth was the name of St. Cecilia's guesthouse. I picked up a pew Bible and waited to be told the passage they wanted me to read.

But the English woman in the pink sweater had narrowed her eyes on me. "Are you Catholic?" she demanded.

The question took me aback. It's not like I was wearing a sign that said I was a non-Catholic; after all no one *looks* Catholic. Put the Pope in civvies, and no one would know he was Catholic.

"No I'm not, but..."

"No. You absolutely can't read. It won't do," Sweater Lady said brusquely. "Should have asked you that first."

Both women hurried away as if they feared contamination.

Well, that was harsh. I picked my humiliation off the floor and dusted it off. I shifted in my seat again and sat ramrod straight, staring ahead at the altar. My chin began to wobble.

A wild clanging of bells started up, not the tidy singular and soft toll to which I had become accustomed at Quarr Abbey, but a veritable racket. Father Luke, preceded by a thurifer casting wispy threads of incense in his wake, strode toward the altar. He was dressed in a green chasuble and looked very priestly.

The clamor of the bells stopped, and an angelic sound rose from beyond the grill, a clear, ethereal sound, the type that gives you goosebumps. The sisters of St. Cecilia's filled the church with their soaring supra-soprano chant.

Yet this glorious and practiced singing did not enchant me: it lacked the warmth and earthiness of the Quarr chanting. As I compared the singing style of both communities, my memory sailed back to Quarr, its church and the monks. The water level behind my eyes began to rise. *Uh oh.*

I remained on the precipice of a meltdown when the service rolled around to Communion. I decided to join the rest of the small congregation at the rail, not because I necessarily wanted a blessing but because I needed to be nearer to Father Luke, the closest friend I had at that moment. If it meant enduring the ignominy of singling myself out as a non-Catholic by crossing my arms across my chest, then so be it.

As I walked down the aisle, arms dutifully in formation, Sweater Lady leaped to her feet and surged like a scud missile through the clot of parishioners to intercept me.

"You're not a Catholic," she challenged in a not very quiet voice, "which means you can't..."

"I *know*," I hissed back with as much righteous indignation as I could muster without someone calling the authorities. "Why do you think I have my damn arms crossed?"

"Oh, jolly good then," she chirped, and she returned to her seat.

There endeth my flirtation with Catholicism.

It was a mortifying experience, but more than that, it angered me that such a rigid and uncompassionate attitude still existed between two faiths that couldn't be more related. What's more, it was an attitude that was obviously condoned because no attempts were made to correct it: in the church bulletins or from the lips of its priest or on the signage there was no invitation to those of other faiths or to the non-baptized to come forth and join what is really a solemn gathering around Jesus' table.

By the time I reached the Communion rail, I could not look at Father Luke. My eyeballs were holding back the Hoover Dam. I bit hard on my lower lip, and with head bowed I accepted the blessing and returned to my seat. I slipped to my knees, buried my face in my hands, and silently wept.

I was still on my knees when Mass ended and the parishioners were shuffling out of the church. I could hear Father Luke making small talk with some of them. I tried to dry my eyes. *Please God, don't let him see me cry.*

"Jane," he called out with a smile in his voice. "C'mon, I'll take you through the special passage."

I got up and walked toward him. Sweater Lady was standing beside him. She looked aghast that I, a non-Catholic, was *actually on speaking terms* with a *Catholic priest, a monk* at that! As I walked past her, I held back the urge to thrust my chin at her and gloat, "You know, he used to be an Anglican."

I trailed Father Luke through the narrow passageway steeling myself from breaking apart while he blithely bantered away.

When we reached the rotunda, a parishioner took Father Luke aside, allowing me to turn my back and pretend to be fascinated by a collage of photos of the convent. Water began to leak dangerously around the edges of my eyes. *Don't. Don't!*

Someone called my name. I turned around. A smiling bespectacled nun strode purposefully toward me, her hand outstretched in greeting.

This was Sister Prudence, with whom I had made arrangements for my stay.

"How good to finally meet you," she enthused as if we were old friends. "Let me show you to the Garth."

We were almost through the door of the church when Father Luke interrupted his conversation with the parishioner and called out to Sister Prudence: "Make sure you look after that one." I could not bear to look back.

By now aware of my emotional fragility, Sister Prudence gingerly asked, "Have you stayed in convents before?"

I had to reply; avoiding conversation would have been rude. As soon as I opened my mouth, the dam burst, and I bawled uncontrollably, gulping out my words like a fish flailing on dry land. One hand was dragging my suitcase; the other was plunging into my purse to grope for a tissue.

"I'm so sorry," I sobbed between hyperventilating gasps. "I'm a little emotional today." That might have been a lie: I'm a lot emotional every day.

We walked up the street a bit and then followed a path to a squat stone building (in a previous life, it was probably a semidetached home). It had small, white modern windows and doors that were unsympathetic to the style of the façade. Sister Prudence unlocked the front door.

Based on the descriptions given to me by everyone at Quarr, the Garth sounded superb, on par with a four-star hotel. Sadly, there was no correlation between those reviews and the reality. It was a pokey, dreary place with low ceilings and no charm. The walls were bare save for the occasional crucifix decorated with a sprig of dried-out something that required the botanical equivalent of dental records to identify its species. The furnishings were so bland and institutional looking, so uncozy, that it prompted another dribble of tears. It had all the warmth of a hospital ward, and it rather smelled like one, too.

"You're the only guest till Friday," Sister Prudence announced, believing that the news would make me feel better. Never have I been so relieved to have privacy; never have I been so in need of company.

She listed the times for the offices and for good measure showed me a list on the bulletin board in the hallway with the same information. God bless women and their penchant for organization.

I gradually regained my composure, and we chatted briefly about the reason for my visit. Sister Prudence regarded me with a degree of curiosity. Or was it skepticism?

"May I ask how old you are?" She asked this as diplomatically as possible, but it pricked nonetheless.

"Fifty-seven," I replied, trying to make it sound like thirty-seven.

She pursed her lips and raised her eyebrows, sizing me up and down.

"Too old?" I asked in disbelief.

There are many indignities that beset a woman in her fifties, but perhaps none stings as much as being told that she is too old to be a nun.

"A bit," said Sister Prudence. "Look, I have to be somewhere right now but can we talk longer about this tomorrow? Say, eleven-fifteen?"

"Yes, that would be great," I smiled.

Then she was gone. I stood alone in the hallway with my luggage not knowing whether to cry or kick myself. *I'm too old to be a nun? To serve Christ? What the hell? And I'm being told this now? Does He know about this?*

I stomped angrily through the Garth trying to decide whether to take the upstairs bedroom or the one on the main level. *Fifty-seven? Fifty-freaking-seven?* I repeated this aloud—practically spit it out—like a mantra. *When did fifty-seven become the new eighty? And who the hell decided fifty-seven was "old"—some thirty-two-year-old? Some tucked and Botoxed "I'm-in-my-forties" sixty-two-year-old?*

I thought of my circle of friends—none of whom you would dare accuse of being too old for anything, not if you hoped to keep your internal organs intact. And me? I was accomplished, educated, healthy, enthusiastic. I had strong communications skills, media connections, public relations experience. I had mentored others, I could cook, I could renovate a house, I regarded God as the center of my universe. And I wasn't worth consideration by a religious order? Hell, if I were a religious order, I would have snapped me up! *Don't these people know who I used to be??*

I poked around the guesthouse and wondered how I was going to survive the next six days.

I wheeled my suitcase into a corner of the main-floor bedroom and reluctantly unpacked. It was such a pathetic room; large enough but without that certain quality that makes strange places feel like home. The ceiling was low; a small sink hung forlornly on a wall in one corner; a wardrobe that looked like it had gone a few rounds with Mike Tyson stood in another. The limp, defeated towel that drooped from a rail beside the sink looked to be older than me. Even the little crucifix hanging between the two twin beds looked lost and cold, and I wanted to tuck a small piece of cloth around Jesus' body to warm it up.

I dropped myself on the edge of one of the beds to take in the staggering banality of it all, and as my bum made contact with it, a crinkling sound emanated from the mattress, like the sound made when you scrunch up an empty potato chip bag. I peeled back the pink bedspread, the bed sheets, and the mattress protector. Beneath it all was a mattress encased in thick, industrial-strength plastic. St. Benedict, who made hospitality a cornerstone of his *Rule,* would never endorse plastic mattress covers. Hospitality is about trust and comfort; it does not presume your guests will wet the bed, unless you are expecting a very young guest. Or a guest with incontinence. *Is that what they thought of me? At fifty-seven? The cheek!*

(4:ii)

ON A shelf in the hallway, I fished out a map of Ryde from a messy slew of travel brochures, all of them extolling cheerful stays on the Isle of Wight that were completely at odds with the one I was having. I studied the map briefly, got my bearings, then grabbed my coat and purse, and took off in search of a grocery store. The Garth was a self-catering arrangement, which meant I had to cook for myself. God, I missed Father Sting.

The weather had turned gloomy and cold. I pulled the collar of my coat tightly around my neck and dug a pair of gloves out of my pocket.

I schlepped along Melville Street pondering my future, which seemed as bleak as the February afternoon. *What if I was too old to be a nun? What then? What do women do when they yearn for monastic life and are rejected by a community because of their age? When did ageism creep into the church? Should I have lied about my age?*

What plausible age-related excuses might there be for turning down a candidate for religious life? Can't get down on her knees fast enough? Might have a hemline preference for her habit? Her singing voice is on the raggedy side? She insists on gluten-free Communion wafers? On the plus side, there were plenty of benefits for taking on older candidates. Brains for one thing. What does a twenty-two-year-old know? An older woman would also bring a steady pension along with a wealth of work experience that could benefit the convent. And let's not forget commitment. Women of a certain age know the value of working together for a common cause.

I raised my eyes from the ground just in time to notice a road sign alerting traffic to road construction: CHANGED PRIORITIES AHEAD. I gave a snort: it rather summed things up.

Across the street a window display of furniture caught my eye, and I crossed over for a closer look. I stared vacantly at the items, alternately admiring them and trying to figure out what to do with my life. I caught sight of my reflection in a mirror; staring back was a sad, colorless little face framed by short, spiky hair that showed more salt than pepper. I suppose all women wake up one day to the reality of their older face, but this was not a case of a few lines and wrinkles, this was Benjamin Button on speed: jowls had pillowed along my jawline, deep crevices were etched around the base of my nose, the dreaded "marionette" lines drew my mouth downward into a permanent scowl. Good grief! Is this what happens when you go au naturel; when your role models are people who have survived sandstorms and lived on twigs? Oh sure, those dried-up desert mothers and fathers had inner radiance, but inner beauty is for amateurs.

In his homily that morning, Father Luke had spoken about how, when we have been wounded by the words or deeds of others, our first reaction is to retreat from the world, which actually makes things worse for ourselves. Better, he said, to use the experience to reach out to others who have also been wounded. Spreading our light lights others around us, as

Matthew had said in his gospel: *"Let your light so shine before men that they may see your good works and give glory to your Father who is in heaven."*

Maybe my desire for invisibility was not what God intended for me. Perhaps my sin was trying to wear the hair shirt.

(4:iii)

SISTER PRUDENCE arrived at the appointed time the following day, flying through the front door in a flash of black and white.

There was a time when I admired the look of the traditional habit—there was nothing that a pair of tall black boots couldn't remedy. I had regarded the habit as a symbol of feminine power and independence. Now, on closer inspection, it struck me as severe and fussy—a sort of Christian burqa: the white-lined black veil (*How do you keep that thing on?*); the tight white wimple gripping the head and face (*Itchy? Hot?*); the starched bib (*Can you eat soup without dribbling on it?*); the full-length black tunic (*Constricting? Bulky?*). At the end of a day, do Sister Prudence and her fellow sisters talk about "getting out of this hot habit" or complain about having a case of wimple hair?

A few strands of wavy strawberry blonde hair had liberated themselves from Sister Prudence's wimple, and as she settled into a chair in the living room, she tucked them back out of sight.

We faced one another on two stiff chairs. It felt like the Inquisition was about to commence.

She remained silent, which made me a bit antsy, so I filled the empty space with chatter, beginning with an apology for my emotional state the day before. I told her that I had been unprepared for the considerable contrast between Quarr and St. Cecilia's. I also told her about being approached in the church to read the lesson and about being intercepted on my way to the Communion rail.

Sister Prudence was appalled, and apologized. She promised to look into it.

"Why can't a non-Catholic read the lesson in a Catholic church or take Communion?" I asked, trying not to sound petulant. "Exclusivity is contrary to Christian teaching."

I mentioned that I had a Catholic mother and an Anglican father, and that our family had freely worshipped and participated in each church. I told her I had often taken Communion in an RC church and that my RC mother had taken Communion in an Anglican church.

Sister Prudence was shocked. She adjusted her large pale-framed glasses; the thick lenses gave her the look of an alarmed owl.

"Why weren't you raised a Catholic?" she demanded, her big eyes zooming in on me. "In those days, non-Catholics who married Catholics had to promise to raise their children in the Catholic faith."

I shrugged.

"Your father must have been a very strong personality indeed to resist that," Sister Prudence said in a serious tone.

"Actually, he was a very gentle and quiet man, a man who respected authority, but who put the rules of God before man-made rules."

"Well, let's talk about you," she said, quickly changing the subject. "Tell me about yourself."

I took a deep breath and gave her the Coles Notes version of my life.

144 AND THEN THERE WERE NUNS

It would have been amusing to see the thought balloons that sprang from beneath Sister Prudence's wimple as she listened. It could not be said that she had a good poker face.

"I have three children," I said at length.

Her big eyes widened and she exclaimed, "You do?"

"I've been married."

"Oh!" Her eyes became saucer-sized.

"Twice."

"Oh my!" She raised her hands to her mouth and averted her eyes.

When I mentioned that I was engaged to be married a third time, she nearly passed out, and it seemed best to stop and spare her more distress.

"Given that background, I don't know how you have the nerve to attend church at all. And *you* want to be a nun?"

The remark was such a slap that I flinched. I barely knew how to respond.

"Yes," I said steeling my confidence. "But you say I'm too old."

"Our upper age limit is forty," she said with a tight smile.

It was clear that this nun thing wasn't going to happen. Not here anyway. And yet I wanted to argue my case with Sister Prudence. I wanted to cite the case of St. Angela of Foligno, who had whored her way through much of her life until she renounced her behavior, founded a religious order, and became a saint. Wasn't the church all about forgiveness? As for divorce and age, those were hardly grounds to deny someone a chance to devote her life to God. Wasn't there dispensation for late bloomers? If I had told Sister Prudence that I had a million dollars to donate to the convent, I'll bet that "upper age limit" would have been dropped pretty quickly.

And yet I desperately sought her approval. I wanted her to ignore the evidence before her and see the big picture. I wanted her to look into my heart and recognize its longing to belong, its desire to surrender its vagabond life for divine stability.

"Look, it's not like I planned my life this way," I finally said. "Stuff happens. Some things are beyond our control; when a partner constantly denigrates you in public or up and leaves you because he's decided that you're holding him back from some greater glory, what are you to do?"

She looked blankly at me, but I could tell that the wheels in her head were churning beneath that starched wimple.

She asked about my previous marriages, and suddenly she arrived at a solution.

"Two marriages would disqualify you from becoming a Catholic, but we could have your first marriage declared annulled because you married under duress..."

"I *didn't*," I countered. "I just..."

"But I don't think there's anything that can be done about the second. You could become a Catholic and you could receive the Holy Sacraments, but you would never be able to marry again."

Removing from the equation my ambitions to become a nun, Sister Prudence saw an opportunity to snag me as a convert to Catholicism, and offer it as a consolation prize.

"What if..."

Anticipating my question she said, "If you marry again, you will not be permitted to receive Communion. Ever."

The statement was delivered like a thick metal door of a vault slamming shut.

I am embarrassed to admit that I sat there for a little bit weighing Communion against sex, but there you go. I wasn't about to give up.

"Why is there such an intractable difference between the Catholics and the Anglicans when both originated from the same root?"

"Because," sighed Sister Prudence, "when the Anglicans broke with Rome they severed the apostolic succession. You do understand apostolic succession, don't you? You know, Jesus laid his hands on his apostles, they went out and laid their hands on others to ordain them as priests, and so on. In breaking that sacred tradition, Anglicans have no God-given authority to ordain others."

"But Jesus was a Jew…" I attempted to interject.

"What's more, Roman Catholics also believe in the transubstantiation of the bread and wine into the actual body and blood of Christ. Anglicans do not necessarily believe this."

Neither do 45 percent of American Catholics, according to a recent poll. What's more, a survey by Milan's Catholic University found that 70 percent of respondents consider themselves "good Catholics" without following the Vatican's rules on sexual morality. About 55 percent have no qualms about contraception, only a fifth of respondents flatly condemn abortion, and 40 percent thought that women priests should be allowed. But it was pointless to start down that road with Sister Prudence. As for her remark about apostolic succession, well, it is a cornerstone of the Anglican creed—"We believe in one holy catholic and apostolic church"—and if she wanted to get technical about it, I could have pointed out that Catholic priests converted to the Anglican faith during the Reformation and ordained others, thereby maintaining the continuity of apostolic succession.

"And another thing: the Archbishop of Canterbury has no authority," she continued. "None whatsoever! All decisions in the Anglican Church are made by committee."

Oh please, not the "committee of academics" metaphor again!

"The Catholic catechism makes it abundantly clear what we believe," Sister Prudence continued loftily. "Decisions come directly from the Pope, who defends the Christian tradition on Earth. Whether you agree or disagree is not the issue: the fact is that you always know the church's position on things. The Anglicans, well! What do they believe? I'm afraid you don't belong to a valid religion."

(4:iv)

THE SUN was shining and the birds were chirping as I set off resolutely on a long walk—just me and my invalid religion.

I took a short-cut through Abbey Lane to East Hill Road and down to the Esplanade and followed the boardwalk along the Solent past the boarded-up carnival rides, attractions, and ice cream stands, hotels, guest houses, and apartment buildings.

My head was pounding with anxiety and confusion. I was apparently too old to be a nun, had too much of a past to be considered a nun or even a Catholic, and I belonged to a faith that was considered "invalid." And that elucidation was the fruit of just one discussion with Sister Prudence. She said she would pop in for more chats every second day during my stay. At this rate, I might not be deemed worthy enough to board a ferry by the weekend, which is why when I reached the ferry terminal I immediately purchased a one-way ticket off the island. Saturday seemed eons away from a Tuesday point of view.

I continued walking, lost in a confusion of thoughts, with my back to St. Cecilia's until the buzz of Ryde gave way to a quiet residential area with well-tended English gardens. The street ended abruptly at a busy road but continued as a footpath on the other side of Spencer Road. I was about to cross over when, at the last moment, I realized where the footpath led—directly back to Quarr Abbey. I glanced at my watch: the monks would be in none, standing in their dark oak choir stalls chanting the office. My heart ached from missing them. If I continued on the path, I could be at Quarr in twenty-five minutes. It was so tempting.

But I did not cross over. Returning to Quarr would only have made me sad, and I could not do that to myself. In many ways it felt like I had come to the end of my own path. I had no idea what to do.

I retraced my steps slowly back into Ryde. I considered ditching my invisible habit and becoming a tourist for the rest of the week, or walking the island's 67-mile coastal trail.

My impression of the Isle of Wight was souring by the minute. It had no doubt left a similar impression on one of my favorite people in history, the bright, busy monk named Bede.

In 686, Bede is said to have visited the Isle of Wight to record its conversion to Christianity. It was to be a momentous occasion because the island was the last part of England to convert, and Caedwalla, king of the West Saxons, was going to do the honors. I pictured Bede in a state of fussy excitement as he prepared to chronicle the events, perhaps arranging his quills in a straight line and neatly stacking his parchment. Or maybe he was nervous because Caedwalla had a reputation as an unpredictable brute. What transpired was horrifying. Caedwalla arrived, duly baptized the island's pagan inhabitants, and then massacred the lot of them. The island's entire population was replaced that day with a boatload of Christians that Caedwalla had specially shipped in.

What a thing for poor Bede to witness.

I had to switch to happier events in the Isle of Wight's history otherwise I would have marched back to the ferry terminal and exchanged my ticket for the next passage. So

I thought about Horatio Nelson sailing off to meet a short French guy at Trafalgar; and Marconi launching the world's first radio station in 1897 at Alum Bay; and Charles Dickens writing *David Copperfield;* and Alfred, Lord Tennyson scratching out his *'Tis better to have loved and lost* lines; and Bob Dylan penning "Like a Rolling Stone"; and Jimi Hendrix playing his last performance before 600,000 tie-dyed and hallucinating fans. And then I remembered that the Isle of Wight is one of the few places in Britain where you can find red squirrels – as rare as people with invalid religions.

(4:v)

I CONTINUED to read and pray over the next few days, but my attendance at the offices was spotty at best.

Not only did I feel unwelcome, I had the distinct impression that my apparently unholy reputation was making the rounds of the cloistered community at St. Cecilia's. Now when the nuns filed into church and bowed to the altar, several had taken to pivoting their heads slightly toward the congregation to look at me. Was Sister Prudence sharing our conversations?

I crossed my arms defiantly and stared right back at them. *Yes, sisters, this is what life looks like on the other side of the cloister wall. It's messy and muddy, and it doesn't always work out the way you hoped. But divorce is not the end of the world; in fact, with the long stretches of silence, the absence of sex, and the slavish obedience to house-cleaning, it looks remarkably like convent life. That's right, sisters: divorce is the new monasticism.*

Without a firm monastic routine, my days turned into lonely stretches of aimless walks through Ryde. I also spent a lot of time reading, but the Garth, especially in the evenings, had all the friendliness of a Stephen King movie.

One night after compline, I returned to the Garth and felt a weird, edgy vibe. I flicked on the lights and paused in the hallway to listen for unwelcome sounds, then tip-toed around the main floor turning on every light possible.

In the kitchen, as I waited for the kettle to boil, I kept looking behind me because it felt like someone was watching me.

I took my tea into the sitting room and sat down at the table to read, facing into the room. The atmosphere continued to be inexplicably charged. It was a struggle to keep bad thoughts from invading my mind. Almost a week had passed since the incident with Wanker Man at Quarr.

I glanced up from the page of my book, and just then something crept into the room and scooted behind a chair.

Was I imagining things? No, I saw it as clear as day.

It was a creature, a bit more than a foot tall, with gray, leathery skin and a head slightly larger than its body. It was walking upright with muscled legs and cloven hooves, and its arms were short and clawlike. Its thin tail, covered with small scalelike protuberances, tapered into a triangular shape, and it flicked like a whip. The creature's face, half human half animal, had large eyes, small ears that looked like horns, and a mouth that was curled in an open smirk. It said nothing and did nothing while it positioned itself behind the chair out of my sight. But I knew it was there. I had not been drinking or ingesting legal or illegal substances, though at that moment I wished I had a crateful of something that would render me unconscious.

Had the devil sensed my fear and, like a wild animal, returned to stalk me? The Quarr Abbey incident began to replay itself in an endless loop in my mind like a made-for-TV movie, each version scarier than the previous one. I began to pray fervently, but the devil wasn't going anywhere. He had found me, weak and doubtful, cowering in the corner with my "invalid religion."

I packed up my books and hurried out of the room, ignoring what was behind the chair. I got ready for bed and hopped in; the crinkling of the mattress cover sounded like I was slipping into a body bag. And there I lay, eyes wide open, heart pounding, with the lights on and the bed covers clutched to my chin. I said the Jesus Prayer aloud over and over: *Lord Jesus Christ, Son of God, have mercy on me, a sinner.* I was scared out of my wits.

At three in the morning, the bedroom lights were still on and I was still shaking, too scared to sleep. By the time the gray February dawn leaked through the curtains, I was a complete wreck. I got out of bed, dressed, and headed to the ferry terminal to change my ticket. I was not going to stay any longer than I had to.

(4:vi)

SISTER PRUDENCE arrived for another visit. I was not sure how to broach the subject of my guest from the previous night or whether to tell her about it at all.

As we moved into the sitting room, I casually checked behind the chair to see if the devil had left a calling card.

"Did you read the catechism?" Sister Prudence asked, having assigned homework during her last visit.

Catechism, Schmaticism! What we need is an exorcism!!

Actually, I *had* scanned the catechism—at three in the morning while I was holding off Satan.

"Yes, some of it," I replied. "The creeds of the Catholic and Anglican faiths are virtually identical."

A pained expression appeared on her face, and she heaved a sigh of frustration.

I was getting mightily frustrated, too. Sister Prudence could never see my side of things. I wanted to tell her that all this baloney about apostolic succession was petty crap. That Jesus would be incensed by our preoccupation with such arcane silliness. As a progressive, creative thinker, He expected us to think and live outside the temporal box. But how do you argue with a nun, especially when you're sleep-deprived?

Sister Prudence soldiered on about the matrimonial obstacles to my salvation. She insisted that I not marry Colin but remain single and make God the center of my life.

I wanted to bang my head on the table.

"God *is* the center of my life," I said with exasperation. "He is all I think about. That's why I want to be a nun."

Honestly, it was like being waterboarded.

She gave me another pained and pitied look. I felt like Madeline being lectured by Miss Clavel (and then my mind, which tends to go off on tangents, wondered, *Why was Miss Clavel, who was clearly a nun, never referred to as Sister Clavel?*)

Back to Sister Prudence.

We were just not going to see eye to eye, so I changed the subject and asked Sister Prudence about her habit. When all else fails, you can usually level the playing field with a woman by talking about her clothes.

"Do you ever wear civvies?"

She looked as shocked as if I had asked her whether she wore a G-string.

"Certainly not!"

I was going to mention that most sisters of my acquaintance rarely wore their habit anymore, but then I remembered that most of those sisters were Anglican, and I could not bear to give Sister Prudence more anti-Anglican ammunition.

"This is the only outfit I have, aside from the shorter version, which is worn when we're doing chores. And the one we wear to bed."

"You wear a habit to bed?"

"Of course."

I wanted details. What does a night habit look like? Was it a stiff black shift, or a long, creamy diaphanous number? Nightgown? Flannel PJs with an angel print on them? There was no time to ask, because Sister Prudence was controlling the conversation.

"I am adamant about wearing the habit," she said defiantly. "We get ridiculed and hassled by people, usually kids, on occasion, but one must stand firm and not back down. After all, Our Lord endured worse persecution, and we need to stand in solidarity with Him."

Our hour was up, and as she prepared to leave, she perused the stack of books I had taken from the Garth's bookshelves, including one on Merton.

"Merton," she groaned, rolling her eyes.

It was not a surprising reaction. Merton challenged traditional Catholics, and many of them were dismissive of, if not openly outraged by, his ideas.

I did not tell Sister Prudence that the devil had dropped by the night before. Doing so might have prompted her to call a priest or a psychiatric hospital. I did tell her, however, that I was leaving earlier than planned. She offered to arrange a taxi.

That night, I headed straight to bed after supper. I got ready for bed and arranged several spiritual books around me like a fortress—the Bible, books by Merton, Vanier, Nouwen, a book of Psalms, Father Luke's book about Quarr Abbey, Shakespeare's sonnets. I scanned the bookshelves in vain for *Vatican II for Dummies.* I did find a weekend magazine from one of the national newspapers and it got added to the pile.

A crucifix hung on the wall behind the bed, so I figured I was well covered.

Gradually, the house descended into a gloom of ominous silence. Floorboards creaked, the tap in the kitchen dripped, the refrigerator shuddered as if it had been spooked.

As I picked up the weekend magazine, I could hear the devil sneer and rub his hands in satisfaction: *Yup, thirty seconds of that and her mind will stray from that religious nonsense and default to furniture arrangement and color swatches. When she reaches the fashion pages, she'll start thinking about what to buy to perk up her spring wardrobe, and the cosmetic ads will remind her that she left her brown eye pencil in Canada, and so she'll make a note to go to Boots and buy one. Ha! Ha! My work is done here.*

I shook the devil out of my headspace. Leafing nonchalantly through the first few pages of the magazine, I was suddenly catapulted back to the land of glossy ads for cosmetic fillers, cranky columnists whining about their self-indulgent lives, fashion spreads, celebrity interviews, and catty restaurant reviews of places where meals cost fifteen times what I had spent on food that week. A quarter of the way through the magazine, the decorating ads got me musing about paint swatches and redecorating Colin's flat. The fashion pages prompted a hasty list of clothes—vibrant, joyful-looking clothes—to buy for spring: *Should I go for the jersey dress with a bright mini print? What about that leopard-print blouse and scarf, or would it make my top half look too big?*—and then I jotted a reminder to myself to drop into Boots in the morning and buy a brown eye pencil.

Feeling more secure, I dismantled the fortress of books, stacked them neatly on the floor beside the bed, turned out the light, and slipped into a blissful sleep.

(4:vii)

I WENT to Mass the next day. I don't know why, but I was glad I did. It was lovely—lots of candles, genuflection, beautiful priestly vestments, and enough incense to justify a health and safety warning. The sisters sang beautifully, the best I had heard them all week.

It was the Feast of St. Scholastica, a saint whom I admire for her pluck. She was born in 480 and died about sixty years later. Her twin brother was St. Benedict. Theologians like to bicker over which one of the twins was the first to embrace religious life.

Scholastica and Benedict were devoted to God and also to one another. Each year, they met midway between their respective religious houses to have a good old chinwag and while away the weekend worshipping and discussing religious texts. One year, brother and sister met as usual, but when Benedict made his move to leave, Scholastica threw a tantrum. They hadn't finished their discussion, she complained, and she insisted he stay one more night. He said no, that he had to get back to his monastery. Scholastica fell to her knees, and as she prayed, a ferocious storm kicked up.

"What have you done?" asked a frightened Benedict.

"I asked something of you, but you would not listen to me," Scholastica pouted, "so I asked God for something and He listened to me. If you want to leave, go ahead."

Benedict could not make his way in the storm, and it is surprising that he even tried. Really, you do not mess around when you are in the company of someone who has a direct pipeline to God.

When Benedict eventually reached his monastery, he saw a white dove circling outside his cell window. Moments later, word arrived that his beloved sister had died.

Despite the celebration for St. Scholastica, I stayed clear of the Communion rail.

Sweater Lady was in the congregation. I wanted to compliment her on her cardigan, which was the color of raspberry sorbet this time, but she kept casting mean church-lady looks at me. She read one of the Bible lessons during Mass in a beautiful soft, clear voice. As she read, I completely forgave her for how she had treated me. Like me, she was a child of God, full of imperfections yet striving for what she thought was right. Despite her penchant for colorful sweaters, perhaps all was not rosy in her life, and I felt a bit sad for her.

Having been denied Holy Communion for two weeks, I headed to a pub after Mass and ordered a bowl of tomato soup, bread, and a small glass of red wine (in honor of St. Scholastica). If I couldn't get Communion served to me in a Catholic church (and all the Anglican churches in Ryde were shuttered up tighter than a miser's purse), then I was going to do it DIY style. I did not intend to be sacrilegious, but it is frankly sacrilegious to withhold Communion from Christians who desire it.

And then I went out and bought a brown eye pencil.

(4:viii)

TWELVE HOURS.

Ten hours.

Six hours.

I had been counting off the hours until my departure for two days, and now, finally, it was down to single digits. I couldn't wait to leave the Isle of Wight.

Father Luke said Mass that day. We chatted afterward, and I recounted my whole sorry adventure, including my scaly night visitor. I'm not sure what Father Luke made of it—or of me—but we hugged goodbye and promised to stay in touch.

I walked back to the Little Catholic House of Horrors and awaited Sister Prudence's final visit.

In a strange way I was going to miss her and her maddeningly blunt conversation, though I wished she had taken me more seriously.

"So, you are off up North?" Sister Prudence asked, settling into her regular chair in the sitting room and smoothing out the skirt of her habit.

"Yes," I replied. "I'm going to an Anglican Order—the Order of the Holy Paraclete—for about three months."

"You mean weeks. Three weeks."

"No, months. Three. Months."

"Months!?"

"Yes." I tried to hide my irritation.

She stared at me as if I had turned into the burning bush.

"You think I'm crazy, don't you?" I finally said.

"I don't think you're crazy." She lingered on the word "crazy," as if trying to find a word that meant crazy but was more polite. "I'm just curious to see how all these strands of your life fit together."

The heart of the conversation that day rested on whether I would tune myself to a life fully committed to God rather than heading into marriage number three. I knew which option Sister Prudence wanted me to choose.

"The problem here is that you're looking at marriage as a bad thing," I said. "Both of these are good and positive options."

"But don't you see that this relationship with your fiancé is an obstacle to God?" she countered.

"Obstacle? Or gift?" I replied. "Colin might have been sent as an anchor of stability. When I was walking the Camino de Santiago de Compostela in Spain several years ago, I had asked God to send me a good man, a man of quality, and He did. I ended up meeting Colin on the Camino."

Sister Prudence was quiet for a moment.

"Haven't you ever been in love?" I blurted.

There was an awkward silence.

"I had an experience once," she said eventually. She had fallen for a priest when she herself was a nun. She wanted it to be purely friendship, but as her feelings for the priest deepened, she realized that would not be possible. "I thought he was sent as a gift," she said. "But I now see that he was sent as a test."

"That must have been difficult for you, but in your case you had already taken your vows, as had he. That would be like a married woman falling for a married man. What you did, pulling away from the priest, was the right thing."

"Yes, it was," she answered thoughtfully. "That's why I wonder whether this new relationship for you is an obstacle."

"Or a gift."

"Well, that is what you must discern. I feel I must speak the truth," she said quickly. "This isn't me speaking; it's the Holy Spirit speaking through me."

"I appreciate your candor, but there was no need to make me feel like a harlot. That was undeserved."

"Oh blimey, I've had worse than you!"

The doorbell rang at that moment. It was a new guest, a young woman from London. She looked to be in her mid-thirties, cute with a shy edge, and with eyes that squinted like Renée Zellweger's when she played Bridget Jones.

Sister Prudence gave the young woman a tour of the Garth, and I went off to my room to pretend to finish packing. In truth, I had been packed for two days.

It was time for Sister Prudence to leave. We hugged, and she glided out the door as the wind turned her habit into a sail of black and white.

"Pray for me!" she called out.

I closed the door and looked at the clock. One and a half hours until the taxi was due to arrive. Why doesn't time fly when you want it to?

The New Girl and I chatted in the hall for a few minutes. She told me she was thirty-seven and was thinking of becoming a nun. I told her I was fifty-seven and was thinking of becoming a nun.

"I'm apparently too old," I pouted. "Did you tell Sister Prudence about your intentions? She'll be all over you."

"No, I didn't tell her," New Girl said dreamily. "I just came to check it out. How can they say you're too old? That's mean. What are you going to do now?"

"I'm heading to Whitby to stay for a few months with an Anglican order."

"Whitby? Bram Stoker got his inspiration for *Dracula* in Whitby," she said. "Think he wrote much of the book there. And Whitby is where the goth festivals are held."

"Why, yes, you're right!" I recalled reading something about goths and Whitby while researching the area. "How do you know all this?" I teased. "Are you a goth?"

"I was," she stammered shyly. "But I wasn't a very good goth, I'm afraid. Sort of a goth-meets-hippy version. I wasn't hardcore."

"From goth to nun. I love it. Hey, if you do join a convent, let me know; maybe they'll let me be a nun there."

I listed off some of the vaguely goth music on my iTunes but admitted to New Girl that a convent guest house had not seemed the right venue to play them. Truthfully, it was too scary a place to play them.

"Oh, I love AC/DC and Def Leppard, too. That would've been fun!" she giggled in her squinty Bridget Jones way.

It was a pity she hadn't shown up a day earlier to brighten up the Garth (or is it the Goth?) and rid the joint of the little cloven-hoofed creature—which I did not tell her about.

I did, however, mention the wonderful collection of spiritual reading on the bookshelves in the sitting room.

"That's good to know," she said in a tone suggesting that she would prefer a colonoscopy over that prospect. "Actually, I brought an *ok!* magazine just in case. And some crisps."

We said goodbye and wished each other good luck. She headed off to none, and I gathered up my things, put on my coat and gloves, and sat on the stairs waiting out the final interminable hour and seventeen minutes for the taxi's arrival.

Then forty-five minutes.

Twenty-five minutes.

Twenty-three minutes.

At five minutes to three—hallelujah!—the taxi light appeared above the stone wall at the end of the walk. I bolted through the front door, locked it, and slid the keys through the mail slot. Incredibly, they popped back out and landed at my feet.

"What the...! Get in there, you bastard," I muttered. I roughly shoved the keys back through the mail slot, and this time I held down the metal flap until I heard the keys hit the tile floor on the other side of the door.

5

The Cloistered Castle

Order of the Holy Paraclete
Whitby, England

I ARRIVED WITH MY confused and broken holiness at St. Hilda's Priory, the home of the Order of the Holy Paraclete (OHP).

My family initially thought I was going to be staying at a religious bird sanctuary, The Holy Parakeet. The term "paraclete" refers to the Holy Spirit, which infuses each of us with character and personality. I was in critically short supply of both.

Rain hailed from the underbelly of a swollen sky, the sort of downpour that nails you the second you step out in it. I made a thirty-foot dash from the car to the shelter of a small canopy above the priory's front door and got soaked despite the effort. Rivulets of rainwater streamed across my scalp and dribbled down my face. My feet made squishing noises in my waterlogged boots. I tugged at my sodden, clinging clothing and tried to make myself halfway presentable.

The priory door was locked. I jiggled the door handle with the barest of hope that doing so would miraculously unlock it. I was beginning to give up on miracles.

To the right of the door were two doorbells with instructions on when and when not to ring each one. It was a layer of complication I did not need at that moment. I pressed one and hoped it would yield a positive result and not a scolding. Thunder crackled, the wind howled, and a fresh lashing of icy rain pelted me. It felt like the beginning of the apocalypse.

I'll give it thirty seconds, I thought, as I shifted impatiently from one squelchy boot to another. *If no one answers the door, I'll leave and give up my convent aspirations. What was I thinking anyway? I'll send an email to the prioress and explain that something had come up. A family emergency. Yes, that's it. I'll say...*

Through the fogged and rain-streaked glass door, a shape instantly materialized. As it advanced closer, I could make out a woman in the gray habit of the order. The door swung open, and I recognized the woman from a website photo: it was the order's prioress, Sister Dorothy Stella.

"Jane? Oh for heaven's sake, come in and get out of this miserable weather. What a day! Real Yorkshire weather, this. Don't worry, you'll get used to it. So glad you arrived safely. Oh, it's good to finally meet you!"

I cannot recall whether we embraced, but I do remember feeling instantly at home: warm, welcomed, relieved, and safe. I was back in Anglican territory.

I tried to formulate a quick impression of the place, wondering whether the next three months would be heaven or hell. I cast wary glances into the dark corners to see if my little Spock-eared friend had followed me from St. Cecilia's.

The interior of St. Hilda's did its best to appear inviting in spite of the limited amount of natural light filtering through huge panes of glass that lined the corridor. Around the corner, a planter containing several pots of primrose in vivid shades of lemon yellow, deep purple, bright red, and bubblegum pink winked a welcome.

The gloomy day actually enhanced the austere Normanesque features: the low arches, the stone floors and walls, and the many doorways and passageways emanating from the entrance. If I was looking for atmosphere, this place had it in spades: more *Nun's Story* than *Name of the Rose,* but a proper priory nonetheless. Even the habit that Sister Dorothy Stella was wearing met with my approval: light gray-brown fabric, mid-calf length, with long, slightly bell-shaped sleeves, and a high but nonrestrictive rolled collar in contrasting white. It was softly tailored and cinched at the waist/hips with the traditional black profession cord. Practical; modest but also feminine. *Yup, I could wear that.*

I paused in front of a wooden statue of a woman cradling a church in one hand and holding a staff with the other; ammonites were arrayed at her feet.

"Our patroness, St. Hilda," Sister Dorothy Stella said proudly. "Let me give you a quick peek at the chapel, since you'll be spending a fair bit of time in there." She led me by the elbow through a rounded wooden door and down a couple of steps. "You've come at a good time: We have a funeral and a first profession this week!" She spoke as if both events were reasons to break out the champagne.

As we stepped inside the chapel, that potent, familiar aroma rushed toward me in greeting, and it warmed my chilled body. I mused about whether the ecclesiastical sector routinely ordered the same scent of incense, placing requisition orders each quarter for a new supply of—what might it be called— Monastic Musk? Holy Halo? Reformation No. 3?

Although constructed in the 1950s, the priory's chapel was designed with medieval sensibilities in mind—a soaring vaulted and buttressed wood ceiling, blind arcades of stone pillars, and Norman arches inset with leaded lancet windows. The walls and floors were brownish-gray stone, and the warm honey-hued oak choir stalls were arranged on opposite sides of the chapel nave to create a spacious open area in front of the sanctuary.

A sweeping chancel arch formed a protective embrace around the sanctuary, but it had obviously been unable to repel an invasion of jarring modern refurbishments in the last decade or so. The sanctuary's back wall was ringed with a built-in bench of alternating dark and light oak panels that reminded me of a piano keyboard; the altar looked like a trestle table, the type used for slaughtering something for a sacrifice, and from it hung a giant disk, like a gong but with soft appliquéd designs. A large electrified crucifix of amber-colored glass and iron was positioned across the sanctuary window, and when it was turned on, it looked like a traffic light.

It was so different from the churches at Quarr Abbey and St. Cecilia's Abbey, and it was a complete contrast to the glass modernity of St. John's, but I liked it.

Several rows of padded conference chairs were set up for visitors inside the chapel entrance.

"Do many outsiders attend your offices?" I asked Sister Dorothy Stella.

"Not during the week, generally, but on Sundays we have a large congregation. They regard us like their parish church."

Sister Dorothy Stella was the eighth prioress of the Order of the Holy Paraclete. She was a tall woman with a soft body, and had a happy, open face framed by short, wavy light gray hair. Her large, pale blue eyes smiled a little wearily from behind wire-rimmed glasses. There was a kind, motherly vibe about her.

The Order of the Holy Paraclete's connection with the Sisterhood of St. John the Divine had come about during the Second World War, when the OHP sisters, who operated a boarding school at the time, evacuated their students to Canada. The SSJD sisters immediately stepped in and organized the billeting and care of both students and teaching sisters. The two communities stayed connected after the war, and thanks to a generous benefactor, they had been able to maintain an annual rotating exchange program that allowed a sister from one community to spend a month with the sisters of the other community.

As Sister Dorothy Stella led me through the priory we exchanged news about sisters we knew in common, and this easy rapport sped up my kinship with the place. My sisterhood aspirations were back on the table.

I tried to remember whether I had given my age to Sister Dorothy Stella; maybe Sister Elizabeth Ann at St. John's had tipped her off. I put a spring to my step, raised the register of my voice slightly, and dropped the word "cool" into the conversation. If I couldn't be younger, then maybe I could appear hipper. (Can nuns be hip?)

We hauled my luggage up four flights of stairs to the top floor of the convent and then down a long narrow unlit corridor. The wing was reserved for novices and aspirants like me, said Sister Dorothy Stella.

My room was charming, and the slanted ceilings gave it the coziness of an atelier. The floor was covered in beige carpet that looked fairly new; the walls were pale yellow. Pretty yellow-and-pink floral print curtains framed the large dormer window. A single bed was pushed up against a wall, a chest of drawers doubled as a bedside table upon which was a small vase of field flowers with a little handmade card welcoming me. A small green upholstered chair was tucked into a corner at the foot of the bed, and a wooden desk and chair occupied the dormer. In an opposite corner, a wall-mounted sink hung near a long white shelf for toiletries. Four or five wall hooks served as the wardrobe.

"I hope this has been turned on," Sister Dorothy Stella murmured as she ran her hand along a hip-high portable radiator. "You're going to need it."

My attention strayed to the view from my window. Between wisps of fog I could make out trapezoids of farm fields stretched like a patchwork quilt across distant sloping hills. Even under a leaden sky it was beautiful.

"This is great," I said, turning to Sister Dorothy Stella. "Thank you."

She cast worried glances at the radiator and periodically laid her hands on it to feel for heat.

"We don't have any novices at the moment, so you have the floor to yourself. I hope you won't be too lonely. The rest of us sleep on the other side of the attic, though one or two sisters are in cells just below you. You'll find your way around eventually."

(5:ii)

I'LL ADMIT it: I was scared of Sister Marjorie at first. She was five-foot-nothing and no more than eighty pounds, but man, she was intimidating.

The job of showing me around the priory and providing my orientation had initially fallen to the guest sister, Sister Gillian. As she guided me along the main corridor, we ran into Sister

Marjorie, attired in oversized wellies and a rain jacket, and about to head outdoors for, as she put it, "a bit of air."

I had glanced through the glass doors: a tornado was gathering steam and tearing off tree branches.

"It's a bit rough out there."

Sister Marjorie had shot me a withering glare, looking me up and down as if I were some alien hot-house creature.

Sister Gillian was gently explaining that I would be staying for an extended period and that she was giving me a tour when Sister Marjorie interrupted her and fixing me with flinty blue eyes said, "A tour, huh? I'll give you a tour, a *real* tour. Ten o'clock. Here. Tomorrow." Then she was out the door, swallowed up by the storm.

"She's indomitable," Sister Gillian had whispered nervously as we walked away. "Just turned ninety. Went sky-diving and abseiling last year."

Ninety? Sky-diving? I mentally calculated how far I was from ninety.

"When you meet with her, be prepared. Her tours are not for the faint-hearted."

And so, the next day I found myself walking briskly toward where Sister Marjorie stood at the end of a long corridor by the back door where we had first met.

From thirty paces, I could spot a perturbed look on her face. She regarded my approach and alternately ran her hands impatiently through her shag-style crop of white hair and checked her watch: I was a minute and fifteen seconds late.

In spite of Sister Marjorie's blunt and feisty exterior and the reports of her daredevil escapades, I figured this would be a short tour: she was old and small; she'd run out of energy in no time.

Boy, was I wrong. She was like a terrier in a habit.

We went up back stairs, down front stairs, through connecting tunnels, up more stairs, then down again, past tapestries and paintings, each with a story quickly told and forgotten. We barreled down carpeted passageways, past offices, rooms set aside for prayer, a conference room, a bar (*A bar? Sweet!*), and a few reception rooms.

"This one is for your use, I believe," said Sister Marjorie, flinging open a door to one of them. "In case you want to watch TV. Or relax." I detected a guffaw when she said the word "relax."

It was an elegant room of pale yellow walls and white trim, a high ceiling, and floor-length windows framed by drapes of a more gracious vintage. There was a TV in the corner, some plump chairs arranged in a semicircle, and a fireplace. It would take me the better part of a month to find the room again.

We then sprinted across the courtyard to the warren of dormitories and classrooms that had been used for the order's former boarding school. Each bend in a corridor left me further disoriented, and had Sister Marjorie abandoned me right there and then, I might still be trying to thread my way back. All the while, she maintained a running commentary about the castle and its features.

Sneaton Castle had not always been a priory or a castle. It was built in 1813 as a lodge to house a seminary for young men, though the idea never got off the ground. A few years later, the stone building was sold to Colonel James Wilson, a Scottish-born surgeon and politician. Wilson plied his skills on the Caribbean island of St. Vincent and was rewarded for his services with a sugar plantation and the slaves to work it (it is a point that still makes the sisters wince). When he strutted back to England with his pockets bulging with money, Wilson decided to establish an ancestral seat. He bought the lodge and hired an architect to convert it into a castle. Two square crenellated towers were constructed to bookend the original building, and the façade was rebuilt with a castellated roofline and parapet. A stone crest was added above the front door, an enclosed garden was landscaped, twenty cannons were lined up across the front lawn and, voila!, instant castle.

Wilson became a British member of parliament and gave generously to the Whitby community, but no one shared his interest in the castle, not even his family. When he died in 1830, the place sat virtually empty for almost a century.

In 1914, along came Margaret Cope, a clever and headstrong twenty-eight-year-old geography teacher who wanted to rent it for her fledgling religious order and its boarding school.

The Archbishop of York at the time, Cosmo Lang, had patronizingly attempted to dissuade Cope from starting her order on the grounds that she was too young. No shrinking violet, she retorted that people felt he was too young (he was about fifty) to be an archbishop.

Not only did Miss Cope, soon to be Mother Margaret of the Order of the Holy Paraclete, follow through with her intention, but within a few years she had bought the castle outright.

Sister Marjorie and I stood below a large oil painting of Mother Margaret staring down her aquiline nose at us with an uncompromising and penetrating gaze.

"When did she die?" I asked.

"Nineteen sixty. Fell down the steps at one of the branch houses. Never regained consciousness."

Sister Marjorie excused herself for a moment, so I sauntered over to a rack filled with the day's editions of the major newspapers and picked one up. It was a perk I hadn't expected at a convent: national newspapers delivered daily.

When Sister Marjorie reappeared, I folded up the newspaper and tucked it under my arm.

"Put that back," she snapped.

"I haven't finished with it." There was still the Lifestyle section to read, the sudoku to do, the crossword to puzzle over.

"Doesn't matter. Someone else might like to read it."

"But there are other newspapers."

She stared me down.

I put it back. Obviously I was not as free of attachments as I thought.

We took a back staircase to the next floor, and then wended our way up a spiral staircase in one of the castle's turrets to the roof.

Sister Marjorie pushed open a door and suddenly I was facing a glorious panorama of pastures, the great North Yorkshire Moors, the town of Whitby, and the shimmer of the North Sea. A thrilling sight, the kind that made me want to spread my arms and yell "I'm Queen of the World!" Except that I didn't because although it was sunny, the wind was buffeting us like boxers in a ring.

It felt as if we were going to be blown through the crenellations, so I grabbed hold of a chimney and began to emit girly exclamations of alarm. But petite Sister Marjorie was unfazed. She did not hold on to anything, and stood stalk-straight, impervious to the wind. *Bring it on,* she seemed to say.

Her fondness for the castle was evident, and no wonder: she had lived here almost her entire life, starting as a student at the boarding school. She had been among those evacuated in 1940 to Toronto to wait out the war.

"When I returned to Whitby from Canada," she said, "I got a job as Mother Margaret's secretary, and eventually I decided to join the novitiate. I've been a sister here for, well, it will be sixty years in August."

There had been long, exhilarating stretches serving in the order's various branch houses in Africa, the memory of which sent her into a dreamy reverie and brought a smile to her face.

"No regrets, then?" I asked, now clinging to a TV antenna and bracing for the next gust.

"Well, of course I have," she said abruptly, returning from her reverie. "It's like a marriage. You're not always happy, but you carry on; you work through the rougher bits."

When I returned to my cell later that day, the question of my vocation was waiting for me, hands on hips and foot tapping with impatience.

Well? Do you like this life or not?

I just got here, for crying out loud. Give me time.

But as I unpacked and arranged my books, I could not help thinking how perfect it all seemed. *Yes, I could see myself in this place for a very long time.*

(5:iii)

THE FOLLOWING afternoon I attended the sisters' weekly house meeting in the community room, a large reception room that was off-limits to all but the sisters themselves. The only reason I had been invited was so that I could be formally introduced. Sister Dorothy Stella motioned me to a chair next to her.

House meetings were held to coordinate schedules, inform each other of medical appointments and days off, and share news about events outside the convent. It was exactly like a family sitting around with a calendar and jotting down who had to be where and at what time. About twenty-five sisters, ranging in age from early twenties to ninety-plus, sat in armchairs arranged in a large circle. They all wore their habits, some with black shoes, others with running shoes. One or two wore the traditional black veil, but that appeared to be optional.

They acknowledged me guardedly; I smiled back nervously.

Sister Dorothy Stella brought up some housekeeping matters and correspondence that had arrived. There was a reminder about the rule of silence in the cloister corridors. I was ruminating about the pitfalls of being the "new girl" in a convent when I noticed that all eyes had swiveled toward me. Sister Dorothy Stella was asking me to explain to the group why I was there.

I told them about the persistent call to religious life I had felt since my teens, about leaving a full-time job to explore the call in earnest, about being at the Toronto convent and about receiving instructions from the talking tea towel with the picture of Sneaton Castle on it.

Their faces remained impassive through all this, which I believe is the correct expression to assume when confronted by a psycho. That, and don't make any sudden moves. What was that adage? If you talk to God, you're religious; if God talks to you, you're psychotic?

I told them that I was divorced, had grown children, and was engaged to be married a third time when this call to religious life began ringing.

A few glances were exchanged—some with raised eyebrows.

"I know it isn't the tidiest of lives, but surely not everyone is blessed with a clean passage through this world." I was getting sick of apologizing for the way my life had turned out.

One or two shifted in their seats.

"If it doesn't work out, then I'll accept that," I continued. "But I need to settle that yearning within me one way or another."

A couple of perfunctory questions followed: What did my children think of this? How did my fiancé feel about it? I said that my children were happy for me and that my fiancé was "understanding."

I also told them I had been a journalist and an author, and that I hoped to write about my convent experience.

After an uncomfortable silence, Sister Dorothy Stella spoke up.

"Since you're obviously proficient with a computer, perhaps you could assist us while you're here."

I nodded, and moved to the edge of my seat to show I was eager to be helpful.

"There is a binder containing the twice-yearly charges that our foundress, Mother Margaret, delivered to the chapter meetings in the nineteen-forties and -fifties. We need them transcribed.

"We also wondered whether you could help us update our history from the last ten years," Sister Dorothy Stella continued. "We already have a book that was published, but we're looking at republishing it with newer information. We'll give you an office in which to do your work."

This was perfect. Just before the meeting I had been thinking about small vocations. Throughout my career I had always gone after the big-bang assignments as much for the praise as for the challenge of proving myself. But lately I had begun to consider the satisfaction that could be gained from less visible work, the type of work that has a direct and positive impact on someone's life, often someone you might never meet.

"Yes," I told the group, pleading in my needy way. "I'll help in any way I can."

That opened the floodgates to more "small vocations."

(5:iv)

THE NEXT day, after a silent breakfast, I cleared my place, took my dishes into the kitchen, and placed them on a rack destined for the dishwasher. I ambled back into the refectory to see if I could be of use. It never seems right to accept food from people without offering to help clean up.

A sister—quiet, intense, about my age, with thick brown wavy hair kept in place with a bobby pin—seemed to be in charge of the post-meal cleanup. She moved very quickly around the refectory, directing the work of a couple of the other sisters and switching chairs among the different tables.

She saw me standing alone and snapped impatiently, "Well, grab a penny." No introduction; no "Please grab a penny."

"A penny? OK." I began to look on the floor for a penny, though I was not entirely sure why she needed one.

"What *are* you doing?" she said, narrowing her eyes as she drew closer. "A *pinny*."

Pause.

"Apron," she said. She tugged at the one she was wearing in case I was too dim to comprehend the word "apron." "They're hanging on the back of the kitchen door."

Aprons. I thought those things had been retired to the Smithsonian.

I scurried into the kitchen letting the term "pinny" roll around my brain—*Was it in the dictionary?*—before plucking an apron from about a dozen hanging from a hook on the kitchen door.

"Oh, I wouldn't use that one," murmured one portly sister who was putting away the breakfast condiments. "That belongs to Sister X, and she might get upset."

I quickly put the apron back and pulled out another one. I looked at her and waited for approval.

"Don't know who that belongs to, so it's probably safe to use. I think."

I tied it on. When I turned around Sister Margaret Anne— someone in the kitchen had by then told me her name—was standing in the doorway that connected the refectory with the kitchen. Her hands were on her hips, and she gave me a look that said *What the hell is taking you so long?* I was becoming a rapid decipherer of body language.

I scurried after her into the refectory. Before I could speak, she thrust a broom, two dustpans, and a table brush at me and instructed me to sweep the floors "on that side."

I set to work with a conscientiousness I had forgotten I possessed. I swept the parquet floors around and under the large oak refectory tables, and then with the table brush I swept the tabletops of breakfast crumbs. Another sister was sweeping the other side of the refectory, so once I finished my side, I helped sweep her side, too. I efficiently gathered all the bits into the dustpan, took it into the kitchen, and proudly dumped it into the bin.

Sister Margaret Anne was at my heels.

"You're not supposed to do that."

"What?"

"You use *this* dustpan for the table, and *this* one for the floor. Don't mix them up. It's not hygienic. Besides, the crumbs from the table can be used to feed the birds. From now on, put the table crumbs in the blue bin on the ledge over by the breadbox, and the dust and dirt collected from the floor into the garbage. Food scraps go into this yellow bin for the donkeys."

Donkeys? What donkeys?

I flushed with confusion.

"Furthermore, when you sweep the refectory you are only supposed to do the side you've been assigned; another person does the other half. Did you notice there were two of you with brooms? You might very well be faster, but that's not the point. We share our tasks, and it is important to make others feel valuable, even those who are slower."

I flushed again.

Sister Margaret Anne had seen right through my so-called diligence and to the heart of one of my major flaws. I'm competitive, and I have a tendency to go overboard when given a task just to prove my capability and efficiency. I call it value-added; others call it sucking up. Ask me to do dishes, and I will wipe down the countertops and kitchen cabinets, too. Ask me to change a bed, and I will gather the linens, put them in the wash, and iron them afterwards. I don't know where this compulsion came from, but somewhere along the road of life I became an approval whore. I swept the other side of the refectory because I wanted to prove my indispensability; I collected the crumbs and dumped them in the garbage to show I didn't need to be told what to do. I hate this too-eager-to-please part of my personality, I really do, and yet whenever I have tried to correct it I end up disappointing people. Flaws: can't live with them; can't live without them.

Next, I was asked to set the tables for the noon meal.

Meals at St. John the Divine in Toronto were served buffet style; at St. Hilda's in Whitby, things were far more formal. A full complement of cutlery was employed—eating and serving utensils, water glasses, coasters, placemats and trivets, various bowls for discarding fruit rinds, and other bowls for collecting certain pieces of used cutlery.

In my previous life as a wife and mother I had set lots of tables—for evening meals, dinner parties, family celebrations—and I had also been fortunate to dine at a few rather fine restaurants in my time, but never have I been confronted with so much hardware as I was at St. Hilda's. It was like ground zero for cutlery fetishists.

My acumen for table setting must have taken a sabbatical without warning me because it became quickly evident that I was incapable of handling anything beyond placing the knives and forks, and even then I got that wrong, having transposed them while struggling to get my flustered state under control. Thank goodness Sister Margaret Anne was there to correct my error.

"We prepare our refectory and set the tables as if Christ was coming as a guest," instructed Sister Margaret Anne, as she swiftly circled the tables and changed the position of the cutlery. The urge arose to mention that Christ might find this layout daunting, but Sister Margaret Anne might have considered the comment irreverent.

I could hardly wait to get out of the refectory that morning. Once the tables were set, I scrambled out of my "pinny"—*Must check the dictionary for that one*—and made a beeline for the sanctuary of my cell so that I could collapse in a heap of pity on my bed.

En route I was intercepted by Sister Katherine Thérèse.

"Can I interest you in a job?" she asked with a smile.

"Sure!" I said with guarded enthusiasm. I did not want to come across as a grumpy-guss, but at the same time I did not want to cultivate a reputation as a doormat.

I made an exception for Sister KT, as she was known, because she had a spark to her. She was in her mid-forties, slender, with shoulder-length brown hair worn in a ponytail. She was from Lancashire and had a cheerful, slightly rough-and-ready quality.

"You see," explained Sister KT as she steered me toward the chapel, "Grace got her foot in a garden pot, so she's off chapel duty. I need someone to take her place."

I had no idea who Grace was or how she got her foot stuck in a garden pot, but I kept my questions to myself. I was still trying to work out how I could have forgotten how to set a table.

"Now," said Sister KT as we walked toward the sanctuary, "all you do is vacuum and dust the Lady Chapel, the sacristy, and the sanctuary. Just clean out to the edge of these steps."

I had never been given a task that brought me so close to an altar.

"Is there a special way to clean the altar, a ritual I should follow?"

"Nah. Just like cleaning your house. I mean, don't go knocking things about, but just clean it, normal like. Here's where we keep the supplies."

Behind a dark brown wooden door at the entrance of the Lady Chapel was a collection of the most basic of cleaning tools: an old Henry canister vacuum cleaner, a couple of thick dusting cloths, an extension cord, and a bucket. There were no cleansers, no furniture polish.

"We don't worry about that," Sister KT replied in answer to my query.

"Do I clean every day?"

"No, silly—once a week. Friday mornings once you've finished in the refectory after breakfast."

Could I do it instead of the refectory? Visions of Sister Margaret Anne flashed to mind.

I took off again for my cell but this time I bumped into Sister Dorothy Stella.

"What are you doing after lunch?" she asked.

I wasn't sure whether to say "Nothing," tell her I was busy, or scream.

"I have to go into Whitby to buy a train ticket," she continued. "I was wondering whether you'd like to come along. It would be fun for you to see the town and...," she lowered her voice before adding, "to get out of here for a while."

(5:v)

WAS THERE such a thing as spiritual jet lag? I was sure feeling it. Three convents in three weeks, all with different landscapes, schedules, customs, routines, and even denominations. If it's February, this must be Whitby. Plus, there were new names to learn, which was complicated by the fact that 75 percent of the sisters at St. Hilda's seemed to be named Margaret or a variation of it, or their names began with M. Who could keep up?

With my senses at various stages of wakefulness, I arrived for lauds the next morning and took a seat in the congregation area of the chapel. *At least I don't have to think,* the lazy monastic in me reasoned. *I can just sit and let the liturgy and the dreamy chants float over me.*

"The sleepy," wrote St. Benedict, "make many excuses." I doubted that ol' Benny had ever contended with this level of disorientation, or set a refectory table with a complement of cutlery that rivaled what one might find in the sideboard of Hampton Court Palace.

I was barely settled in my seat when Sister Dorothy Stella caught my eye and cocked her head toward a choir stall.

Are you sure? My quizzical look asked.

She responded with a nod and a confident smile.

I moved tentatively from the congregation area to the choir stalls and took a seat in the double prie-dieu she had indicated. *A prie-dieu à deux?* I chuckled to myself. My humor drained when I saw the small shelf in the prie-dieu crammed with an assortment of books: a psalter, two hymn books, a binder, a couple of spiral-bound booklets, a prayer book, and a few loose booklets and sheet music. *Oh dear.*

The next thing I knew, Sister Margaret Anne was standing beside the stall staring at me with a similar look of panic, only hers wasn't about the prayer books; it was the fact that The Incompetent One was sharing her choir stall. *What the hell?* her look screamed. She spun toward Sister Dorothy Stella, whose head was conveniently bowed and her eyes shut tight in prayer.

I met Sister Margaret Anne's gaze with a sheepish shrug of my shoulders. She did not look pleased but took her seat anyway. She shifted uneasily, looking at me, then turning away, then looking back several times as if not quite believing this intrusion.

Resigning herself to it, she pulled a few books and binders from my shelf, deftly leafed through the pages, and marked certain ones with greeting card covers and postcards that had been repurposed as bookmarks.

I mouthed "Thanks" many times. Angels do not always come in the guise of cooing, ethereal beings: they sometimes reveal themselves by their steadiness and their quick, no-nonsense help. Sister Margaret Anne was one such angel.

I was hopeless during the office. I flailed like a dog in a bathtub. Everything was inexplicably strange, only marginally familiar to the office said by the sisters at St. John the Divine.

I glanced at the cover of the prayer book to make sure I hadn't inadvertently walked into the Lutheran Church.

I messed up the psalm by not pausing between lines, as is the monastic custom. I stumbled over the chanting of the Venite, which I have known by heart for years but which now struck me as foreign. As for the Lord's Prayer, had someone rewritten it? I did not dare sing. It was like being presented with a new language.

The learning curve didn't stop there. An infinitesimal number of things had to be remembered not only *in* chapel but *about* chapel: the times of the offices, how to decipher the abbreviations of the weekly chapel schedule that indicated what hymn book to use, what psalms to recite (and which verses), which version of the Magnificat to chant, which Eucharistic prayer was to be used for Holy Communion.

Around me the sisters flipped effortlessly between multiple books, landing on the right canticle or antiphon, locating the proper responsory, hymn, and prayer. Each office began with a vocal recitation of the Angelus to accompany the tolling bell. Would the day ever come when I could recite it without needing a cheat sheet?

(5:vi)

A PLACE of silence tunes your antennae to the observation of body language and of mood. At St. Hilda's, you had to keep your head bowed in prayer and humility and still be able to gauge facial expressions and gestures to know what was going on or whether you were messing up.

Example: At breakfast, I initially helped myself to a bowl of cereal. So far so good. Then I walked to the fruit bowl at the far end of the refectory, plucked a banana from the bowl, and returned to my seat to slice it on my cereal. Sometimes I added a piece of bread with marmalade to this repast.

It took a few breakfasts before I clued in, not by what was said to me but by the widened eyeballs of the sisters, that this amount of food was excessive. You could have cereal or bread or fruit, but not two of the three, and certainly not all three. I managed to figure out that two cups of tea were permitted with breakfast only because I saw Sister KT go up for seconds.

The noon meal was more structured. We assembled in the refectory after the midday office, found our places at table, and stood until grace was said. Then we sat down, and those sisters assigned to serve the tables would fetch the food. The sister at the head of the table would serve the main dish and pass the plates to each person. Once you had your plate, you could help yourself to potatoes or vegetables. When everyone at your table had been served, you could begin eating. When you were finished, you waited until others were finished. Occasionally, you might be offered a second helping. This was all conveyed through a series of head nods and eye and eyebrow movements. When everyone had finished eating, the prioress would ring a small bell. A cacophony of moving chairs and clanging dishes and cutlery would erupt as dinner plates were removed to a trolley and taken into the kitchen. The same trolley would re-emerge laden with dessert—"pudding" as the Brits refer to it. Again, the head sister at each table would serve the pudding, and again you did not dig in until everyone at the table was served. When you finished, you waited for the rest to finish. The prioress would ring the bell again. Dirty plates and bowls were heaped onto the trolley and wheeled into the kitchen. When the sister who had taken the trolley to the kitchen came back to the refectory, we stood and bowed our heads for a parting grace.

Supper was sometimes formal and sometimes not, and periodically the vow of silence was relaxed at these meals, but I was at a loss to explain how this was determined. I did manage to retain the fact that Sunday dinner was a "talking" meal.

By evening I could not get into bed fast enough. As I waited for sleep, my brain neurons continued to fire like pistons with the eternal question cycling through my draining consciousness: *Are you or are you not going to be a nun?*

I was too tired to think about it. All that mattered was to stay out of everyone's hair and do as I was told.

(5:vii)

SISTER HEATHER Francis was off to York for the day and invited me along for the ride.

We set off after lauds under moody skies across the scrubby moors, our small silver car navigating an undulating landscape of dense fog like a small tugboat rising and dropping in choppy water.

There is a disturbing beauty to the North Yorkshire Moors in February. With its clots of brown prickly shrubs studded across a vast no-man's land, it seems ideal for two things—getting lost, and being able to scream without disturbing anyone.

Sensing my thoughts, Sister Heather Francis piped up, "You can't tell now, obviously, but later in the year, this becomes a blanket of purple when the heather blooms. It is a marvelous sight."

Her hands gripped the steering wheel as the car hugged a sharp turn.

Sister Heather Francis was a tall, thin, precise type with a degree in biology. She was unnervingly quiet but always perked up when the conversation came round to plants. On our way to York, I made an admiring comment about hedgerows, and she proceeded to give me a master class on their care, their uses, their ecological value, as well as legislation relating to them.

I am fascinated by hedgerows and how decades, sometimes centuries, of careful cultivation and grooming have managed to create these enormous foliated fences, giving the British countryside a look that seems sprung from the pages of a story-book. There is much to know about hedgerows. From Sister Heather Francis, I learned that hedgerow maintenance is expensive, that pruning requires tractor-mounted cutting equipment, and that in some regions there are bylaws concerning hedgerow stewardship. Cuttings are harvested and used to construct and repair thatched-roof buildings; hedgerows protect the fields from flood damage and erosion, and they provide shelter and nesting places for birds and small critters such as the great crested newt and the dormouse. And here I thought hedgerows existed merely to make the landscape pretty.

When we arrived in York, Sister Heather Francis continued my education by taking me on a walking tour along the top of the ancient city walls and then down through the park bordering the River Ouse.

We stopped in front of the strange, reptilian-looking monkey puzzle tree—"*Araucaria araucana* is its botanical name," she said. "You probably noticed lots of shops in Whitby selling jewelry made of a black stone called Whitby jet? Well, it is from the compressed and fossilized wood of the monkey puzzle tree that Whitby jet derives."

I felt as if I should be taking notes.

We gravitated toward the Old Quarter and meandered through the narrow, winding cobblestone streets where Elizabethan timber buildings teeter overhead. And there were shops. Lots of them, all with tempting window displays of vibrant and colorful clothing like I had never seen: long multi-textured and multi-colored scarves, tailored velvet jackets, long, gored skirts, and almost all of it on sale to make way for spring wear. I thought of my 2011 Winter Nun Collection and felt a pang of—what was it? Longing? Regret? Desire? Greed? And yet it wasn't as if I could tug on Sister Heather Francis's arm and say, "Hey, let's check that out! There's a sale!" She was enviously free of the world of skinny jeans and chunky jewelry.

I liked the feel of York. It was a proud city, not arrogantly proud but proud in a genteel and protective way.

When it was established in AD 71 as a Roman fortress and given the name Eboracum, it was a trade hub, but over time it became a key player in ecclesiastical matters.

During the Anglo Saxon period, Edwin, King of Northumbria, made York his seat of power, and re-introduced Christianity to the region with the help of Paulinus, a priest who served Edwin's very religious wife. Whether Edwin's conversion was due to faith or politics (or pressure from his wife) is a question still batted about by historians, but what is undisputed is that it was a seminal event. Edwin was baptized along with members of his family and court on Easter 627, in a small frame church. The occasion proved auspicious on several fronts: that small frame church was the genesis of magnificent York Minster; Paulinus the priest became the first bishop of York; and among Edwin's family was his thirteen-year-old niece, Hilda, who would play a pivotal role in Christianity's rise in Britain and become one of its major northern saints—the same Hilda whose statue graced the reception area at St. Hilda's Priory and who the Order of the Holy Paraclete had adopted as its patroness.

There was so much about York I wanted to know, and I had an urge to hop on a tour bus and get the lowdown on its chocolate history (Rowntree and Terry's both started here), its Viking roots, and its reputation as the most haunted capital in Europe, but Sister Heather Francis was several paces ahead of me, her black veil fluttering in the breeze. She was one of only a handful of sisters in the order who continued to wear the veil.

"I like people to know who I am and what I do," she replied matter-of-factly when I asked her about it. "The veil is instantly recognizable. People say they never hear about religious orders anymore, and a lot of that has to do with the fact that we do not make ourselves visible. I wear it to promote religious life."

It seemed to be working, at least in terms of making her visible. In the streets of York several people did double-takes when she passed by, and a woman in a café pointed her out excitedly to her companion as if Sister Heather Francis was the Queen of England. Maybe nun-spotting was the new thing.

Again I was reminded of the remark by former Archbishop Carey about nuns being "the best-kept secret of the Anglican Communion." Which prompts one to muse, if a nun doesn't wear a habit, does her vocation truly exist?

We walked to the order's branch house, a smart-looking townhouse across from the Minster, to have lunch.

Most religious orders have branch houses where sisters live when their work and ministry makes it impractical to live at priory HQ. The Order of the Holy Paraclete had eight branch houses—five in England and three in Africa.

The two York sisters were engaged in duties connected with the Minster such as serving as tour guides and helping run the Sunday school.

They had prepared lunch for us, and over salmon sandwiches, a bag of crisps, fruit, tea, and a Kit Kat bar (a York invention, by the way, that pumps out a billion bars a year locally) we chatted away. It did not feel as if I was among a group of nuns; it felt like a neighborly coffee klatch with women who had extraordinary experiences.

Joining us at lunch was a woman visiting from South Africa, and that got the sisters reminiscing about their work in that country.

From 1950 to the mid-1990s, the Order of the Holy Paraclete had a branch house—it was called St. Benedict's—in the Rosettenville district of Johannesburg. At the height of the apartheid era, St. Benedict's was a locus for hospitality and refuge. The sisters adopted a passive-aggressive resistance to the apartheid law, and fed, comforted, treated, and advocated for those who were being terrorized by the regime. Desmond Tutu and Trevor Huddleston, both priests during the struggle, were frequent visitors. Not surprisingly, St. Benedict's was subjected to midnight raids, random searches, intimidation, arrests, and phone tapping. At the time, Huddleston was surreptitiously working on the manuscript for *Naught for Your Comfort,* his excoriating critique of the regime. The sisters took turns hiding the manuscript under their mattresses and one of them ultimately risked her life to smuggle it out of Africa and deliver it into the hands of Huddleston's English publisher.

Huddleston's book had taken aim at the apartheid regime but it also took a strip off Christians who used the shield of patriotism and religion to defend odious government policies. He felt Christians should be held to a higher moral and ethical standard. I wondered how the experience he related in his book squared with his fellow clergy today and the barriers their own regime had erected against women and gays.

As memories were excitedly traded around the kitchen table the sisters' eyes lit up. It was clear that their work at St. Benedict's had shown the order at its finest, living its calling to the fullest. When the order had handed over St. Benedict's to another religious order, the termination of its work and the loss of connection to the place had been traumatic for the sisters, as well as for those in Johannesburg who were recipients of the nuns' courage and kindness.

After lunch, I wandered across the road to York Minster, a monster cathedral of soaring pillars and mammoth tracts of stained glass. The stories reverberated in my head of the sisters' descriptions of life under apartheid, the muddy over-crowded squalor, the horrific treatment of blacks, and the emotional brokenness that swept through the shanty towns like a plague. I tried to reconcile those images with the Minster's glittering interior.

A cathedral can be as distracting and as gaudy as a shopping mall, and pilgrims can easily get as swept up by the artistic and architectural wow factor as shoppers do over displays of handbags and housewares.

I was as transfixed by the Minster as everyone else, but when I tore my gaze from its splendor, I noticed brokenness amid the perfection. While the tourist throngs had been admiring the ornamental ceiling bosses, other souls had slipped through to tend to their world of big and small traumas. Some stared ahead at the altar; others buried their faces in their hands; a few were weeping.

My strident attitude toward the church's organized structure softened, and I became appreciative of the silent and largely unsung service churches provide to those who come not to worship or to gawk at majestic architecture but to sit and come to grips with the pain and the muck of life. If not for churches, where would people go to safely unburden their souls? Where would I go to confront the memory of my rape?

(5:viii)

A CELEBRATORY mood rippled through the priory as the sisters fussed with flower arrangements and prepared for the first profession of Sister Samantha.

There are several steps in a woman's journey toward becoming a full-fledged nun: aspirant, postulant, novice, first professed, and life professed. There are generally three years between each of those last three stages. Theoretically, you could become a doctor faster than you could become a nun.

Sister Samantha was young, in her early twenties, and as I observed the ritual along with the rest of the congregation, I wondered how I would respond had it been my daughter, of similar age as Sister Samantha, making her profession vows. Would I have been overjoyed that she had found a passion for this life, or would I have been sad that she was cutting herself off at such a young age from experience and discovery?

The Anglican ceremony is far more low-key than the Roman Catholic tradition, in which the profession ceremony involves a bridal gown and mimics a marriage to Christ.

Dressed simply in the order's habit, Sister Samantha fearlessly approached the presiding priest and made her vows in front of her community:

Priest: *Do you believe that you are called by God to serve Him in this way of life?*

Sister: *I do.*

Priest: *Do you promise to live by the Rule of this Order and to observe its customs for the next three years?*

Sister: *I do.*

Priest: *This life to which you are called involves a steadfast intention expressed in the three-fold vow of Poverty, Celibacy, and Obedience. Will you undertake to be bound in this way during the period of First Profession?*

Sister: *I will, God being my helper.*

After signing the register, Sister Samantha held it open, displaying it to the congregation, and repeated the verse from Psalm 119: "O stablish me according to Thy word that I might live, and let me not be disappointed of my hope."

She knelt before the priest to receive the first-profession gifts of the silver cross of the order, the black girdle or cord, and the veil. Only at life profession does a nun receive a gold wedding band and have three knots put in the girdle to signify that her three vows are being made for life.

It made me think what a sensible arrangement this might be for secular marriage: have the partners pledge to love, honor, cherish, and live responsibly for three years, after which they can renew their vows for life if they wish. (St. Francis of Assisi is reputed to have remarked that "if marriage were an order having a Novitiate, not nearly so many would enter it.")

After the ceremony, we adjourned to the refectory for cake and wine.

A few days later, the chapel was decorated for a different celebration: the funeral of one of the sisters. For those in religious life, funerals are not sad occasions but a time to rejoice because the deceased has transcended the earthly realm to rest with God.

Six tall, thick candles stood sentinel around the coffin, the blazing reflection of their flames shimmering off the walls of the chapel like beating angel wings while clouds of incense billowed from a censer.

We trooped out to the small cemetery behind the priory, huddled under umbrellas against the cold drizzle, and watched the coffin being lowered into the ground.

And once again, we adjourned to the refectory for cake and wine.

(5:ix)

THEY HAD chocolate digestive biscuits by the cake tin-full. I could not believe my luck.

Nor could I believe I had reached the stage of life where this was all it took to make me happy. There was a time when I wouldn't have thanked you for a chocolate digestive biscuit. Now I wasn't sure I could live without them.

I fell in step with the priory's busy but ordered life. My usual frantic and chaotic state had been transmogrified into one of serenity and balance. The stress from that horror show at St. Cecilia's was well behind me.

Every morning I got up, washed, and chose an outfit from the five-outfit 2011 Winter Nun Collection.

The bland wardrobe cut down on getting ready in the mornings. Make-up? That was for shallow sissies. This no-fuss regimen put me in a state of readiness for God. I now understood that conversation I had had with Sister Sue back at ssjd about why nuns couldn't wear lipstick, bangles, or earrings. It was all about making life less complicated to allow you to focus on God.

The conversion from consumer to a contemplative was not going to happen overnight, but I could see how it was transforming my personality. The time I saved by not primping was spent on admiring a sunrise or in tending to a chore or having a few extra minutes for a leisurely chat with someone. I began to feel like a better person.

There was an overwhelming desire—not an obligation or a demand—to attend, to be present in everything put before me. The secular world calls this "living in the moment," something I had never had time to do when I lived in it. I was too busy multitasking and art-directing the moment in which I could "live in the moment."

In the secular world, the hours bled into one another indiscriminately, whereas in the convent, each hour had its purpose. This is where the Benedictine system was brilliant. It gave you space, and if you didn't follow it, you would find yourself crazy busy. Gone were the days of working through the lunch hour or grabbing a bite at my desk. For the first time in my life, I was taking tea breaks.

I had never been a clock watcher, but I became one in the convent in order to pace myself and avoid getting involved in anything that might cause me to be late for office. Two hours was the longest block of time devoted to work. At the sound of the bell, I shut the lid of my laptop and headed to chapel. This was such a departure from my normal mode of work that initially I felt like a slacker.

As the sun drifted down to the horizon I never asked, "Where did the time go?" because I knew exactly where it had gone. The day had not been sucked up with checking or responding to email, answering phone calls, or performing myriad domestic tasks that cause the day to vaporize like bits of ash. I could account for every hour of my existence, and this brought a wonderful clarity and appreciation to life.

My schedule at St. Hilda's was arranged like this:

6:00 a.m.	Wake-up, dress, quiet prayer
7:15 a.m.	Lauds
8:00 a.m.	Breakfast/cleanup
9:00 a.m.	Work
11:00 a.m.	Tea
11:20 a.m.	Work
12:00 p.m.	Midday office/Eucharist
1:00 p.m.	Dinner/cleanup/quiet time
2:30 p.m.	Work
4:30 p.m.	Tea
4:45 p.m.	Work
6:00 p.m.	Vespers
7:00 p.m.	Supper/cleanup
8:00 p.m.	Read/free-time
9:00 p.m.	Compline
9:30 p.m.	Bed

(5:x)

A LETTER arrived from Colin. We had reverted to old-fashioned pen and paper because access to the Internet wasn't always reliable in certain parts of the priory. The ping of a computer's inbox heralding newly arrived email did not come close to the thrill of receiving a handwritten, stamped, and posted letter.

The letter was left for me on the table in the cloister corridor as I entered the refectory for dinner. I put it in my pocket quickly, and when the meal was over and the dishes were done, I hurried to my cell, shut the door, and tore open the envelope.

There was a sensual quality to snail mail that I had long forgotten.

I first scanned the letter to analyze Colin's penmanship—*Was he ill, rushed, or happy when he wrote it?*—and then I returned to the top of the letter and read it slowly, as if deciphering a coded message. I digested each word, parsed each emotion expressed, as well as those unexpressed. He was chattier in writing than in person. I scrutinized his choice of words, pondered the subjects he chose to tell me about, and noted those he avoided or neglected. His parents and siblings were all well; work was OK. He described an interesting television program on an area of England that he thought we could explore—together. He said he missed me.

I examined the envelope for signs of a scribble or a hidden message, perhaps a coffee spill. I checked the way the stamp was affixed because there were clues there, too: perfectly lined up with the corners of the envelope meant he was being precise and careful; if it was somewhat angled, it might indicate that he was hurried or had other things to do.

When I was done reading and ruminating over the contents of his letter, I pressed my cheek against the paper he had touched and tried to capture some of his scent.

(5:xi)

"WELL, AREN'T you a great wally," Sister KT scolded good-naturedly as she elbowed past me to correct my mistake. I always joined the sisters in cleaning the kitchen and refectory after meals. I wanted to be helpful—these women worked so hard—but I also wanted to be around them when they let down their metaphorical wimples.

I had pretty much sussed out the kitchen routine and figured out everyone's chosen chore. I had also learned not to horn in on someone else's chore unless I was prepared to have my head bitten off, so I stuck to the ones where I was needed.

I had also mastered the setting of tables and I knew where the cutlery and dishes were kept and where the condiments were stored (in the same place as the chocolate digestive biscuits), so I figured I could handle the dishwasher. Sister KT normally loaded the dishwasher, but on this day she hadn't arrived in the kitchen, so I took the initiative.

Naturally, I messed up, or rather I did not do it the way she did it. She shook her head good-naturedly and corrected my mistake. And she called me a wally. Like "pinny," "wally" was an unfamiliar term.

"What does 'wally' mean?" I pestered her. "Where does it originate? Is it a term of endearment, like 'pal' or 'buddy'?"

She paused in the midst of rearranging the plates in the dishwasher rack. "Um, yeah, that's it. Endearment," she said, and then she quickly turned her face away.

The little scamp. It was only when I called another sister "wally" a few days later and was met with an offended look that I realized it was definitely not a term of endearment.

"See? That's what makes you a wally," chuckled Sister KT when I confronted her about my faux pas. "But look, if it makes you feel better, I'll be nicer. I'll call you Ms. Wally, OK?"

"Fine. And I'll call you Sister Wally," I said, whipping the tea towel at her in mock offense.

It was the sort of easygoing camaraderie found in kitchens everywhere when two or more women are gathered in the name of cleaning up.

As each sister migrated to her station to load the dishwasher, scrub the pots and pans, wrap up the leftover food, restock the stores, scrape off the plates, or whatever, the banter would start up. The interactions were relaxed: invariably someone would say something funny or tease someone, or you could catch up with someone about how their day was going. Soapy water and tea towels bring out the playful side of women.

But as soon as everything was cleaned up and back in its place, as soon as the pinnies were hung back on their hooks, we all left the kitchen, and once again silence reigned and communication ceased.

(5:xii)

I SKITTERED along the cloister corridor toward the chapel for lauds. The gauzy morning light of winter slanted through the large windows and made a weak attempt to warm things up. I rubbed my hands together and blew out puffs of breath, like smoke rings, which evaporated into the frigid air. Yes, it was February; yes, England has a northern climate; and yes, as a Canadian, I would be expected to show a bit more hardiness where the weather was concerned—but how can it be this cold *inside* a building? The day before, a few of the sisters had given me a peek at the extra layers they wore under their habits: some had cut the feet off a pair of long, thick socks and wore them as arm warmers. I made a mental note to drop into a charity shop the next time I was in town and buy a pair of long socks.

On the way to the chapel, I passed the furnace room and was tempted to nip inside. It was the toastiest place at St. Hilda's, as I had discovered when Sister Margaret Anne sent me the other day to fetch the brooms to sweep the refectory. The moment I unlatched the large wood door, it was like stepping off an airplane that had just landed on a Caribbean island. I always offered to fetch the brooms after that. At certain times of the day, when the wind's direction shot blasts of cold air through the cloister corridors, or in the dark evening before compline, I would get the urge to pray in the furnace room. It wasn't a fear of being caught that deterred me—no one would have minded at all—it was the fear of finding others huddled there in the dark.

The other place that was warm was—big surprise—the chapel.

As we stood at our prie-dieux to recite the Hail Mary, the Angelus ringing in accompaniment, cold hands and feet were forgotten. The prayers and vibration of the chants unlocked our hearts and opened them to the divine. Our voices came together and rose and fell, drew back and surged forward like the North Sea tides. During those exquisite moments when our voices gelled, when our vocal pitch and register aligned, a shiver of joy would shoot through me.

Invariably, so would a pang of hunger. Stomachs never rumble during a loud hymn or a semi-loud prayer but only when there is a pause in the homily or during quiet moments of reflection.

There was little chance of being sated today. It was Friday, and Fridays were abstention days, which meant that only tea and bread with butter or marmalade were allowed at breakfast.

The true work of a contemplative nun is praying. I had never appreciated the power and intensity of prayer until I prayed with nuns.

On the surface, praying seems easy. Knit your eyebrows in concentration, mutter a few words, and then get on with your day. It's not like that in a convent. Think of the hardest job you could do—mining comes to my mind—and then imagine doing that in silence and in a dress.

Every day the sisters descended into the Pit of the Soul, picked at the seam of despair, sadness, tragedy, death, sickness, grief, destruction, and poverty, loaded it all onto a cart marked "For God," and hauled it up from the depths of concern to the surface of mercy, where they cleaned it and polished it. It was heavy, laborious work.

In my secular life I had learned to inoculate myself with the usual distractions against soul-tearing news stories, but there was no such luxury at the convent. No skimming the newspaper, tallying up the dead and distressed from the headlines, and uttering something banal like "Poor guy" or "Poor gal" before closing the newspaper and getting on with my day. Nuns do not allow themselves such things. Every crime, every death, every lost child, every inhumane action by a government, every potential tragedy is brought before God in prayers and meditations.

If you were praying for a woman who was badly injured in a car accident, for example, your prayers focused on the physical and emotional pain the woman had experienced until you almost felt it; you considered how the injured woman's body would respond to treatment, the possible medical setbacks, and the advances that would hopefully restore her to wellness. It was sort of like the Ignatius method of prayer. You prayed for her family, the worries of her children, husband, elderly parents, friends, work colleagues—the entire circle. You prayed for the person who caused the accident and for his or her circle of family and friends, too.

The sisters' prayers were real and specific. They interceded on behalf of the unemployed fishermen in Whitby and those up and down the coast, for those in prison, for single mothers who were about to lose a vital community service because of government cutbacks. One prayer that by its sheer honesty always pulled me up short was, "We pray for those who will lose their lives violently today." And I would reel back and think of the ways people die violently these days. In battle on a desert road, in street gangs, in a robbery, in a traffic accident, from suicide, from a broken heart. The images were too terrible, the possibilities too numerous.

Prayer requests to the sisters arrived by mail, email, and phone and were posted on the bulletin boards at the entrances to the chapel and the refectory. They covered a range of needs: for a son looking for a job, for a woman awaiting the results of a breast biopsy, for workers facing a factory shutdown, for a religious person who was reconsidering his or her vows.

Whether in their chapel stalls, their rooms, the corridor, or the garden or whether walking, eating their meals, or sipping tea, the sisters prayed. They did it because prayer works, and the proof came in the form of emails and cards from people reporting that their prayers had been answered: a baby had recovered from an illness or a student had done well on a critical test or an operation had been successful.

It is hard to imagine what would happen to the world if people stopped praying.

Here's the thing about prayer: It doesn't require fancy words, or a theology degree. It doesn't even require you to be articulate on any level. Sometimes my own prayers are so scrambled and banal that I wonder whether God thinks English is my second or third language. But therein lies the beauty of it. Vocal articulation is unnecessary. You can sit in silence and sputter out your thoughts telepathically. Still, it doesn't come easy for everyone. A priest I know admitted that he couldn't pray; it just didn't work for him, he got tongue-tied and could not muster the attention for it.

Jesus had a word or two to say about how to pray, and one of them was to keep it short and simple: God's not impressed by your MA-level vocabulary. The other thing about prayer is that it is to be done in private. Like Jesus says in Matthew's gospel, "When you pray, do not be like the hypocrites, for they love to pray standing in the synagogues and on the street corners to be seen by men... When you pray, go into your room, close the door, and pray to your Father who is unseen."

Being in a place conducive to prayer, where prayer was not just a way of life but was *the* life, began to change the way I prayed. My prayers became less of a laundry list of thanks and requests, and more of an encounter.

Praying sometimes left me empty or weak or ravenous. And sometimes it left me speechless and frightened of the world.

But it was always a profound experience, a privilege even, to pray with the nuns. When we prayed together, I could feel the energy coalescing and being transmitted into the universe like telepathic waves.

(5:xiii)

SILENCE WAS a language in the convent. In time I came to recognize its various dialects. Facial expressions—a quiet smile, a cocking motion of the head, lowered eyes, an impassive face—were the easiest to decipher, but there was also communication to be gleaned from a purposeful stride, a slack posture, fidgety hands. It was like possessing a supernatural capacity to pick up birdsong and using it to deduce a change in global environmental patterns.

The language of silence required intense and focused listening with both the brain and the heart, and the sisters' tacit connection to one another made them alert to the slightest frisson of anxiety, the deepest source of pain, or the withholding of a secret. They would never say anything aloud or pry into the source of another person's concern—this might be due more to the British sensibility than to being religious in general—but they would still know intuitively if all was not as well as a stiff-upper-lip sister might let on.

It was with this sixth sense that I tuned in to Sister Margaret Anne's frequency. By virtue of the fact that we shared a choir stall, I probably spent more time with her than most of the other sisters. And although we did not talk a lot and rarely communicated with one another outside of chapel, I probably knew her better than any of the others. She had become a tremendous help in steering me through the liturgy, and she kindly assisted me when I lost my place in the prayer books and hymnals.

Sitting next to one another in chapel, we could gauge each other's health or mood in seconds. I became hypersensitive to her breathing, singing, enunciation, the way she stressed a syllable or a particular word during the recitation of a prayer. I would experience a jolt of concern when she blew her nose, and would worry about whether she was coming down with a cold or flu. She must have shared the same concern for me, because when my voice dropped out of a hymn or the singing of the "Te Deum," she would quickly glance over to see if I had lost my place or if I was OK.

One day in the kitchen we found ourselves across from each other stirring our tea, and we both reacted with surprised laughter: "Oh, this is what you look like from the front," Sister Margaret Anne exclaimed. "I'm so used to seeing you in profile in chapel!"

(5:xiv)

TO BE or not to be a nun, that was the question. I could not make up my mind. One day I was in; the next, I was out.

I decided to stop fretting about it. After all, if God the Father Almighty, Maker of Souvenir Tea Towels, had directed me to St. Hilda's, He would surely speak to me again. I wondered when and how He might appear this time. No burning bush for me; maybe the tea kettle? A cereal box? A chair? This is how I know God has a sense of humor: He's like a pop-up store.

At times, I wondered whether God was trying to tell me something through the Bible passages that were read in chapel. In Matthew 19, Jesus speaks about marriage and divorce and says that those who divorce and remarry are guilty of adultery. Each time this passage was read—and since the beginning of my spiritual quest, it had been read half a dozen times and twice so far at St. Hilda's—I would feel prickles of discomfort. I wasn't sure whether it was intended for me or for the priest reading the passage: he was about to be married for a third time. Maybe the hat-trick marriage was the new thing.

Multiple marriages are more acceptable these days, a sort of life-stage thing: you have your starter marriage, your kids-and-mortgage marriage, your midlife marriage, and perhaps a retirement marriage and then a nursing-home marriage. Gosh, that's what, five marriages? Three marriages seemed an almost naïve level of experience. Seriously, no one, or rather no one with a heart, dreams of being a serial bride. Each misfire makes you wonder where the fault lies—with your personality or with your skill at choosing a partner. I was embarrassed by the prospect of a third marriage, and part of the draw to monastic life was a way to atone for my failure in that department.

Another Bible passage that was on heavy rotation was the parable of the Samaritan woman at the well (John 4:7–27). It has always made me chuckle, because it revealed—I'm sure not intentionally—Jesus' sense of humor. When Jesus tells the woman to "go and get your husband," the woman replies that she does not have a husband. This prompts Jesus to say, "You're right. You don't have a husband, for you have had five husbands and the man you're living with now is not your husband." Talk about a biblical gotcha moment.

I felt sorry for the Samaritan woman and her multiple marriages, and I wished that John, in writing his gospel, had been more of an investigative reporter and had ferreted out the reasons for them. Were they due to adultery on her part? On her husbands'? Had her partners died? Had one or two walked off without so much as a goodbye, or "I'm just stepping out for a skein of milk"?

Like an epoch, each marriage has its reasons for blossoming and for dying. If I had had only one marriage or if I had never married, I might have indeed looked askance at people with wedding albums cataloged under the Dewey decimal system.

That winter, marriage was in the air and in the media every single day. While I dithered over whether to enter the convent, Prince William and Kate Middleton were picking out china patterns and mulling over guest lists and wedding menus. Part of me missed not knowing every delicious detail of the wedding plans or not being able to weigh in on the relative merits of fascinators versus traditional hats. That is, until I dipped in one day to the online comments about the upcoming nuptials. The snipes were vicious, especially those aimed at the bride-to-be's family. The British media were no better, as they feigned disdain for the entire event and offered people holiday getaways to escape the celebrations. What a way to react to a couple of kids who announce their wedding!

Reaction was far more civilized at St. Hilda's. Once a week, we prayerfully included the betrothed couple in our intercessions.

(5:xv)

SISTER GILLIAN cornered me in the kitchen after breakfast to inform me that I was to have a day off each week. The news was like a lottery win. At first I tried to make out like I didn't need a day off. Sure, I was tired and I was working hard, but sweeping the refectory and praying four times a day wasn't exactly breaking my back.

Sister Gillian was adamant.

"You cannot keep working like this and remain here all the time. All of us have a space day. You can do what you like: go for a walk, go into Whitby; you don't have to attend office..."

"Any of them?" I might have asked that too eagerly.

"... any of them. You can use the day to do errands or as a retreat day. You don't even have to show up for meals. Just indicate it on the sign-up sheet in the refectory, and I'll keep a plate for you that you can microwave when you get back."

I adored Sister Gillian. She really took her role as guest sister to heart. She was diligent in her duty, but she also radiated happiness to such a degree that you could not help but feel better just by being around her. She would move through a room and deftly accomplish several tasks en route, chatting amiably as she did so and never giving the impression that her tasks were more important than you were.

I took my tea into the parlor and mentioned my impending day off to the sisters gathered there. They were all keen to know what I was going to do, since it was only two days away.

"I think I'll go and explore Whitby."

"Have you got a bus schedule?" one inquired.

"No, I was going to walk into town," I replied.

Eyebrows shot up, glances were exchanged, and cheeks puffed out as if to say, "You think so, do you?"

"Well," began another sucking air between her teeth to indicate that the prospect was doable but somewhat foolhardy, "you want to go through the castle gates, turn right, and just opposite the bus stop you turn..."

"No, that's not it," interrupted another sister. "You go out the gates and then two streets down on The Avenue, you turn past the mini-roundabout..."

"No," injected a third impatiently. "She wants to go through the housing development along Westbourne..."

"No, the fastest is through the path off High Stakesby..."

I politely excused myself to top up my tea and steal a chocolate digestive biscuit. (I was considering giving them up for Lent.) My hand was in the biscuit tin when Sister Patricia walked in.

Sister Patricia was a doll. She had a thick frothy cloud of white hair and the sort of ethereal aura that often gets mistaken for flakiness. During some of our casual conversations, Sister Patricia had revealed a sharp insight, and the combination of her wisdom and free-spiritedness was enchanting.

"Don't mind them," she said in her soft, slightly shaky voice. "I'll show you a shortcut to the sea where the road leads straight into Whitby. We'll go for a walk tomorrow afternoon if the weather's fine."

The next day after the noon meal, Sister Patricia and I met in the coatroom and girded ourselves against the cold with an armor of thick coats, scarves, and gloves. She pulled a black toque over her white hair.

We threaded through a residential area, the wind knocking us about and howling so loudly that it made talking virtually impossible.

At the end of Upgang Lane, on a small lookout, we clung to a metal railing and stared out at the choppy, leaden North Sea. Far below us on the beach, appearing to be roughly the size of ants, were people enjoying a Sunday stroll. Dogs fetched sticks thrown by their owners, young tots in bright-colored jackets waddled as close to the water's edge as their parents would permit, couples walked hand in hand, and children kicked around a football using scavenged rocks as goal posts. It was a joyous sight.

Down the beach to the right of us was Whitby; to the left as far as the eye could see was a cluster of white stucco buildings.

"That's Sandsend," said Sister Patricia. "It's a rather pretty village. You can walk along the beach to it. Maybe we'll do it together one day. Shall we walk down to the beach?"

We started down the precariously steep, narrow asphalt path to the beachfront when Sister Patricia suddenly turned to me and asked with immense concern, "Are you sure you are up to it, my dear? I don't want you to get too tired."

Bless.

There were little gullies along the stony route to the beach, but Sister Patricia skipped lightly over these. Her face wore a look of childlike delight, and she treated everything and everyone she encountered as a source of wonder. Like Sister Gillian, her face was in a perpetual smile.

As we walked along the beach, Sister Patricia told me about her years growing up in Derbyshire. She had taken a degree in literature from Oxford and migrated into teaching jobs, one of which was a teaching exchange to Pretoria. She had fallen in love, but it had not worked out, and she intimated that that was the reason she had chosen a job far away from England. It was only when she returned to the U.K. and got a job teaching at St. Hilda's boarding school that she decided to enter the novitiate. She made her life profession vows in 1964 and had spent long periods working at St. Hilda's branch houses and at missions in Ghana and South Africa, which she had loved as much for the work as for the sun and the heat.

It was good to get out and feel the sea air. The intensity of the wind combined with the mighty roar of the waves blunted my senses and filled me with a wild and pure energy.

On the way back to the priory, we chatted about the funeral that had taken place a few days earlier. Sister Patricia was as excited as a child on Christmas Eve at the prospect of her own funeral.

"I can't wait," she enthused, clapping her hands with glee. "I've decided that at my funeral reception, people will be served soup and a roll and the rest of the meal will be puddings! All types of puddings!"

"You get to choose the food that will be served at your funeral reception?" I asked.

"Oh yes. We fill out a form listing all the particulars that we want—the menu, the type of funeral, the music we want played, the hymns we want sung—and it has to be followed. To. The. Letter."

She told me that the order had never had a nun reach the age of one hundred.

"Maybe you'll be one of the first," I said.

"Oh gracious, no! Please, no!" she laughed. "I'm ready to go now. I don't want to wait *that* long."

(5:xvi)

I LEAPED out of bed the next morning. *Woohoo!* It was the last day of February—I dislike February intensely: the shortest month of the year feels so damn long—and it was also my day off. I couldn't wait to see what mischief I might get up to.

When I heard the Angelus and was certain everyone was at lauds, I scampered downstairs from my attic cell, dropped my laundry onto the cart in the corridor, had breakfast alone in the refectory—bliss—and then sailed out the front door of the priory. The sky threatened rain, and the wind threatened to hurl me off the planet. Perfect conditions to hunt for Dracula.

Not exactly Dracula, but his creator, Bram Stoker, the Irish-born journalist/personal assistant/business manager/novelist.

Stoker had been smitten by Whitby during a holiday one year. He loved its narrow streets; the tall, skinny, imperious-looking terraced houses that loomed like disapproving aunts; the dense, rolling fog; the wild North Sea storms; the nefarious activity along the docks.

Charles Dodgson, a.k.a. Lewis Carroll, also stomped through this town, and I wondered whether Stoker had come to the town to mop up some of the muse dust left by Dodgson/Carroll.

In 1885, during a storm, a Russian schooner crashed into Whitby Harbour, and the event became the catalyst for Stoker's dark tale of coffins, vampires, and a pair of innocent girls—Mina and Lucy—on a seaside holiday.

The good folks of Whitby are not the least bit offended to be associated with a blood-sucking count, and both Stoker and Dracula have pride of place in its tourist industry.

I sat down on a bench to take in the landscape and the atmosphere that had inspired Stoker. The River Esk bisects Whitby, dividing it into two steep cliffs known—none too imaginatively—as East Cliff and West Cliff. They are linked by an iron swing bridge (in *Dracula* it is referred to as "the drawbridge," across which Mina makes a breathless dash toward the churchyard to save her friend Lucy). Directly across from me on the opposite cliff, high above the Esk, was the churchyard of St. Mary's, and behind it loomed the eerie, skeletal remains of Whitby Abbey. Seagulls soared and dipped agitatedly through the moody skies above the harbor, their high-pitched screeches sounded like screams. All that was missing was a fog machine and a bat.

Several gulls landed nearby and strutted muscularly toward me like hoodlums. As if to reinforce their territorial prerogative, they set about using the patch right in front of me for their morning shit. I moved on, their beady little eyes following me. Has anyone noticed that certain species of birds—gulls, geese, swans, pigeons, crows come immediately to mind—seem to have interbred with a biker gang?

Once a thriving shipbuilding and fishing center, Whitby, like many mid-sized towns in Britain, was floundering through the New Economy with high levels of underemployment and unemployment along with the ancillary social wreckage. Another round of job cuts to the decimated fishing industry had just been announced in the local newspaper.

With Stoker and his toothy creation in its back pocket, Whitby had repurposed itself as a tourist destination. About 90 percent of the working population now toils in the service industry.

I made my way through twisting passageways and subways, down steep steps, past Victorian brick homes with their red pantiled roofs snuggled together along quiet, wet narrow streets.

I crossed the swing bridge to Church Street, a narrow, cobblestone street jammed with quaint tea rooms, sweet shops, and jewelry boutiques selling creations fashioned with Whitby jet. There were also goth shops galore stocked with skull jewelry and vampy-looking lingerie and feather boas, and goth-inspired housewares. Looking for a set of vampire bookends or a toilet brush with Dracula's head as the handle? You will find it here. The goth-nun I had met at St. Cecilia's was right about Whitby's goth reputation.

Church Street ended at the base of the 199 Steps, which Mina clambered up on a dark and stormy night to warn Lucy before Dracula planted his incisors in her neck. I started up the steps myself. It is one of the "things" you do when you visit Whitby.

The steps—pedantic locals will remind you that "stairs" are made of wood and "steps" are made of stone—have existed for four hundred years. In the early 1800s, the wood treads and risers were replaced with stone, and handrails and landings were added to make the journey easier for pallbearers hauling coffins up to the church cemetery. Judging from historical accounts, the refurb had not entirely solved the problem: in several instances the coffin had slipped from the pallbearers' grip and torpedoed back down to the base.

At the top of the steps in the graveyard of St. Mary's Church, I wandered among the worn, battered gravestones, their inscriptions all but erased by time and the elements, and then nosed around the twelfth-century church before crossing the churchyard to Whitby Abbey, site of a thirteenth-century Benedictine monastery.

For tourist and goth potential, you could not wish for a more dramatic landmark. The ruins are noticeable the moment you enter the town, and they follow you everywhere you go in Whitby: in fact, I could see them all the way from St. Hilda's Priory. The iconic silhouette of Whitby Abbey is festooned on almost every piece of tourism material, on the ubiquitous Whitby jet jewelry, on café menus, on souvenir tea towels, and in books. In the last eight hundred years, the Abbey has been subjected to climatic battery, pillaging vandals, and war bombs. It is remarkable that so much of it is still standing. Up close, the lacey ruins of mottled charcoal stone stand like an old soldier before a cenotaph, damaged and scarred but resolutely upright.

Weeks earlier in York, I had stood near the site where thirteen-year-old Hilda had been baptized with her uncle King Edwin. Now I stood on the site where her spiritual journey had brought her, and where she had founded a mixed religious community in 657. There is nothing left of the build-ings from that era—people mistakenly think the Abbey ruins are from Hilda's time—yet she is inextricably linked to Whitby, and to Northern England.

It was said of Hilda that she was a patient woman, energetic and blessed with the ability to recognize the paraclete—the spirit of personality—in people. It was Hilda who overheard a young cowherd named Caedmon singing to himself, nurtured his gift, and turned him into one of the great Celtic poets. It was Hilda who schooled five monks who eventually became bishops. And it was Hilda who hosted the first synod, the Synod of Whitby, in 664, at which a heated debate ultimately decided the way we calculate the date for Easter.

How sadly ironic, then, that the site where Britain's first recognized female priest established her community and where many believe Christianity officially took root in Britain had been appropriated by the cult of a fictional demon.

6

The Winter Desert

Order of the Holy Paraclete
Whitby, England

"A MONK'S LIFE SHOULD always be like a Lenten observance." So declared St. Benedict. No wonder his monks tried to poison him.

Lent is the desert season, an intense, bleak period requiring more spiritual vigilance, deeper introspection, and greater resistance to self-gratification than is demanded during the rest of the Christian calendar. The grand reward is spiritual transformation.

From a liturgical point of view, I could not have chosen a better time than Lent to continue discerning my vocation to be a nun. From a psychological point of view, it almost did me in.

I have always thought the church misses an opportunity at Lent to encourage people, regardless of their faith, to use the forty days and forty nights as a personal challenge—to quit smoking, lose weight, volunteer in the community, and otherwise set goals to change or improve their lives.

Lent appeals to the part of me that likes rigorous self-improvement, so when one sister cautioned, "If you can survive Lent in a convent, you can survive anything," my reaction on the morning of Ash Wednesday was, *No sweat, baby,* followed by a cavalier chuckle. That blithe attitude lasted until suppertime, when I discovered that the bun-and-tea menu from breakfast would be repeated at supper. Almost every night. Until Easter.

At first I was stoic, but by the second day, I was ready to bail. Now I was cold *and* hungry. *This isn't Lent; this is the gulag! This is Scott's expedition to Antarctica!*

After compline, I sat on the edge of my bed in flannel pajamas, pulling on multiple pairs of socks to cover my feet and hands and whimpering for a hot water bottle and a steak.

I had made two Lenten vows—to give up the Internet and to read the New Testament—but by Day Two, the first one was out the window, though this was Sister Gillian's fault.

"That's a rather impractical vow." Her smile showed more than a trace of concern. "You need the Internet and email because your work for us involves visiting the sisters in the branch houses, and how are you going to arrange your visits without email and without the Internet to check the bus schedule?"

I could have suggested to her that I use the telephone, but frankly no one, not even a nun, gives up the Internet these days. I could also have done a swift amendment to the vow and given up chocolate digestive biscuits, but my rampant consumption was keeping a factory in Harlesden in business, so as I saw it I was doing my bit for the economy.

Lent also meant that the liturgy would be changing. When Sister Margaret Anne dropped the new prayer book on my prie-dieu I felt my resistance mounting. *Why can't things just stay comfortably familiar?* It was like arriving at work and being told you had to learn a new computer system. No one expected me to know the lay of the liturgical land as well as, say, Sister Margaret Anne (who had been a sister for thirty years) knew it, but my own high standards insisted on it.

Sister Margaret Anne wordlessly took my books and methodically began juggling various binders and inserting bookmarks into specific pages to help me navigate my way through it all. Even then I lost my place, and she had to point to the page number in her book to get me back on track.

All this demanded the sort of mental agility that put my self-confidence in question. Maybe Sister Prudence had been right: maybe I *was* too old to be a nun. I might just as well have laced up a pair of toe shoes and presented myself to the Royal Ballet.

It would have been easier had there been someone with whom to commiserate about all this. I could have gone to Sister Dorothy Stella, but she had her hands full enough with nearly fifty women to placate. The last thing she needed was a wimpy aspirant clinging to her ankles.

As for the others, they swept into chapel for the offices and then vamoosed until mealtimes. Sometimes I would come down from my cell to see if I could button-hole someone, but there was no one about. Were they watching TV? Having secret nun meetings? Praying?

The nuns were all genuinely kind, like a coterie of caring maiden aunts. They offered smiles in the corridors, the odd wink of greeting in the chapel, light conversation in the kitchen and the parlor, but that was it. I needed more. Silence and solitude were beginning to have a shelf life as far as I was concerned.

Perhaps a walk was what I needed. I went into the coat room to fetch my coat from its hook. Sister KT was there zipping up her jacket.

"Going outside?" she asked. "Has anyone showed you the new trail? No? I will then. It's really lovely."

Yes! Someone to talk to! I was glad it was Sister KT. The other day, she had been helping me in chapel to mark the pages for the next office when we came across a bookmark that showed the statue of a black angel. We had paused to admire it, and turning it over I read aloud the name of the gallery where the statue was exhibited.

"I know that place," Sister KT had casually remarked. "My ex-husband worked there."

Ex-husband? I hadn't said anything at the time but I was dying to ask her about her transition from divorcée to nun. What had led her to religious life? Had she tired of the bar scene? Given up on Internet dating? Couldn't find a satisfactory responder to her SWSCF (single, white, straight, Christian, female) profile? Or had she been scratching at the crannies of her personality?

But now that we were on the trail together, I was afraid to ask her anything in case my questions scared her off.

She mentioned her divorce again and said that she had decided to enter religious life after her marriage broke up. *Out of anger? Out of pain? Out of a long-held longing to wear a habit? Because convent life was unthreatening? Had she been in an abusive marriage?* There were so many possibilities, but it felt smarter to let her take the lead in the conversation.

"You'll never guess what I did before I joined this place," she said.

"Um, were you a truck driver? A doctor?"

She snorted.

"Oh, I know... a fashion model!"

"Get outta 'ere. Hah!" She gave me a good-natured shove. "You're trying to take the mickey out of me, aren't you?"

"OK, so you weren't a fashion model. What were you?"

"A secretary."

I pictured her in a pencil skirt and black heels, her slim legs crossed beneath a desk as she typed something for the boss, her posture erect, just as it was when she sat in her choir stall.

"And were you a good secretary?"

"Oh yes, I quite enjoyed it."

I'll bet she was one of those secretaries that everyone liked, the kind who teased and got the others in the office laughing.

"And now you're here," I said enthusiastically, in hopes of encouraging her to tell me more about the kind of secretarial work she did, the town or city she worked in. Had she been there long? Did she rock out with her friends at the pub on Fridays after work? What music did she like? Did she like to read? It's the sort of information you gather easily and quickly when you are getting to know someone.

But when that someone is a nun, it isn't so easy. Just as I feared, Sister KT fell suddenly, inexplicably quiet. She ducked back into the silent zone like a spooked turtle retracts into its shell.

(6:ii)

I TOOK my tea into the parlor and joined the others gathered around the table.

"Did you see that article in the paper about the nun who was refused her state pension?" I asked. A British Court of Appeal judge had ruled that the nun did not deserve a pension because she was supported by her religious order. Many nuns worked as qualified teachers and nurses without pay and were regular volunteers in youth centers, eldercare centers, soup kitchens, and children's playgroups, and yet they were denied a state pension. It was another indication of secular society's misinformation about how religious orders supported themselves.

"Well, what do you expect," scoffed one sister. "People think that we come from wealthy families."

"Or that we have big pensions from when we worked before joining the order," said another.

"Or that because we live in a castle, we're rich," added a third.

"My father took me out of his will because he assumed that since I was in a convent, I wouldn't need the money," said a fourth.

"You do know that people assume that religious orders get financial support from the church," I said. The issue still confounded me as to why a Mother Church did not fund or at least subsidize its religious orders.

The weary smiles and collective rolling of eyeballs reminded me of Father Luke's reaction when I had raised the issue with him at Quarr Abbey.

Yet it wasn't as if the monks and nuns in Britain or anywhere else for that matter go out of their way to set the record straight.

"What do you do to correct that assumption?" I pressed. My question was met with uncomfortable silence and lowered eyes.

I knew why, or rather I was learning why. Members of religious orders do not speak up because the tacit vow of humility forbids complaint. Complaining is contrary to the example Jesus set when He suffered on the Via Dolorosa. There had been another news item about elderly nuns at an English convent who silently endured a decade of abuse by their caregivers, the details of which only emerged when one of the caregivers who had been sacked by the convent took her case to an employment tribunal. Through the nun-vine, I also heard about a community that had been robbed of its savings by a wily secular couple who had been entrusted with the community's accounts. Such stories will never make the newspapers or be brought to the attention of the police or the courts because of this infuriating submissiveness by the nuns and monks themselves.

"What about discounts from local businesses for your regular housekeeping purchases?" I asked, trying a different tack.

The sisters responded with puzzled looks.

"All the beds you have here—and you must have at least fifty—did you buy them without negotiating a discount from the furniture store?"

They looked at one another. "We didn't think to ask," one of the sisters said. "We did order ten beds once, but the merchant never offered us a discount."

"And all the supplies you order in bulk—toilet paper, soap, shampoo, jams, that sort of stuff—you don't negotiate a discount?" My Warrior Nun was rising.

Again, their eyes dropped to their hands folded politely in their laps.

One of the sisters piped up helpfully, "If I have a large purchase at the greengrocer's, I might get ten or fifty pence off."

"That's not enough," I said. "Every business negotiates with its suppliers. You need to approach things like a business and demand best-price discounts from your suppliers."

The days of wealthy patrons footing the bill for religious orders had long passed. Nowadays, donations are modest, not the sort of dosh that puts food on the table for several months. If churches do not support religious communities, who does? Who will?

I'm no economist, but surely it made sense for convents and monasteries to pool some of their resources and maximize their purchasing power. The adage "God will provide" only works so far: God did not create us to be completely dependent on Him; He gave us brains to find solutions to our problems.

I understood that the *raison d'être* of a religious order was to withdraw from secular life, but the sisters couldn't exactly live on grass and berries. Besides, with a modest amount of self-promotion, they might encourage new recruits or find a benefactor or three. There is nothing sinful about self-sustainability.

As it had at Quarr, my brain scrambled into marketing and promotional overdrive. How about a retreat aimed at women, or publishing or promoting some of the controversial bits of Mother Margaret's addresses, or hiring out the priory as a movie location or the chapel as a concert venue, maybe a cookbook called *Puddings from the Priory* or *Cookies from the Cloister,* selling the farmland to an enterprise that could train unemployed youth to be farmers and at the same time produce food for the local community? There was no end to the possibilities. But there didn't appear to be much enthusiasm for new ventures. Perhaps the ideas had been tried before and had not succeeded, or perhaps that was the point of the contemplative life that eluded me: that you really do focus on prayer and nothing else.

The absence of freewheeling, idea-driven conversation tugged at my heart like a primitive longing. Could I really surrender to a creative gag order, even if God were my boss? Surely He had something better in mind for me. Maybe I could become a life-professed shit-disturber.

(6:iii)

BRAIN CANDY: that's what I needed. All this thinking about how to save the nuns and monks from penury and avoiding the issue of my rape was making my head hurt. The inability to express myself within the cloistered world was beginning to chafe like an itchy sweater. I needed a respite from religious reality, something that wouldn't break the rules, the bank, and local bylaws.

I had become rather good at finding my way around the castle and had learned a few shortcuts. One evening after supper, I trod across the squeaky floorboards of the attic passage next to my cell, careful not to bang my head on the thick, low-hanging rafters or trip over the Henry vacuum cleaner. (Britain must be the only country in the world that puts a happy face on a vacuum cleaner and makes it look like a character from *Thomas the Tank Engine*.) I emerged into a corridor of closed dark wood doors. I tiptoed down the long, narrow, threadbare-carpeted hallway, past the sisters' cells, past assorted offices and storerooms, past the prioress's office, and down a wide and graceful staircase. To the left was a door, and as I turned the knob, I looked over my shoulder at the looming portrait of Mother Margaret sternly staring down at me. She must have known that I was going to skip compline.

This was the sitting room that Sister Marjorie had showed me more than a month earlier during our whirlwind tour. I had stumbled upon the room again only the day before and remembered that she had said it was available for me to use.

It was a large reception room, the type you would associate with a country home. Original plasterwork decorated the ceiling, and there were very tall windows flanked by heavy curtains hung from large brass rings. The furnishings were a little faded and worn, which made them all the more cozy. There was a television in the corner along with the usual intimidating array of remote control devices. I picked up one of them and, remarkably, the first button I pushed switched on the TV.

A house-hunting program that I knew of was just beginning, and the sight of its two hosts prompted me to let out a little cheer.

The British media frequently ridiculed this pair, but I adored them. They were warmth and comfort itself. The man was always seizing a chance to duck into a pub, ostensibly to counsel nervous homebuyers; the woman in her plummy, bossy voice and impractical stilettos would herd them from home to home like a mother hen.

I curled up in one of the chairs and prepared to put my brain on "stun" when the door behind me suddenly opened. It was Sister Gillian.

"Just doing the night rounds before compline, and I saw a light on," she whispered. "No, no, don't get up; you need to relax. Maybe you should have a lie-in tomorrow if you're not feeling... Oh! Is that Kirstie and Phil?"

For a few seconds the possibility hung in the air that Sister Gillian would capitulate to the dark side and say, "Well, no harm in missing compline for one night, right? Here, shove over. Should we make popcorn?"

But, of course, she did not. She cooed goodnight and, like the good nun that she was, scooted off to compline. Like the bad nun-in-training that I was, I snuggled deeper into the soft upholstery and aimed the remote at the TV to turn up the volume.

(6:iv)

"GOOD MORNING, sister!" one of the worshippers arriving for Sunday Mass called out to me. I did not bother to correct her; it was a relief to know that I blended in with the nuns and that my being a sister was in the realm of possibility for at least one person. A few days earlier, a guest at the priory who had been told that I was discerning a vocation had exclaimed to all around her that I looked the part: "She has the eyes of a nun!" *Not when they're outlined in black eyeliner and three coats of mascara,* I considered tossing back.

I looked forward to the Sunday Mass in our chapel when the local population attended. Sister Jocelyn played the organ at the services and the sound of diverse voices belting out heroic-sounding hymns would cause my eyes to well up as memories were awakened of attending church as a youngster with my parents. Church music has such an ability to ennoble our sentiments and memories.

It was also nice to hear some male voices for a change. On this particular Sunday, one man's stout and practiced baritone boomed above the rest. I don't think I will ever hear the hymn "Lift Up Your Hearts" without being reminded of his singing.

"What a fabulous voice," I whispered to Sister Margaret Anne during the hymn.

She beamed back: "That's my brother; he's visiting me for a few days."

The afterglow of a good hymn lasts only so long, however, before it all collapses at the Peace.

I detest the Peace. Or rather, I detest its placement in the service.

The Peace occurs after the prayerful confession of sins and absolution from the priest, when worshippers are called upon to demonstrate their reconciliation. They do this by greeting their pew neighbors with words—"The peace of Christ"—and a handshake. The custom originated with the early church and has over the centuries been removed and reinserted with various revisions of the Anglican prayer book. What never seems to change is its ability to summon feelings of immense awkwardness among the congregation. (I could be cynical and suggest that the Peace was reinserted as a way to butter up parishioners just before the Offertory, but I won't.)

The intention of the Peace is good and uplifting and even necessary. But it is a ritual that has completely got out of hand. Even the restrained Brits, who I had counted on to wrestle this beast with their usual abrupt tact, had let it run amok. Anglicans have turned the Peace into intermission, a time to mingle and stretch their legs. No sooner has the priest said, "The peace of the Lord be always with you" when the place devolves into a raucous affair, responding en masse like a dog who hears the word "walk."

I had made the mistake of reverting to my Anglican sensibilities at Quarr Abbey when the Peace was invoked during Mass one day. (Roman Catholics convey the Peace with a perfunctory nod to their pew neighbors while remaining fixed in place.) As I moved from pew to pew dispensing my bonhomie to all five people in the congregation like a politician on the campaign trail, people reeled in alarm. They must have thought I had lost my mind.

During the exchange of the Peace at St. Hilda's chapel, all hell broke loose. Worshippers struggled over pews to shake hands with all and sundry, one woman lost her footing and fell, and there was much hugging and catching up with neighborhood news, commiserating about the previous night's football match, extending of invitations to dinner or drinks at the pub, and avuncular forays into the state of the economy. Total and prolonged mayhem. The priest loudly called everyone to order and directed them back to their pews and on to the next hymn, but even then people continued to chat, greeting one another as if they had been displaced by war for several years and had only recently returned.

The Peace is anything but. It is the Grand Interruption that fragments the solemnity of the service. If there is another revision of the prayer book, we can only hope those vested with the undertaking will review this ritual and provide some rules of sanity or find a less disruptive, more amenable place for it in the service. The post-service coffee hour, perhaps?

(6:v)

MORNING DAWNED in striated layers of pale orange, light green, and deep blue that bled into one another like a Turner watercolor. The town and surrounding farms were silhouetted in darkness. Soon the sun would be up, the landscape would be illuminated, and people would be rushing about their day, forgetting that they had glimpsed a beautiful sunrise, or worse, oblivious to the fact that one had occurred at all.

The days and weeks were passing quickly inside the cloistered cocoon, but at the same time it was as if life stood still. The outside world took on a surreal quality, and as each day flipped over to the next, I felt the world I once knew slip from my grasp like filaments in a spider's web.

From my cell window I observed with a bemused detachment the cars zipping along Guisborough Road. Cars had become an alien species now. I walked everywhere, and on the few occasions when I was a passenger in a car, the experience was akin to boarding a spaceship.

In Lidl, as I stood in line waiting to pay for a couple of packages of chocolate digestive biscuits (a full-blown addiction that I felt obligated to pay for out of my own pocket), I watched people as if they were part of a stage play. Their frenzied conversations were a curiosity, even though I had been part of that crazy world not that long ago. *Rushing off to fetch the kids from school? Have fun with that! Fretting about what to cook for dinner? Good luck!* That world was but a hazy memory now.

All my needs were met at St. Hilda's, but the loss of human contact affected me the most, like a sharp, deep stab. I missed the touch of another human being—a pat on the arm, a friendly hug, a kiss. But more than that, I longed for meaningful social interaction, both light and in-depth conversations. I appreciated that silence was paramount in a convent, but the balance was so heavily weighted toward it that it engendered a form of isolation.

I thought it was me, that I was defective or somehow inferior because I felt this need, but when I looked around me it seemed that there were more than a few sisters who could have benefited from more social interactions and physical contact. You can never overstate the healing power of human touch. Some struggled emotionally, and their problems were manifested by ultrasensitive personalities, chronic stomach problems, and eating disorders. One sister confided that she felt left out, that everyone seemed to have a buddy except her. I wondered whether the same type of social isolation would befall me if I joined a religious order. Social connections are vital whether you live inside or outside the cloister, and breaking into a new social circle works the same way in a religious community as it does in a secular community. Today's "new kid in the convent" is tomorrow's "test of my patience."

The loneliness was most acute on Saturdays.

Saturday morning in a convent was business as usual. There was no lazy breakfast, no steaming mug of coffee while sitting in your pajamas poring over the weekend newspaper. No random comments to lob at someone such as, "Well, did you see this story about…?" or "I can't believe the government thinks it can revamp the health service by slashing jobs! Insanity! What do you think?" or "Look at that fabulous hotel in Spain. Wouldn't it be great to go there?" No, there are no conversations like that at a convent. In fact, there are rarely conversations, period.

Long ago, when I was living off the fumes of a consumer lifestyle fueled by fashion and home-decorating trends and multiple trips to big-box stores located in vast asphalted wastelands of suburbia, I never appreciated the little freedoms inherent in a Saturday. Saturday was a day of sundry domestic responsibilities, but it was also a day that was your own to design.

Here, Saturday morning was about silence, just like the other six days of the week. There was a vague sense, an intuitive whiff, if you will, that the world was operating on weekend mode, but that was the extent of it. A million creature comforts I had taken for granted in a secular Saturday morning began to assemble into a chorus line of longing: the smell of coffee, the ring of the phone, the crackle of a fire, the rustle of a newspaper, the homey discussion about the day's errands and chores, the hum of the washing machine, music from the radio, and mostly, companionship. Without these, I felt very poor indeed.

I left the refectory after breakfast, and when I passed the newspaper rack stocked with the weekend editions—*The Times,* the *Daily Telegraph,* the *Independent,* the *Guardian,* the *Yorkshire Post,* and periodicals such as the *Church Times* and the *Tablet*—I was overcome with a greedy desire to have a newspaper of my own. Especially a complete, untouched newspaper.

The newspapers—"intercession material," as Sister Marjorie called them—never made it to the cloister rack intact. They were disassembled by one of the sisters, who felt that the sports sections from all the newspapers should be lumped together, as should the real estate, business, travel, commentary, and arts sections. The glossy weekend magazines disappeared completely, only to materialize days later in the parlor.

The slap on the wrist that first day from Sister Marjorie about hogging the newspaper had made me more circumspect. I would take a section of one of the papers to my cell or the library and read it, then return it immediately and take another section. But now I craved a newspaper to peruse at my leisure. On my way to post a letter that morning, I went into a shop and bought one. As I walked back to the priory clutching it to my body, it felt as if I had scored dope.

I smuggled it into my cell, then stretched out on the floor, the newspaper in front of me, and read and lingered over it while the sun poured in through the dormer window. It was close to heavenly.

That night, I sat in my prie-dieu awaiting the start of compline, and a different longing returned. This time I thought about all the people who were out on a date or channel-surfing at home or uncorking a bottle of wine with friends or making last-minute plans to see a movie or curled up in their PJs with a book in front of a blazing fire. Ah, Saturdays.

(6:vi)

A DUSTING of frost had coated the ground, but by midmorning, the sun had melted the evidence and was beaming its heart out.

A small stone patio and rockery behind the priory proved to be an excellent suntrap, and in good weather the sisters often took their tea or said their prayers and meditations there.

Passing through the main corridor, I spied Sister Patricia sitting on one of the wooden benches on the patio. Her eyes were closed, and her white hair shone like an aura. Her face was inclined toward the late morning sun, welcoming its warmth, and I could tell that she was in that zone of listening to God. Occasionally her face broke out in a smile, as if God were telling her a joke. Perhaps it was this one: A Sunday school teacher was leading her young class into church when she turned to them and asked softly: "Now class, why do we need to be quiet in church?" In a loud whisper a little girl piped up, "Because people are sleeping."

I opened the patio door and tiptoed past Sister Patricia toward the gardens.

The cold of the previous weeks had been replaced by sun and warmer air. Spring was never my favorite season; I always wanted it to hurry up and get to the hot days of summer. Now I saw the gentle beauty of it, the reawakening of life.

I walked around the rockery and admired the new growth. The garden was tended by Sister Heather Francis, under whose diligent care flowers had begun poking up—purple and yellow crocuses, periwinkle, and a raft of other species that she would know by their Latin names. A few pigeons were strutting around. This particular species always made me smile, because its plumage—grayish brown with a white band at the throat—was identical to the nuns' habits.

Scattered around the gardens were stone troughs, some containing plants, others heaped with shells, fossils, and stones that the sisters had found on their excursions.

Many of the fossils were ammonites. Depictions of St. Hilda almost always show her with ammonites at her feet—a nod to the welcome legend in which she battled a plague of snakes and turned them all to stone.

I picked up an ammonite and rolled it around in my hand, feeling its weight and running my thumb along its hard, ridged surface. Its coiled spine conjured many images—a spiral staircase, a labyrinth, the starting point of Dorothy's yellow brick road—and the images splintered into word association: the reversing of life, the rewinding of memory, the unraveling of trauma. *Uh oh.*

(6:vii)

WE WERE deep in Lent now. Fog had stealthily crept in and coiled itself around the convent, and it did not look like it had plans to move on any time soon. The cloister corridors were dark and empty, and the wind—the unforgiving, swirling, ever-present, abrasively loud wind—was a bitter reminder that we were still in the throes of winter. A winter desert.

Lent had turned everything into a metaphorical desert: the food in the refectory looked the same from one meal to the next; the silence was oppressive and brought a sense of foreboding. Grayish brown was the dominant hue: it was in the stone walls and floors of the priory, in the sisters' habits, in the weather, in everyone's mood. It was like living in a sepia-toned photograph.

The sisters themselves were as drained of color as a March day. They moved like a whisper through the corridors, enveloped in a cloud of constant prayer and without offering the barest nod of acknowledgement to those they passed. Their brows were etched with worry, and for good reason.

A catastrophic earthquake and tsunami had hit the eastern coast of Japan, causing a massive loss of life; an explosion at the region's nuclear reactor was imminent. When it seemed things could not get worse, heavy snow had begun to fall, adding to the confusion and rescue efforts.

The disaster was on everyone's mind and on everyone's lips; it was heart-crushing. You do not know where to begin with your prayers with something like that.

The deadly riots in Libya and Syria had also become constant themes in our prayers, as had the state of the world's nosediving economy. With so much heaviness and so many world crises, an extra half-hour of silent intercessions was added to the evening schedule.

You couldn't avoid the pain of the world. From inside the convent, the blunt terror of the world was more horrifying, especially when viewed under the lens of Lent. There were no little distractions to save you from tumbling into despair: you had to absorb it and deal with it.

I had come across a story about a doctor in Misrata who had hustled his wife and four kids into the car to escape the bullets raining down on his neighborhood. He had hoped they could find safer shelter at his in-laws' home. The family had driven into the street but had to stop the car because the gunfire was so fierce. When the doctor looked over his shoulder to check on his children in the backseat, he saw that two of his older children had had half their heads shot off; the younger two no longer had heads at all.

I had read the story with my hand over my mouth. In a world of such unremitting horror, how do people keep their faith? How do you pray when something like that happens to you? I had been whining about the deprivations of Lent while parents were coping with their headless children.

I arrived in the chapel with the barest of light as guidance and groped my way to my prie-dieu. As my eyes grew accustomed to the darkness, I made out silhouettes of the nuns sitting still and silent in their stalls like apparitions shrouded in mourning and praying their souls out for the dead, the living, and those who wonder if there is a God.

(6:viii)

THE TWISTED branch of a vine slapped against the window of my office, its scrawny, dry tendrils scratching the glass pane like a clawing rodent. The screams of the wind were unbearable. My office was located at the inside corner of the building, a wind trap, and the wind seemed to take this as a personal affront, tearing and raging like a caged animal and threatening to shatter the windows completely.

Its fury mystified and terrified me. I had never been affected by the wind before, but now I could not escape it in my office, in chapel, or in the library. I was safe from it in my cell until I went to sleep, and then it invaded my dreams, in which every scene featured the wind at its most furious.

In the daytime, it was so voluble that my only escape was to go outside and face it. Then it would become more playful, blowing me toward Whitby Beach and the rugged, ancient North Yorkshire coastline.

I was helpless against the wild landscape: the disheveled grass, the shivering trees, the swelling, tempestuous sea beneath smoky puffs of clouds that sailed swiftly through the blue and white sky like a flotilla setting off for the New World. It was alive and unpredictable. One minute the sea would dazzle with sapphire clarity; the next, it would be smothered in dense fog. The week before, I had watched a rainbow materialize, one of its ends dissolving into the shimmer and sparkle of the sea.

I frequently took the steep asphalt footpaths that switchbacked precipitously down the cliffs to the beach and waded through uneven drifts of sand to the water's edge. I would stand there feeling the drumbeat of the waves, letting them permeate my senses and push my anxiety to the side. This was where my Aquarian nature felt most at home.

When I exposed myself to the elements, especially to the sea, I could come clean with myself and admit—as much as I did not have the courage to admit at other times—that I was forcing myself into religious life. A square peg trying to fit into a round hole: I was manipulating that square peg to plug the hole of my pain.

My faith wasn't flagging, but my struggle against my willful and possessive nature was.

Even my vocabulary had a possessive quality. Colin's weekly letters carried references to "our garden" and "our flat," when in reality it was *his* garden, *his* flat. All my references were to "your place" and to "my place." In a monastic culture, where all things are held in common, there is no "I" and "mine." Perhaps I wasn't fit for marriage or a monastery.

As for the other part of my nature—the one that likes to talk, question, and probe—was it realistic to drive it underground and take on a new personality? Was that even honest?

My thoughts returned to Thomas Merton and his natural proclivity to communicate, the tension he felt between wanting to be a monk for God and a man of the world. He could not stop himself from writing letters or spending long afternoons in conversation with visiting friends. I hate to think how he would have coped with email.

I had read about how one of Merton's friends would pick him up at the abbey under the ruse that they were going to attend a religious function. Merton would have a satchel with him, supposedly containing religious material. A few miles down the road, Merton would tell his friend to stop the car, and while the car idled, Merton, satchel in hand, would dash into the bushes in his cassock and emerge dressed in denim and leather, his cassock stuffed into the satchel. The two friends would then hit the bars, and the monk, the one who craved silence and solitude, would be yakking to everyone and buying rounds of beer. The contemplative contradiction. That was me: the dual personality, the elastic monastic, trying to adapt to a monoculture.

(6:ix)

"ARE YOU sure you know what you're doing?" a worried Sister Gillian asked as we sat in the car at a bus depot in Pickering. "You get off at Malton, remember, and transfer to the bus to

York. Then at York you have to transfer buses again to get to Bishopthorpe. Oh dear, are you sure you can handle it?"

Who could blame her: I was after all putting myself into the hands of the British public transportation system.

"Yup, I'll be fine. And if I get lost, I can just ask someone."

Sister Gillian looked dubious.

I gathered my purse and my overnight bag and patted her arm. "Don't worry so much."

I was off to York. The prospect of traveling on unfamiliar buses and making transfers in unheard-of places had a strange thrill to it. At times I hoped I would get lost.

The previous week I had taken another bus trip (Sister Gillian had been more relaxed about that one since it did not require transfers) north to Dormanstown as part of my job collecting information for the historical update the order asked me to do. Two sisters, Anita and Pam, worked with the poor in this former steel-making powerhouse—Dormanstown steel had built the Sydney Harbour Bridge. During that excursion, Sister Anita and I discovered we were both Bede freaks, so we made an impromptu road trip north to Durham Cathedral to visit the monk's shrine. Standing in front of Bede's tomb was like visiting Graceland.

Sister Anita had been a chatty companion who augmented my fledgling education about early Christianity's formative years in Britain and the Northern saints who shaped it. Hilda was one of them, of course, but so was Cuthbert, Northern England's patron saint. I was always game to learn about a new saint, because invariably they had wonky career trajectories (which made me feel better about my own peripatetic path) and because there was usually something bizarre about them. Cuthbert did not disappoint.

A contemporary of St. Hilda, Cuthbert was a shepherd, a monk, a prior, a soldier, and a priest. It was said that he was a kind and cheerful sort, and this proved as much a blessing as a curse. When he retired to his hermit cave on Inner Farne Island, pilgrims and hangers-on refused to leave him alone, and they would row out to talk to him. Among them was King Ecgfrith, who pestered Cuthbert to take up the post of bishop. Worn down by the request and well into old age by this point, Cuthbert agreed. He was ordained at York around AD 685 and died less than two years later.

A dozen years after Cuthbert died, monks pried open his coffin and found his body to be perfectly preserved. (It makes you wonder what propels people, aside from lurid curiosity, to open a coffin.) The monks were rather pleased because they had also preserved the head of King Oswald, who had been killed and dismembered in battle thirty years earlier. With two grisly relics in their possession, they fled an imminent Viking invasion and took the remains on the road for—and this is just weird—three hundred years, lifting the lid on their macabre exhibit to curious passersby, pilgrims, benefactors, anyone willing to pay handsomely for the privilege.

The monks finally buried the pair at Durham Cathedral, once the building was completed, in 1130. Cuthbert remained undisturbed—his shrine survived the Reformation—until the 1820s, when the poor fellow was dug up again, probed and prodded, and relieved of his cloak and pectoral cross, which is now displayed in the Cathedral museum. The last (and let's hope final) exhumation was in 1899.

I didn't expect to find a story to rival that one in York, despite York's reputation as the most haunted capital in Europe.

My business in York and Bishopthorpe, as it had been in Dormanstown, was to interview the sisters posted there for the Order of the Holy Paraclete's historical update.

As the bus approached York, I checked my watch and realized I had a chunk of time before the arrival of my connecting bus.

I ambled across Lendal Bridge to a café, a former toll house, ordered lunch and settled into a window seat overlooking the River Ouse.

Whenever I would go out for lunch in my secular life, I would order what appealed to me—a tasty entrée, maybe a glass of wine, and invariably a scrumptious dessert. On the days when I was feeling particularly expansive (usually on pay day), I would take a gander around the shops and maybe splurge on a pair of shoes. There was always the confidence that another paycheck was around the corner. Now, my postulant persona kicked in. I ordered the cheapest item on the menu—a bowl of soup—and a glass of tap water. I was watching my pennies like a pensioner.

In Bishopthorpe, a small, tidy suburb a few miles outside York, I was met by two charming sisters whose mission was to provide a presence of prayer at Bishopthorpe Palace, the official residence of the Archbishop of York.

It was a mild March day, and the three of us strolled the grounds of the palace, where drifts of daffodils shone in the late afternoon sun, their nodding blooms resembling yellow-bonneted women having a good chinwag.

We said vespers in the palace's thirteenth-century chapel, with its floors of black and white marble; its ceiling studded with bosses painted with heraldic shields, and its thick stone walls of blind arcades inset with stained-glass depictions of the saints. It was the prettiest chapel I had ever been in. Edward II apparently worshipped here just before he signed a truce with Robert the Bruce in 1323, following the Battle of Bannockburn. If a chapel like this were located near my home, I would be in it every day, if not multiple times a day.

It made me wish that more people were aware of such stunning spiritual oases but also that they recognized the abundant calm that an office such as vespers affords. Vespers, a mere fifteen-minute office, provides an elegant transition between a frantic day in an office cubicle or on a factory floor and the soothing familiarity of home. It would be a nicer world if churches resurrected vespers and people attended in enthusiastic droves.

There were four of us at vespers—the two sisters, the palace chaplain, and me.

The chaplain was a young woman possessed of a gentle manner that I hoped was an indication of her true personality and not the result of being browbeaten and bullied by those antagonistic to the idea of women priests.

"Ah, Canada," she nodded sadly when she learned where I was from. "It is so much easier for women priests there. Here, it is . . ." Her voice trailed away. There was no need for her to finish her sentence.

Not long after I had arrived at St. Hilda's, I had been asked whether I minded having a female priest officiate at the Eucharist. I had chuckled by way of response until I realized that the question was not intended as a joke. It would certainly be a joke in North America, where more than 35 percent of active Anglican clergy are women and fourteen of its bishops are women.

In the U.K., I had to continually remind myself that I had not fallen through a crack in the space-time continuum and been sucked back to the Pleistocene era.

The visceral opposition to female clergy in the U.K. from both men and women is as mystifying as it is scandalous. It made my blood boil, roused the Warrior Nun in me. What's the fear? That women will do a fantastic job? That they will cause far fewer sexual abuse scandals? Bring some humanity back to the church?

Those Christians who scoff at the notion that God sits on a fluffy cloud overseeing creation will assert with a perfectly straight face that female priests don't belong in churches because they weren't mentioned in accounts of the Last Supper. And my response is, how do you know for certain that Jesus had only twelve apostles and that they were all men? The Bible is a collection of selective and in some cases heavily edited anthologies of stories and letters that were handpicked by the burgeoning hierarchy of the organized church centuries later. It might be "the gospel," but it doesn't mean it's the whole story.

A section of the Bible that often gets overlooked because scholars debate whether it is canonical is the Apocrypha, or Book of Wisdom. It contains riveting stories of heroic women who were no strangers to temples or to preaching (even during Jesus' time). It is a shame that the Apocrypha is often left out of editions of the Bible and that it isn't read more in churches, because it contains many terrific female role models. Then again, maybe that explains its exclusion.

There are still many U.K. parishes where churchgoers refuse to accept Holy Communion from a female priest, never mind a female bishop. The Church of England actually suggested a compromise in which female bishops would be ordained but male bishops would be brought in to dispense the sacraments and other religious ceremonies such as weddings, funerals, and the like—so that a woman could be bishop in name only but not in procedure. It was beyond ridiculous.

There is a Church of England group with the ironic name of Forward in Faith that actively campaigns against the ordination of females. Replace the word "female" in that last sentence with "blacks," "homosexuals," "people with disabilities," or any other such label and you have a human rights case.

The Church of England's two archbishops, York and Canterbury, had handled the situation badly. They vacillated (such an Anglican thing) and played the consensus game rather than assert their unequivocal support of female clergy at every level of the ecclesiastical hierarchy and denounce the opposition as both patently wrong and definitely un-Christian. Their dithering alienated people on both sides of the argument, in particular women, who have done the grunt work of the established church for eons.

It was mind-boggling how the same church that preaches the liberation of the poor and the oppressed in Third World countries can't accord equal rights to women in the so-called First World. You cannot be a Christian and exclude others; nor can you cherry-pick those groups you wish to admit and those you set aside while you "study the theology."

It's not enough to be the smartest man or woman in the room nowadays: you need to be the most compassionate and the most vociferous defender of human rights.

And speaking of "studying the theology," if we are to be absolutely true to biblical theology, then all priests should be required to start off as Jewish rabbis before they can be baptized as Christians and then ordained as Christian priests. Of course, the idea is preposterous, but no more preposterous than banning women from ordination and leadership.

The glimmer of hope is this: more women than men are entering the Anglican priesthood in the U.K. In 2010, there were 290 women and 273 men ordained.

I was also detecting a streak of paternalism cropping up in other areas of the church, specifically a kind of slavery among the religious class. Many of the sisters I met had exceptional executive-level skills but were largely relegated to the status of handmaidens. At important church functions, nuns were used as servers and dishwashers rather than encouraged to circulate, offer their insights, participate in intelligent discourse, and at least make their vocations visible. Instead, sisters were trotted out by churches on special occasions and used as spiritual window dressing, only to be packed away along with the bunting after the events. You do not see monks setting tables and drying dishes at church functions, so why is it OK to make nuns do it?

That evening back in York, as I sat in the Minster for compline with a full choir chanting and singing the liturgy, I wondered about this attitude toward women and why it has been allowed to go on for so long in the English church. The real theological scandal of our time is not whether God exists but why women have been shut out and in some cases obliterated from full inclusion in the church—both the Roman Catholic Church and the Church of England. Perhaps it was time to establish a new Anglo-Catholic denomination, entirely led by women. St. Hilda—that Celtic trailblazer—would surely approve.

(6:x)

THE NEXT morning after finishing my interviews, I found myself with some time to kill before the bus arrived to return me to Whitby.

The term "time to kill" suddenly sounded awfully harsh.

Was "time to waste" better? No, "waste" is so un-Benedictine.

"Time to spend"? Too much of a material ring.

"Time to bum around"? Yes, it had just the right balance of self-effacement and no fixed address. Like Jesus.

I wandered into the old quarter and sat on a bench in the square near Holy Trinity Church. The sun shone brilliantly and the sky was the clearest of blues. Stall keepers were arranging their wares, people were hurrying to work, and young mothers were corralling children who were running and squealing with the delight of their freedom. People ambled into cafés for a morning coffee, then returned to settle around the outdoor tables hastily set up to take advantage of the unseasonably warm weather. It was a mundane sight, ordinary in the extreme, but it gave me so much pleasure. I sat on the bench mesmerized by people jumping, running, laughing out loud, squealing with happiness.

Added to this was the profusion of color everywhere. There was such a kaleidoscopic swirl—in the sky, in the clothing people wore, in the shop window displays, in the enormous urns of flowers, in the brickwork of the buildings, in the almost blinding glint of light from the chrome café tables. It made me smile in a way I hadn't for a long time.

It occurred to me then how much I would miss not being a part of this if I disappeared behind the walls of a convent. Would I be content to pray for these people and for this life in my intercessions, or would I prefer to be in the thick of things, where I could muck in with them and pray alongside them? The hurly-burly of life is exhausting and maddening, but it is also invigorating, and a rather large part of me needed that stimulation.

A year of wearing virtual nun's weeds of black, brown, and gray and nearly three months living in the monochromatic-toned world of the Lenten cloister began to fall away from me. It was like regaining my sight.

I got up and walked along the main artery, and at a side lane, I came across a boutique with a riotous display of clothing in its window. I could not resist. Or rather, I did not resist. Among the racks of gypsy skirts with their Kaffe Fassett–like explosion of variegated patterns and textures, one caught my eye.

It's not exactly nun wear, the Voice Inside warned as I held the skirt against my body and admired it in the shop's full-length mirror.

And I'm not exactly a nun, I shot back.

When I emerged from the shop, the sun was beaming full strength. Everything around me was so intense and alive with laughter and movement that I had to sit down and catch my breath.

Why can't monasticism be a wee bit more colorful? Surely embracing color and being devoted to God aren't mutually exclusive.

I wanted my monasticism with a side order of materialism. Would that make me a material monastic? A monastic materialist?

The bus back to Whitby deposited me at a garden center at the far end of the priory grounds. I walked through lonely and uneven fields of wheat stubble as dusk descended. A grove of poplar trees, their bare limbs uplifted, seemed to hail me in greeting. Between their thin branches, the backdoor light near the priory kitchen twinkled "welcome home." I sped up my pace, one hand clutching my overnight bag, the other a shopping bag of new clothes.

(6:xi)

A GUEST arrived at the priory: John Sentamu, the Archbishop of York.

In simple terms, the Archbishop of York is the Church of England's number two. His jurisdictional responsibility covers the territory north of York, whereas the Archbishop of Canterbury looks after Anglican matters south of York. Matters pertaining to the Anglican Church outside Britain fall mainly in Canterbury's domain. It's all very Anglican and therefore completely confusing and unsatisfactory.

The Archbishop of York had arrived at St. Hilda's to conduct a visitation, which is basically an audit to ensure that the Order of the Holy Paraclete was sticking to its mission and hadn't branched out into arms smuggling or wasn't running a casino. *Although, come to think of it, there's an idea for a new revenue stream...*

Archbishop Sentamu sat across from me at dinner. He appeared to be a hearty, good-natured man. He had a shaved head that revealed a hint of gray stubble and a charming gap between his front teeth. His deep magenta cassock looked rich against his black skin and set off the hand-painted pectoral cross of wood that hung from his neck.

Sentamu—he prefers people to refer to him by his surname— came to the U.K. from Uganda, where he had practiced law. His judicial independence caught the attention of Idi Amin, who threw him in jail and had him beaten. When he was released, Sentamu fled to England, studied theology, and was ordained a priest in 1979. He was appointed Archbishop of York in 2005.

Dinner that day was a "talking meal." There were so many things I wanted to talk to Sentamu about—the attitude toward female clergy, the redacted sign boards I had seen outside Anglican churches on the Isle of Wight, the lack of cohesion within the Church of England, the church's attitudes toward religious orders—but this was not the time or place. Instead,

I told him how much I liked the chapel at Bishopthorpe Palace.

"Ah, you mean the St. Paulinus and St. Hilda Chapel!" he exclaimed in a deep, booming voice. It was the sort of voice given to exclamation marks.

"I wasn't aware it had a name," I stammered.

"It didn't, until recently. In seven hundred years no one had bothered to give it one, so I did!"

When the Archbishop learned I was from Canada, he regaled those of us sitting near him with the story of his visit a few years earlier to a conference in Winnipeg.

"It rained the entire time—all week! Rain, thunder, lightning! Never experienced anything like it. At one point we wondered whether God was trying to tell us something!"

I remarked that Winnipeg was not known for its fair weather and that the city is nicknamed "Winterpeg" on account of its bitter, snowy winters.

Suddenly I felt a little sad for Winnipeg—some cities just cannot get a break from the ridicule of outsiders—so I related a positive anecdote about how a Canadian serviceman on his way to England had impulsively purchased a small black bear and named it Winnie, after his adopted hometown of Winnipeg. It was the First World War, and when the serviceman, arriving with his unusual pet in England, discovered that he was being sent onward to France, he donated Winnie to the London Zoo. Frequent visitors to the zoo happened to be A.A. Milne and his only son, Christopher Robin. So captivated were they by Winnie that Christopher named one of his toy bears after it. Thus was born Winnie-the-Pooh.

Well, I blush at the memory of how transfixed my tablemates were by this story. Sentamu himself let out an enthusiastic "Incredible!"

Afterwards, a few sisters who had been seated at the adjoining tables cornered me in the kitchen and begged to know what I had said to capture the attention of the Archbishop of York.

(6:xii)

IF SISTER Patricia had not become a nun, it is quite possible that she would have become a goth. She was fascinated by goths and by the subculture lifestyle.

The previous day I had wandered into the Whitby Pavilion to discover that the place had been turned into a veritable goth mall. You know you're on your way to reaching your nun potential when you encounter men wearing more makeup than you own and who are able to apply it with more skill than you ever could. It was depressing.

I mentioned the goths to Sister Patricia as we started out for what was intended to be a short walk. She stopped in her 85-year-old tracks, and her hands began fluttering: "The goths are in town? Oh! We must go into Whitby and see them. Right now!"

She loved the costumes, preferring the Edwardian goths to the vampire-cult version. "They look rather harsh," she said diplomatically. As we waited at a traffic light, a tall, husky man stood beside her in a long black leather coat, a spiked dog collar sans shirt, black leather trousers, and black platform boots with studs and spurs. What was this guy's inner life like? Was he a cerebral type, perhaps an aficionado of Gorey and Poe, with a helping of Lovecraft and Gaiman thrown in for lighter fare? Did he hold down a regular day job—an investment banker perhaps?—and don his goth gear on weekends, or was this a full-time personality? When he raised his arm to brush back his curtain of dark brown hair, his sleeve retracted and exposed two bracelets—one of thick brown leather with Iron Maiden's logo burned into it, the other of instantly recognizable pink silicone. *Mother, sister, lover?* I said a quick prayer.

Along Church Street, near Sanders Yard, an Edwardian goth couple was posing for the tourists. The woman wore a fitted black lace-trimmed jacket over a black ruffled-lace dress with a bodice that had its work cut out for it keeping a set of creamy breasts in place. Her hat was a frothy confection of black lace, black feathers, and red ribbons. Her partner was attired in black breeches and boots and a mottled purple ankle-length waistcoat topped by a tricornered black and gold hat.

"Now *that's* lovely," said Sister Patricia, clapping in enthusiastic approval.

We repaired to a pretty café in Sanders Yard for tea and cake and sat for a while in a kind of blissful sugar stupor, watching people watching us—it is surprising how many people gawk at the sight of a nun—or turning our attention to young parents helping their tots in and out of strollers and jackets. Oh, how I remember the days of directing squirmy, reluctant arms into stiff coats and snowsuits as chubby legs kicked impatiently to be released. A family with older children came into the café to take a break from goth watching, and suddenly I felt homesick for my own brood. I wondered what they were up to. Would they ever visit unusual places like Whitby? Would they ever feel compelled to make journeys that might help them reconcile themselves with God? A few years earlier, I had taken them to the Bahamas as a sort of "last family holiday." I had never been able to afford to take them away together before, and now I wished I had been less careful with my money and more reckless about traveling as a family.

(6:xiii)

EARLY ONE morning in mid-March, after ten hours of solid, blissful sleep, I opened my eyes, and without any sort of prompting or prior knowledge of what I was about to do, I spoke aloud to the ether: "I am not going to be a nun." Full stop.

I turned my head toward the wall and let my tears fall until they soaked my pillow. The disappointment was crushing.

For more than a year and a half I had pursued this path with all I could offer. I left my family, gave up a steady job, jeopardized a romance, and alienated some friends just so that I could seize the brass ring of my spirituality. I had been so certain of its veracity, so determined to square my life and lay a new foundation for my future, but even the most fanciful side of my personality had to admit that I was forcing myself into something that was unnatural for me. It was one thing to be an elastic monastic and another to be a spiritual contortionist.

Why isn't it meant to be? I wailed petulantly to God.

But I knew why; I had just been too stubborn to concede defeat.

It had nothing to do with my commitment to God or my failure to adapt to community life. Nor did it have anything to do with my marital status—I had met a few nuns my age who were divorced with grown children and had taken easily to a nun's life. It was my inability—no, let's grind that down to more honest terms—my unwillingness to play by the rules. The disciplined routine clashed with my nature, and it was breaking me apart.

There had been small clues that pointed to my reluctance to unequivocally embrace religious life. When I returned from my walks, I had begun to stall at the little wooden gate leading to the back door of the priory and would often then set off on another long walk as a way to delay my return.

I took more and more walks of greater distances and greater endurance. One day I walked all the way to Lythe, a small village above Sandsend. The long, steep road that twisted up to the little church of St. Oswald's had nearly winded me, but I hadn't cared; I needed to hear my heart pounding to know that I was wildly alive.

Another litmus test had occurred in the parlor several days earlier at tea time. Two magazines sat on one of the tables; on one magazine cover was a dusty African village overlain with cover lines heralding articles about peace and justice conferences and water treatment projects; the other magazine cover showed a close-up of a disgraced fashion designer overlaid with cover lines promising a juicy exposé. As I restrained myself from grabbing the one with the fashion designer on it, another sister came into the room and grabbed the one with the African village on the cover, gasping as if it were the September issue of *Vogue*.

And then there was that obedience vow.

The other day, in the kitchen, Sister Heather Francis had pulled me aside to tell me that she had added my name to the rota for meal preparation. I was to do a breakfast and a supper each week. I almost choked, *"Are you crazy? For twenty-five women?"* Instead, I rhymed off—as patiently as I could without my eyeballs bleeding—the many tasks that were already on my plate. She was nonplussed and repeated the instructions. I could not bow out. I might not like what was assigned, but I did not have the luxury of saying, "No way" or even "No, thank you."

I had left the kitchen to go to my cell and punch something when I had bumped into Sister Marjorie.

"You're looking thin and tired, my dear," she said.

No kidding!

Ironically, my love for Colin, not for religious life, had grown and deepened in the convent. I wanted to be in community with him. I remembered something that a friend, a former nun, had said to me when I told her of my intention to explore a religious vocation: "Whether you choose God or Colin, both are valid; both are good. One is not better than the other. It's about where you fit, where you feel authentic and comfortable." I felt most authentic and comfortable with Colin.

I got up, dressed, and went down to chapel. I went about all my duties as usual and did not confide my decision to anyone. I needed to sit with it a bit longer just to be sure, but by evening my mind was still unchanged.

That night I stared up at a magnificent perigee moon, the gullies and mountains of its surface preternaturally clear, forcing a change in the soundtrack of my brain. It still seemed to be on *"Nun, Nun, Nun."* I was tired of introspection, tired of thinking this through.

ok, I declared to the moon, *I give up. I'm not meant to be a nun.*

I sat on the edge of the bed and finally accepted the decision. And then I tried to formulate a plan on how best to leave the convent. There was no good reason to stay any longer at St. Hilda's, but I felt a sense of responsibility to finish the work the sisters had assigned me. The transcription work on Mother Margaret's speeches was complete; the historical update could be wrapped up in several hours of solid, uninterrupted work, which meant missing the offices. If I did that I could catch a train to London and be back to Colin within seventy-two hours. I could be wading through throngs of rabid shoppers on Oxford Street or sitting in a cinema with a tub of popcorn on my lap by the weekend.

And yet, the prospect did not excite me; nor did it seem right. There was a sense of unfinished business.

I looked back at the moon. It appeared so close, almost within reach. Its corona pulsated with an almost audible energy, as if it were saying, *How much bigger do I have to get, how much closer do I need to be for you to realize what you have to do?*

And then, as one issue was laid to rest, another took its place. A flare of understanding settled on me, and I realized that the reason I had been called to St. Hilda's was not for a religious vocation but to confront once and for all the traumatic residue of the rape. It was time to surrender to it. But still I couldn't bring myself to face it.

(6:xiv)

THE WIND returned with a vengeance. Naturally. Whenever I began to deal with the big issues in my life, the wind would show up like an uninvited guest. This one was fierce, the kind that could uproot a home, break windows, fell trees, and kill wicked witches from the East. It even unsettled the Archbishop of York, who stopped mid-Eucharist that day to express alarm at its ferocity.

Sister Patricia had asked me to join her afterwards for a session of *lectio divina* in the small room above the chapel.

She was there when I arrived, sitting beside a small leaded window as the wind whipped outside. A Bible was on her lap and she had already picked out a passage for us to focus on: John 7:45. In this section a group of temple guards appear chastened before their leaders, the priests and the Pharisees. The guards had been ordered to arrest Jesus but returned to their bosses empty-handed, explaining that it hadn't seemed right to arrest a guy who hadn't done anything wrong. The priests and Pharisees were furious and accused the guards of being wimps and of being seduced by Jesus' teachings.

Sister Patricia and I read the passage aloud together, and then we sat in silence to contemplate the words and imagine the scene. I could see it vividly: the officers breathlessly reporting to their masters, desperate to please them but also trying courageously to reason with them; the gruff and fuming voice of the lead Pharisee shouting "Idiots!" before dismissing his subordinates with a flick of his chubby hand, inwardly worried that he was running out of opportunities to arrest Jesus.

After about twenty minutes of pondering this passage, I said to Sister Patricia, "Well, what did that passage say to you?"

She laughed embarrassedly.

"I did not think of the passage at all, I'm afraid. I was thinking of you the whole time! Yes, it was extraordinary! I could see moments of extreme joy in your life and moments of great despair and hurt."

Oh dear. Where was this conversation going?

"For heaven's sake, poor Jesus is about to be nailed to a cross and you think of *me*?"

She chuckled and her hands fluttered.

"I know, but it's what I saw. Your life appeared to me as a merry-go-round, a carousel. Do you have those in Canada, dear? There was lots of chaos, but happy chaos, but then also frightening chaos..." Her voice trailed off, and she looked at me sadly and then at her hands resting in her lap.

Sister Patricia would make a good psychic.

For several seconds, which felt like minutes, neither of us said anything.

I drew Sister Patricia back to Nicodemus and the Pharisees, suggesting that the Pharisees seemed to be on a crazy carousel, too—*Yeah, that was it*—and they were desperate to find someone, anyone, to pin the blame on Jesus.

As I managed the mood between Sister Patricia and me, I engaged in a psychological tug-of-war about whether to tell her about the rape or not. *How could I lay something so heavy on gentle, serene Sister Patricia? How would she react?*

We wrapped up our session, and I immediately went into the chapel and got out the vacuum and the dusters to clean the sanctuary. Sister KT was cleaning, too.

"Hello, Sister Wally," I said brightly. But she did not reply. Her eyes were red, and she kept snatching a tissue from the pocket of her habit. I asked if she wanted to talk, but she just shook her head. How we love to hold on to our pain. In a sudden flash of insight, it dawned on me that Sister KT would not be a sister much longer.

7

When Silence Knocks

. . . .

Order of the Holy Paraclete
Whitby, England

I WAS RESENTING LENT. It was making everyone crazy, just like the wind was making me crazy.

In the kitchen, I put on the kettle for tea. As it came to a boil, a plume of steam shot up, loud and seething. It was a metaphor for everything and everyone around me.

I had had it up to here with austerity and misery. It wasn't the fasts that irked me anymore—in fact I could now stretch out a bun and a tea and make it feel like a four-course meal—it was the constant and oppressive solemnity. I kept checking the calendar and counting the days to the end of Lent.

The divine office that I had loved so much had lost the joy that had initially inspired me. I privately began referring to the "Te Deum" as "the Tedium." The psalms of David that previously had been moving in their eloquence and sonnet-like lyricism now sounded whiny, and I had to bite back the urge to wish David would "man up."

The routine and repetition were getting to me, too. *If I want repetition, I'll get a skipping rope.* The tyranny of silence was pushing me to the point where I wanted to scream and listen to heavy metal.

But I couldn't blame this gathering tension entirely on Lent; I intuitively knew—though I would have refused to admit it then—that I was projecting the foreboding nature of Lent onto "that other issue"—the rape. I could sense the showdown approaching. Something had to give.

As if recognizing the early onset of Lent-overload, Sister Dorothy Stella suggested we go for a drive. We talked about lots of things as she steered the car through quaint weather-beaten fishing villages along the craggy North Yorkshire coastline, but soon the conversation returned to "the life" and its demands, stresses, and pressures—the very opposite of a model designed to repel such things.

When we returned to the priory, we remained in the car a long time chatting. Eventually, I mustered my courage, took a deep breath, and delivered my bombshell.

"I'm afraid I've come to the conclusion that I am not nun material."

"You're kidding," Sister Dorothy Stella deadpanned. "I could have told you that ages ago."

"Wh-What? Why?"

"There was a time when people could look at a woman and say, 'She has a vocation in this,' but now no one says that, because you just cannot tell. As for you, it's no surprise. You have so much happening in your life and so much awaiting you."

Funny, that was one of the reasons for my being there in the first place—too much going on. But in true contradictory fashion, I wanted it all, and I wanted none of it.

At breakfast the next morning, there was a note tucked in my napkin from Sister KT asking if I would help load the dishwasher at dinner. She appeared to be over her sadness because she was more upbeat and had resumed calling me "Wally."

I couldn't help feeling a bit sad for her. She was well-liked at St. Hilda's, but was she truly happy? Then again, maybe a convent saves you from the hurt and disappointment of marriage and from the fear of spending the rest of your days alone. Maybe silence becomes your friend and soulmate. But while silence offers you space, it doesn't offer you a place to hide.

"That's why some people hate silence, because they don't want to own up to their own emptiness and their vulnerabilities," said Jean. "They keep the noise level up and the activity level going so that they don't have to deal with their deep problems."

I had met Jean my first week at St. Hilda's while she was there as a guest. I gravitate toward unconventional-looking people, and Jean was every bit that with her shoulder-length brown hair streaked with gray, her funky glasses, jeans, and cool earrings. Now she was back in Whitby for the day. We sat on a bench outside a café, and as the sun warmed our faces we talked about the contradiction of silence—its ability to impart both peace and turmoil.

"What the silence does," said Jean, "is bring the unresolved, the troubling things, to the surface, because eventually the problems rise up within you until they start knocking on your head, as if to say, 'C'mon. Let's deal with this.'"

And knock they did.

(7:ii)

"THE RAPE! Look!"

The next morning, I could hear the commotion before I opened the kitchen door. One of the sisters excitedly grabbed my arm and urged, "Go look!"

I flinched. My muscles tensed and my breathing became shallow. A sick feeling radiated through my stomach. My eyes warily followed her pointed finger beyond the kitchen door, toward the window, and far up into the hills beyond. A cluster of sisters was already at the refectory window. Everyone was staring at the rape.

And there it was, a vivid chartreuse slash that appeared to have been magically shoehorned overnight between two lush dark green fields. *Like a bright stain.*

In the U.K., it's called rape; in North America, the plant goes by the less inflammatory name of canola. Regardless of how innocently it is presented—as the name of a plant, in the title of a poem or a work of art, or as the French word for "grated"—those four letters positioned in that order had an effect on me.

I stood there dumb and paralyzed, unable to join in, unable to flee, trying to hold back the emotional squall that was about to smack me. A throb of panic pulsated through my body: *Deal with it now.*

With all the grace of Frankenstein, I unplanted my feet from the kitchen floor and plodded unsteadily back to my cell. To deal with it.

(7:iii)

THE JOURNALIST in me was able to articulate the events of the rape—the who, why, what, where, and when—and recite them without falling to pieces. But it was the effect of the rape that undid me. Imagine a tangled garden of emotions—some of them with short roots and thorny stems; others with deeper, more entrenched roots intertwined with other deep roots. Doing spadework in this plot was tricky, and in the past thirty years it had been easier to survey what needed to be done and then rest my shovel against the shed of procrastination.

From time to time, I have hauled out my shovel and started digging into the impact and ramifications of the attack, but each attempt brought on a visceral paralysis, physical and emotional. The ugly details would rise to the surface until it made me sick to my stomach. Each retch was a purging of the violation.

The memory of the rape disturbed me so much that a random remark could send me reeling into shame and depression. My normally high-spirited, jokey side would go quiet. Sometimes I would stop eating; other times I would start gorging. On the outside, I would be politely listening to someone or even smiling; on the inside, I would be screaming and kicking away memories of the rape that would replay in my head like the scary part of a film you try to avoid. The rape itself lasted perhaps five minutes; the memory has stalked me for thirty years.

As everyone who has suffered a traumatic event knows, memory can't be put on pause or erased. It is a bit like locked-in syndrome: you can see the world going about its merry business but you are incapable of fully joining in because the neural switch that triggers a sense of normalcy has been overridden by constant wariness.

Sometimes I have tried to confront the memory of the rape by writing down my thoughts, only to become obsessed with finding a flawless sheaf of white paper or a pen with a specific color of ink. It is all very OCD.

This time there was no pristine paper or colored pens. It was just me and my silent cell.

I lay on the floor and closed my eyes. Warm spring sunlight streamed in through the dormer window. *Just be silent. Wait for God to speak.* If nothing else, I figured I might get a tan.

"Where do I begin?" I mused aloud.

How about with a question?

"Oh. OK. Here's my question: How do I get to the root of this overriding sense of shame?"

I allowed the question to play around in my head like a child playing hide-and-seek in a garden, peeking under bushes and around corners. I repeated the question: *How do I get to the root of this?* In the midst of this gentle meditation the answer arrived:

You begin at forgiveness, the Voice Within said.

My reaction was instantaneous.

Nope. I am not forgiving him, I replied, shaking my head resolutely. *No can do. I can't believe you even suggested that. Besides, forgive him for what? For violating me? For robbing me of my ability to trust anyone again? For hollowing out a cavity within me where fear and bitterness have comingled so completely that my personality has altered from being happy and trusting to being high-strung and restless?*

In the midst of this rant, I took a breath, and that's when the small, steady Voice Within interjected: *No, not him,* said the Voice Within. *Forgive yourself.*

My eyes sprang open. I stayed on the floor and let the words sink in. It was not exactly a forehead-smacking epiphany, a glorious dawn of understanding complete with an angelic choir belting out the "Hallelujah Chorus," but it made enough of an impact to make me utter in a rather surprised tone, "Oh."

A process of softening slowly took hold, and like the tightly coiled ammonite fossils in the rockery garden and around the feet of St. Hilda, I started to unfurl.

Forgive yourself.

For nearly thirty years, I had beaten myself up about something I could neither have controlled nor have anticipated. I had held myself responsible for answering the urgent knock at the hotel door without thinking about my safety, for not expressing my anger and outrage, for not going to the hospital or to the police immediately after the attack, for letting the guy get away with it.

Instead of fighting back, which is what I should have done with every ounce of my being, I cultivated a posture of confidence and humor to cover up my weak spots and to convince myself that I was A-OK. It takes work to maintain that strong, impermeable exterior. That armor of invincibility that I had forged so skillfully as self-protection had kept at bay those who might have helped me. At the time, I didn't want anyone's help: I was afraid they would think less of me.

Ah, that old, deadly sin Pride. It had slithered under my skin, snaked its way into my heart and made a bed there. It was feeding off my life force and suffocating my relationships. The denial and the pain was infecting everything in my life.

What people do not understand is that the more you avoid something, the more it will torment you and rip you apart and also rip apart those you love who do not understand why they are being ripped apart.

(7:iv)

A NOTICE went up on the bulletin board informing the sisters that private confessions would be heard the following week. Fulton Sheen, the late U.S. archbishop, once said that hearing nuns' confessions was like being stoned to death with popcorn.

I penciled my name into one of the available slots. If years of prayer, sporadic therapy, medication, binge eating, and binge drinking had not worked, then maybe confession would ease the trauma of rape.

Confession in the manner practiced by the Roman Catholic Church is not usually done in the Anglican faith, but some Anglican religious communities adopt the Roman tradition during Lent as a way to start fresh. Easter is the Christian new year.

I went back to my cell and had a sudden urge to clean it. It was only when my arms were up to their elbows in warm, soapy water that I recognized the pattern and the symbolism it conveyed. There's something about a rape memory that sends you into Lady Macbeth mode.

Sister Patricia had asked to meet for another session of *lectio divina*. I was pretty sure she knew I was hiding something, but while she stayed on topic this time, her insight was prescient.

She had let me choose the passage, so I randomly picked Saul's conversion on the road to Damascus (Acts 9:1–18). I read it aloud, and then we sat back in our chairs to have a good think about it. The sun filled the little room above the chapel, and its rays landed on our faces, momentarily blinding us as we drifted into our meditative trance.

I pictured angry, vindictive Saul storming off to Damascus in a blaze of self-righteousness—in the heat of the moment, in the heat of the sun—to exterminate some Christians. It got me thinking about journeys, both small and large, and how we set out with our agendas and expectations, like Saul had, only to discover that the journey ends with an entirely different result. Through the reversal of expectation is wisdom gained.

Sister Patricia felt that Saul's blinding by a lightning strike and the eventual restoration of his sight went beyond vision.

"The attack itself was physical, but his healing came with the gift of insight." She raised her eyes and held my gaze. "The attack went right to Saul's heart to change his thinking and his attitude."

(7:v)

FATHER P., looking a bit like Friar Tuck, smiled as I entered the small room off the chapel's narthex. It was a plain, cramped space with two chairs facing each other and a crucifix on the wall. A small clock ticked away on a side table beside a box of tissues. I patted the side pocket of my dress to make sure I had a supply of my own.

From the moment I signed up for confession, I had been a wreck. The rape memory tormented my every waking moment and catapulted me back into the shock zone. I felt the same queasy sick-fear that had overwhelmed me when the rape first occurred. Once again, I felt violated, raw, exposed, like a big open sore. It made me pine for the good old days when all I had to worry about was whether or not to be a nun.

After we exchanged a few pleasantries, Father P. asked what was on my mind.

I took a deep breath, exhaled evenly, and glanced at the little clock on the table. We had each been allotted fifteen minutes. Could I explain my situation in fifteen minutes?

Remember, the Voice Within gently chided, *this is confession, not a therapy session. Got it?*

I unfolded a scrap of paper on which I had scribbled my points.

I gave Father P. the nuts and bolts about the attack, about how I had kept quiet about it because I had been too ashamed.

How by turning the blame on myself, I had allowed someone to get away with a crime. How I had become harsh, anxious, distracted, and angry to those who deserved a more present and loving person. How the secret had kept me imprisoned for nearly thirty years in a cell of shame.

"Thirty years," said Father P., shaking his head. "That is much too long to have carried this, my dear. It is time to let go of that burden. God forgave you long ago. End this hardness on yourself now."

He said some more words, then made the sign of the cross and said the prayer of absolution, and as he did I became aware of a sudden and clear breeze whistling through me, blowing into the corners where some of the shame had collected and dispersing it like dust bunnies.

And then I stumbled from the room like blind Saul with tears clouding my sight.

(7:vi)

BACK IN my cell, I sobbed out the residue of pain, and when that was done I sat up and breathed in deeply and expelled the air in great whooshes. Then I prayed.

I splashed cold water on my face and went down to the cloister to reintegrate myself with humanity. There was lightness in my step, but I also felt numb. Healing would not be instant, I was under no illusions about that, but at least a poultice of relief had been applied, and it put me in the mood to celebrate.

And yet it was still Lent. Would it ever end?

I was so done with Lent. I had stopped attending my much-loved compline because the Passiontide liturgy—we had moved into yet another liturgical season with its accompanying set of new hymnals and prayer books—was too depressing. Sister Margaret Anne had warned me that the liturgy would be more solemn. It was worse: the hymns were like funeral dirges, and the chants rose and fell like sighs and sobs.

Palm Sunday had brought an interlude of joy and a bonus of sunshine. Sister Jocelyn had tucked palm crosses into the harnesses of the two rescue donkeys in her care, and they led the procession of sisters and congregants from the courtyard of the castle to the chapel doors. But Palm Sunday had fluttered in and out like a butterfly, and now Holy Week had arrived, the death march to Calvary with its stories of misery and betrayal, and its rituals and rites.

The first rite was Tenebrae, which is held during the last three nights of Lent.

Tenebrae is seldom practiced in the Anglican Church any-more. It is a demanding and complex passion play of three nocturnes, each with three psalms and three readings of Scripture. Most of it is chanted, and all of it is conducted by candlelight. The central piece of Tenebrae is the unfortunately named hearse, an inverted V-shaped wooden stand that sits in front of the chancel blazing with twenty-five candles, representing twelve apostles, twelve prophets, and Christ. On paper, it sounds like a Christmas tree; in reality, it looked like a KKK burning.

On Maundy Thursday, the altar was stripped of its linens and candles, and the Reserved Sacrament shrouded in a purple cloth. The ritual always reminds me of what the world would look like without faith and religion, without the glorious, head-scratching, unreal, stirring, aggravating dimension of the spiritual, and without churches as portals of sanctuary and redemption.

The Reserved Sacrament was moved to the Lady Chapel to sit in repose, surrounded by fourteen blazing candles, until Easter Sunday. Over the next three nights, I joined the sisters for the vigil.

During one such session, I had an extraordinary vision. Saying you experienced a vision to anyone who does not believe in the spiritual realm leaves them wondering whether you've been dipping into Timothy Leary's medicine cabinet. I make no apologies for visions. Not only do I believe in them, I have experienced them before and will no doubt experience them again.

There were about a dozen people in the Lady Chapel as I took my seat in one of the prayer stalls. The Lady Chapel was a small room, and some people were sitting on the carpeted floor or leaning against the wall. I closed my eyes and prayed that I would not be transported to the wasteland of unholy and inappropriate thoughts to which I am sometimes prone. I also hoped I would not nod off. Aside from that, I had no expectations whatsoever. The nuns had taught me that it was OK to be empty of prayers, to present myself to God and to Jesus without having anything to say, to listen rather than talk, which I think God and Jesus rather appreciate on occasion.

But within seconds of closing my eyes, I was speedily transported to a desert. *Oh, this can't be good. Why do I always get deserts?* I found myself walking along a path on a dusty hill in a Middle Eastern landscape. The place was devoid of vegetation, a true desert. It looked eerily similar to the vision I had had of Elijah in the wilderness. I plugged along until I saw a man sitting on a hill beside the path. As I got closer I realized that it was—*good gracious!*—Jesus. *The* Jesus! What were the odds of that? He seemed to have sensed that I was approaching, because although He did not look at me, he patted the area beside Him as a signal for me to sit down, which I did quite excitedly.

Jesus, however, did not look as thrilled to see me as I was to see Him. He was staring off into the distance and looked sad, weary, and beaten. I looked directly at His profile, realized that He was talking (like His Father, He's a low talker), and I leaned in to listen to what He was saying.

He began talking about my time at St. Hilda's, and He thanked me for heeding His call back at St. John the Divine. I told Him that I had been a little worried that the summons might have come from, well, "another source" was how I worded it. Jesus turned His head toward me and gave me a wry smile. I was going to mention the satanic presences I had confronted at Quarr and St. Cecilia's—*Who the hell sent those weirdos!*—but He probably knew all about them.

He launched into something about the fact that the sisters and all religious orders regardless of denominations needed help. They were struggling. They were worried that there would be no one to carry on their work. He thought I could help.

Moi?

I was about to mention the nifty marketing schemes I had come up with, but He sort of cut me off, and in fact He probably already knew all about them, too.

"About my vocation . . ." I started to say.

This time He turned His head and looked directly at me.

"I already gave you a vocation," He said wearily. "Why do you want another one?"

I looked at Him like I didn't understand.

"You mean writing? Writing is my vocation?"

It wasn't that I was displeased, but I have always regarded writing as self-indulgent.

"But it's not a proper one," I insisted. "All I do is sit on my backside and type. Shouldn't I be doing something more productive in, say, Africa?"

"Africa?" He said, fixing me with a penetrating gaze that made me feel uneasy. "Others will go to Africa, but not you. They're using their skills to do what they need to do. You need to use your skills to do what you need to do. Obviously, people are not signing up in droves to be nuns or monks. Part of the reason is because most religious orders don't know how to get the word out; the other reason—as you've discovered yourself— is that it's a hard, demanding life."

Jesus continued: "The nuns, they are not part-time Christians—they live and breathe their faith through their work, their worship, their vows of self-denial. They do what they do best; and you need to do what you do best to help them. Did you sense the depth of their devotion?"

"Yes, I *saw* that they are devoted. And I now *understand* the sacrifice that nuns and monks make, though I couldn't exactly *feel* it, to be honest."

"This is what it feels like," He said, and instantly I was filled with a warm, golden light, along with a sensation of deep and profound love. Not a longing or a sexual love, but something beyond that, an intelligent love; genuine and balanced.

I gripped the edge of my prayer stall. I heard myself whisper "Wow," and I hoped no one heard me. *Is this really happening? Is it really Jesus speaking to me, or is it me talking to myself?* A skeptic might agree with the latter, but people of faith know that visions can and do happen.

At that point, someone entered the Lady Chapel, distracting me momentarily, but I quickly got back to the vision and to my conversation with Jesus, and I asked—oh, I am such a greedy woman—if I might experience the sensation again. Almost immediately it came over and through me exactly as it had before.

It was then that I understood completely, albeit briefly, what it meant to be a nun, how the prayers and chants repeated over the course of a day, every day of every year until they take their last breath, allowed them to experience that profound rush of devotion. It does not come always, nor does it come easily, but it was a taste of what was possible to those who chose the path.

"So? Could you really give up everything and follow me?" Jesus asked.

I was afraid He was going to ask this.

I shook my head. "No, I could not. I can be a faithful follower, and I will try to make sure that it directs my witness and my writing, but could I abandon everything for God? No, not to the extent that your disciples did or that the sisters have. I'm sorry."

Just then, the bell in the main chapel rang, summoning us to compline. I was disappointed about leaving the vision and Jesus. When I reached my prie-dieu, I realized that my face was wet with tears.

The vision had rattled me but not in a bad way. In fact I was grateful for it. Whether it was God or my subconscious speaking, it did not really matter (though I will always assert that it was God). What mattered was the honesty and the directness of the words, the unmasking of myself and the acceptance of what and who I was.

Even so, I had begun to count the days until my departure. Evidently, so had Colin. A card had arrived from him with a melancholy message, and I could tell he was getting fed up with waiting for me. It had indeed been a long stretch. How many other men would wait a year and a half while their fiancées vacillated between marriage and the nunnery? On the phone the previous week, he had likened it to my having an affair, with him waiting on the sidelines for it to run its course.

(7:vii)

EASTER DAY. Never had I been so happy to see the back of Lent. Good riddance to it.

I was already awake, showered, and dressed when Sister KT came by my cell ringing a bell at 4:10 a.m. and calling out the words from Luke 24, "Surrexit Dominus vere, alleluia!" To which I responded, "Pax vobiscum."

As if sensing the tension of Holy Week, the universe had sent an overnight thunderstorm to relieve the pent-up anxiety.

I gazed out my cell window into the pitch-black, silent spring air. The rest of the population of Whitby, and no doubt of the majority of the U.K., were still snuggled in their beds. For Christians, Easter is the big day, bigger than Christmas.

We entered the chapel that morning in a mood of uncertainty. The lights were purposely turned off, and we groped our way in the dark to our stalls carrying unlit candles. The Pascal flame was lit and the chapel flickered with the barest of light. A human chain formed as one candle lit another and another until every candle was lit. It was a surprise to see the chapel was filled to capacity.

The pageantry of the Mass was ancient and moving. Incense suffused the place. Halfway through the service, the electrical lights were flicked on, and the chapel was brought to life again. Alleluia!

After breakfast, in keeping with OHP tradition, a group of us walked to the beach, and a few of the braver ones waded up to their ankles into the frigid North Sea.

I hung close to Sister Margaret Anne. She was in a good mood, having heard that her request to be a solitary had been approved. She hoped to be in her hermitage by fall.

We laughed as we reminisced about my awkward arrival all those months ago, and her obvious discomfort at the sight of me sharing her stall in chapel.

"I was only surprised because no one told me that I would be getting a seatmate," she said. "It's an occupational hazard of being a nun: you learn to expect the unexpected."

We talked about my decision not to pursue the life of a nun.

"You've fit in so well here," she said.

"You're kidding, right?" I chuckled.

"No, seriously. You did really well."

I paused to consider whether being told I had done "really well" meant I would make a good nun after all. But I was done with the self-interrogation. Besides, I understood the deeper reasons for the journey.

"I wasn't sure whether I needed more silence or more God," I said. "I do need silence, but not to the extent of what a traditional cloistered order offers. Plus, I am a rebel at heart, and I need to fight—not in a violent way, but in a positive way. I need to find a battle."

I thought for a moment and then spoke again.

"Have you ever had visions? I've had one or two in the last three months."

"Not visions per se, but I frequently feel a sense of disruption, that things are not right with a person or a situation."

She mentioned a specific incident involving an international celebrity and said that she could feel the turmoil in this person's life long before it came to the attention of the mass media. She could also, she said, hear the cries of people far away, on the other side of the world; sometimes she was awakened by it at night and would immediately get out of bed and start praying for them.

I had had time to ponder the vision in the Lady Chapel, as well as the creepy events in St. Cecilia's, and the voice from the tea towel at St. John the Divine, and I did not regard them as nonsense or mental illness, nor did I dismiss them as the neural equivalent of the "undigested bit of beef" that Scrooge blamed for the visitation of the three ghosts. After all, Albert Einstein's theory of relativity was inspired by a vision; Robert Louis Stevenson's *The Strange Case of Dr. Jekyll and Mr. Hyde* came to him during a head trip; and Jack Nicklaus's method of holding his golf club was based on a dream.

God turns up in the silence. He doesn't come when we expect or as we expect, and when He does, He gives us more than we can control or handle. That's probably why we so often avoid silence: we fear losing control.

We returned to the priory in time for dinner. The table had been assiduously laid with the full complement of cutlery and dishes, along with baskets of rolls and a variety of condiments.

After so much grimness, the gaiety of Easter seemed almost obscene, but when a plate of roast lamb was passed to me, I dug into it without a smidgen of guilt.

There was lots of happy chatter during the meal, as wine was passed around and people were offered second helpings. It was a celebration that was as much about reaffirming our common faith and the importance of community as it was about reminding us that it is possible to move beyond the dark past and be hopeful about the future.

I helped Sister KT in the kitchen, unloading the trolleys of teetering stacks of dirty dishes and transferring them to the dishwasher racks.

"I'll miss you, Ms. Wally," she said. "The place won't be the same without you."

"I'll miss you, too, Sister Wally. Promise to stay in touch."

By five o'clock, the cloister was empty and silent again. As I walked along the main corridor, I noticed that someone had returned the vividly colored primrose plants to the planter. I went over to them and welcomed them back.

I slept with the curtains open on that last night so that I could watch the sky move from vivid blue to subdued blue to deep blue and finally a fade to black. The window was open too, and I could hear the distant swoosh of cars, the barking dogs, the life in the night grass blending together as ambient silence.

I glanced at my bags, packed and stacked, ready to be hauled down four flights of stairs. The journey had been overwhelming; I hardly knew how to process it all. Before I could think too much about it, I fell into blissful sleep.

(7:viii)

I WAS in the kitchen staring down a plateful of chocolate digestive biscuits when one of the sisters poked her head in to tell me that two people were waiting for me in the priory reception area.

I raced down the hall. Colin was standing there with my daughter, Zoë. I almost cried at the sight of them. I cupped their beautiful faces in my hands, stroked their skin, and inhaled the familiarity of their love and presence in my life.

I hugged Sister Dorothy Stella goodbye. It was fitting that she, who had been the first to greet me when I arrived at St. Hilda's on that cold, soggy day, was the last to wave me off on a stunningly beautiful sunny day.

There was another peculiar symmetry to my departure from St. Hilda's: I had arrived as a stranger, and in a sense I was leaving as one. In the three months I was there, no one had asked me much about myself beyond the most superficial questions of name and country of origin. It is not that I had expected an interrogation, but I had hoped for a bit more give and take, a bit more curiosity; after all, I had asked some of them about themselves. Maybe it says more about the British reserve than it does about the social skills of nuns in general, but as I discovered during my stay, many of the sisters did not know that much about one another despite living together for decades, some for thirty or more years. Then again, people called to the contemplative life do not enter for the promise of sparkling conversation or in the hopes of finding intimate friends. It would take several months before I understood that the silence of the sisters had played a tremendous part in helping me come to terms with the rape. Had they given me the conversation I craved, I would have fallen into distraction rather than intention.

As we stood in the car park finishing our small talk, I could feel the wind change direction. It felt like the end of a prolonged drought.

I thought it would be difficult to leave St. Hilda's, that I would weep the moment our car began its journey down the long driveway toward the opening in the castle's stone wall, but I did not cry; I felt renewed. Hopeful. And I did not glance back, because I knew I would be back.

(7:ix)

SIX MONTHS later, I was in Toronto standing before the altar of the Sisterhood of St. John the Divine, its chapel infused with a wheat-colored October sun.

The sisters were there in their long royal blue habits and large black and silver profession crosses. So was my Roman Catholic–Anglican mother, who beamed from the front pew. I smiled back, grateful that she and my late father had given me a healthy, catholic attitude toward religion, but more importantly that they had given me a faith.

Sister Anita, who had taken me to see Bede's tomb at Durham Cathedral, happened to be visiting from England, and she was there, too. It was the Feast of St. Luke, a nod to Father Luke who was an ocean away, likely in his choir stall at Quarr Abbey saying vespers at that moment, but aware of the importance of the day to me. In some form, all the religious communities who had helped me along the way were there to support me.

I prepared to take my vows in a clear, resolute voice.

One of the sisters approached me and asked, "What is it you desire, Jane?"

"I desire to be received"—I paused to make sure I would say the correct words—"as an associate of the Sisterhood of St. John the Divine."

Sister Constance Joanna put her hands over the small silver cross that lay on the altar and blessed it. She handed it to Sister Sue, who brought it over and hung it around my neck.

Before the service, Sister Sue had brought me four crosses from which to choose. I had chosen the most tarnished.

"That's the one I chose for you initially, but I wanted to be sure you were OK with it," she said, as she reached for the silver polish and worked it into the corners where the tarnish was darkest.

OK, so a lay associate isn't a full-fledged nun, but it was as close as an elastic monastic like me was going to get. And I was fine with it. As a lay member of the community, I would be required to live by a Rule of Life. I might not have been able to live with the nuns, but I knew I could not live without them.

A few months before I had made my associate vows with SSJD, I stood with Colin before a priest on Cape Breton Island, Nova Scotia, and we exchanged vows. After all the time I had spent discerning a traditional religious vocation, ours was a decidedly untraditional and unconventional wedding. It wasn't held in a church or a convent but in the sitting room of a small hotel. With a CD of the Quarr monks playing in the background, we pledged ourselves to a community of two, a community that intersects with many other communities.

Epilogue

. . . .

London, England

THE FIRST THING I did when I got back to London after leaving St. Hilda's was bake bread. After a long, bread-filled Lent, you'd think I'd never have wanted to look at the stuff again, but the opposite proved true. Before I left, the convent's cook wrote out the recipe:

OHP BROWN BREAD *(Makes two loaves)*
4¾ cups strong wholemeal bread flour
1 ounce of lard or butter
1 7-gram sachet of fast-action yeast
1¾ cups of very warm water

Empty the yeast into the water and let sit. Mix all dry ingredients and break in the fat creating a crumbly mixture. Add the yeast and water mixture and mix well into a dough. Knead for 12 minutes. Halve the dough,

shape into loaves and place on a greased baking sheet.
Cover with greased plastic wrap. Let rise for one hour.
Bake in a preheated oven (350 degrees) for 20 minutes.

MAKING BREAD from scratch—sans bread machine—is both
therapeutic and holy. The gathering, careful measuring and
blending of ingredients, the kneading, the leaving-it-alone-to-
rise stage, the baking, are like the stages of prayer. Kneading
is the heart of the process and therefore the trickiest part
because it requires patience and attentiveness, which are not
my strongest traits. It would be easy to flick on the radio and
lose myself in news or music while kneading, but the convent
taught me the virtue of discipline—not the whip-twitching
type, but the kind that blooms from serenity. Silence floods
into my space and twelve minutes of kneading becomes twelve
minutes for prayer and for keeping an ear out for God. Tea
towels, pictures, and anything that might serve as a possible
spiritual portal are purposely kept out of my sightlines. He
hasn't called on me to do anything lately, but I suppose He's
already given me my marching orders.

The second thing I did was join Women and the Church
(WATCH), an organization fighting for female bishops within
the Church of England. WATCH's battle had been long
underway, so all I could offer was my name to the growing
email list of supporters, write letters of outrage to newspapers,
and attend occasional meetings. I met many inspiring,
dedicated, and learned women priests through this association.
And I also met a number of male priests who were apoplectic
about the treatment of women by the church.

I had once regarded the church as a lover who seduces
with lyrical prayers and liturgies, heart-tugging hymns, and

mystical art and architecture, and whose goodness is evident in its hand-wringing pleas to aid the poor and the outcast. But as I became better versed in the issue of women bishops in the U.K., the church appeared more like a controlling husband who excludes certain people from your circle and who will not tolerate discussion or dissent.

The way women are treated by the church reminds me of my rape. Like rape, exclusion and bullying are emotional violations intended to punish, to subdue, to "teach a lesson," and to assert the oppressor's domination. A harsh metaphor perhaps, but maybe it needs to be articulated in those terms for people to understand the deep hurt it causes.

In the summer of 2012, during the U.K.'s General Synod (a sort of big AGM for Anglicans), the proposal to accept women as full-fledged bishops was routed.

"Women will become bishops with full parity eventually, but perhaps not for a few more years," sighed one female priest as we gathered in a church hall to discuss the verdict. I flopped and thrashed about in my seat like a sea lion on dry land. I didn't exactly want to suggest we transform ourselves into a foaming-mouthed rabble and march on Lambeth Palace with blazing torches, but I did want to turn up the heat.

I wanted women to use tougher tactics, withhold their money, their support, and their volunteer labor until satisfactory change is made. Or maybe the time has come for women to start their own female-centric church. After two millennia of scorn by the church, isn't enough enough? Our group did not opt for the kick-ass approach. Instead, we faffed about and wordsmithed yet another amendment we hoped would find favor with the male-only House of Bishops.

While I was writing this book, a new Archbishop of Canterbury, Justin Welby, was elected. His first order of business was to reconvene General Synod in July, 2013, to deal with the matter. He's either a master mediator or he's got compromising photographs of people in his briefcase because the majority of the House of Bishops now endorses the idea of female bishops, and more miraculously Forward in Faith has done a complete about-face on the issue, which makes many of us in WATCH cautiously hopeful, if not nervously perplexed by this sudden reversal.

An interesting remark about power and religion jumped out at me when I was transcribing the speeches of Mother Margaret, the founder of the Order of the Holy Paraclete. In the early 1950s, a committee had been struck to work toward reunification of the Anglican and Roman Catholic faiths. Wise Mother Margaret saw it as a hoary exercise. Unification, she said, would never happen for the same reasons there would never be unification of all Christian denominations: the church's desire for power and its leaders' tendency toward self-interest. That sort of frank admission needs to be aired more and responded to by church leaders.

As for that other howler of hypocrisy—the attitude toward gay clergy—I cannot be the only person to notice that the church is the gayest sector on the planet. I'll bet it surpasses the fashion industry in the gayer-than-thou stakes. Yet, to hear the church speak, you wouldn't think there was a gay person in its ranks.

Accepting gays and women on equal footing with the current patriarchy is not about being populist or "moving with the times"—this never guarantees a rise in church membership—it's about doing the right thing.

The institutional Christian church has survived on a long wave of entitlement. A spiritual reformation is overdue to recalibrate its values and purpose, and to apologize to a long list of people. Does it possess the humility to do that?

On the other side of the Communion wafer, my attitude toward priests in general has softened. The bloody hard work being done by the church's middle management, AKA the parish priest, is a testament to the faith of those who are drawn to that vocation. They sure aren't drawn to it for the money. Parish priests work under demanding conditions to keep their churches buoyant and relevant—and, yes, happy—and integrated with the larger community. They are up against time crunches, scarce resources, frayed emotions, the usual workplace tensions, but with the additional workload of visiting their flock and praying with them through times of crisis; they organize committees to help parishioners out of debt and the homeless off the streets; they galvanize soup kitchens and drop-in centers and homeless shelters; they liaise with other social services to find ways of improving the community. They stay up late at night figuring out how to save a person from losing their home, or to find someone a job. Frequently, they help those who don't even go to church or might not even share any form of faith. On top of all that, many have families of their own to look after. I have a lot of time for parish priests now.

There are good churches and not-so good churches. If you happen to be blessed with a wonderful and supportive church, consider yourself lucky, but if you have been burned by a church and are skittish about returning to church, then seek out a convent or a monastery. Make it the physical home of your faith.

If not for monks and nuns, I would have bailed on church. I simply would not be interested. But a religious journey allowed me a peek under the rock of institutional faith, and it matured my attitude toward it. I clawed back some of the power I had vested with the church, and began to accept it with more compassion, less deference.

Which brings me to another thing I did when I left the convent. After marrying Colin, I moved to England and to a new church. Initially, I was frustrated in my attempts to replicate the monastic schedule I had lived by for so long. The nearest convent would have taken half a day to reach by public transport. A happy discovery was that my local church in London had a midweek service. The Wednesday morning circle was welcoming, and in short order, I was asked to assist with the sacristan duties (Sister KT would be proud), which involves laundering and ironing the soiled altar linens and preparing the bread and wine for Communion. On the rare occasion that there were Communion leftovers, I had to dispose of them reverentially, which basically meant I had to consume them. Every job has its perks.

(ii)

SPEAKING OF Sister KT, she left St. Hilda's, as I had predicted. The last time we emailed, it sounded as if she was adjusting well to secular life. Similarly, Sister Margaret Anne appears to be happy with her new life as a solitary. Two other sisters asked to be released from their vows. About six sisters died in the year and a half since my time at St. Hilda's, including, quite suddenly, dear Sister Gillian, whose funeral I attended.

SSJD in Toronto, too, lost four elderly sisters and then gained a few postulants. Life in a religious community mirrors the secular world in this regard, with its unavoidable loss and gain of cherished individuals. The Sisterhood has also begun testing an alongsider program. For a fixed period of time, women can live with the community but also move between the convent and the outside world. It is a brilliant, progressive idea. It allows women to deepen their relationship with God, learn about monastic life, and take some of those lessons back to the wider world. It gives the sisters a pool of women to assist them in running the convent and responding to the needs of the secular world.

In Bruce Chatwin's *Anatomy of Restlessness,* one of his characters talks about her plans to retire to the bush. "Some people die in a convent, and I shall die in the bush. I have seen many jungles, and the worst jungle is a convent. Very unhealthy place. In a convent people hate each other all the time. In the jungle they hate each other sometimes but not always."

It is sad that most people's image of convents leans to the negative. Yes, there are no doubt monastic communities that are dysfunctional, but they are human communities, and like our own families and workplaces they, too, go off the rails. If I have learned anything from nuns and monks, it is their humanness. They bear the same emotional wounds and scars from difficult upbringings, rejection, abuse, and bereavement as the rest of us, and they wrestle with demons like we do, too. What sets them apart is that they have found a way to use faith and sacrifice to transform scars and imperfections into something less burdensome.

Life was so ordinary until there were nuns in it. My inbox now pings with their newsy updates, their grumblings about their work load, their insight into something they heard or read or witnessed. That vow of silence vanishes pretty quickly when we visit one another in person. During the summer, I spent an exhilarating week in Paris with Sister Helen Claire—tidy, poised Sister Helen Claire. Who knew I'd be traveling with nuns?

Father Luke is among my new religious friends. When he visited Canada the summer following my time at Quarr Abbey, we spent a few days together, during which he managed to convert me into a fan of Leonard Cohen.

(iii)

MY OTHER new monk-buddy, Thomas Merton, the temperamental Trappist, once wrote, "One has to leave the world to discover it." Which is another way of saying that we don't appreciate what we have until it is taken from us.

It takes leaving the familiar to really understand the familiar. We get jaded about life; we get caught up in our routines and prejudices; our minds slovenly default to old but comfortable sentiments and practices. Our alarms go off at the same time each morning, we get up, get dressed, grab a coffee, and go out the door to repeat what we did the day before. Most people will live blissfully without ever knowing what life would be like without their creature comforts and the people who populate their lives.

I would take Merton's aphorism further and say that one also has to leave the self to discover it. At some point—and it can happen a few times in a lifetime—we are called not only to try something new but to *be* something new. In my case, that's what happened. I could not cope with being who I was while the trauma festered inside me. I had to physically remove myself from my life, had to take up the cross (literally in this case) to travel into the heart of my own darkness.

Maybe that's why Merton liked to deke into the woods, shed his monk's cassock for denim and leather, and head for the bars. He didn't want to sink into complacency in the monastery. He wanted—he needed—to take his jagged-edged self into the public arena and connect with other jagged-edged folks.

(iv)

LET'S TALK about rape for a moment, shall we? Because it needs a public airing, and it doesn't help that when we speak about rape, the conversation is more about shame than outrage. I don't know how we can move beyond this, I just know that we must.

While writing this memoir, I assiduously avoided mentioning the rape aspect when people asked about my book, because I felt more shame than outrage about my own attack. But I discovered something interesting when I eventually opened up to a few people. Of the six I told, two confided that they, too, had been raped and had not reported it; a third person told me his mother had been raped. That's 50 percent of my tiny random focus group that had an experience of rape.

In Canada, as in the U.S. and the U.K., about 90 percent of rapes go unreported. Rape statistics defy the economic divide. The so-called "civilized" countries have nothing to be proud of: a woman born in South Africa has a greater chance of being raped than of learning to read; 5 percent of the female population in the U.S. are raped each year; in 2006, 85,000 women in the U.K. were raped—that's about 230 cases a day. What's more, women who report a rape are considered liars until proven otherwise. Unless they've been literally raped to death.

Silence is the reason rape is so prevalent. For every woman who has been raped, there are children, parents, and friends whom she is protecting by her silence. Most women know their attackers; I knew mine, and I still know where to find him.

When the rape memory invaded my discernment period, blame and shame were my immediate responses. Gradually, a serenity as subtle as the whisper of God settled over me, and that could only have happened by being among the nuns. I never wanted the experience of rape to turn me into a Trauma Queen; but what I didn't know then, but know now, is that when you don't forgive yourself, you keep gnawing—even subconsciously—at your own scar tissue.

(v)

I DIDN'T know how my experience would turn out or where it would take me. It was never going to be the type of journey that comes with a map and reservations (though there were plenty of reservations of another sort). Faith is not for sissies. Then again, the best journeys are the ones that scare you a little and provide the opportunity to examine your direction and reset your compass.

Maybe the call wasn't to *be* a nun but to *serve* the nuns or *be among* the nuns. Whatever it was, I have found the nuns, and that was probably His point. If I can't be a full-fledged nun, then I can try to behave like one. It wouldn't be such a bad thing if we all tried to be nuns of the world.

You know that moment in a tense round of charades when, after a series of frustrated guesses, someone finally shouts the answer just as the time-clock buzzes and the person acting out the clues collapses with relief into her seat, completely spent from the effort? That's how I imagine God feels about me at the moment, flopping with exhaustion into His big comfy cloud chair, patting His broad damp brow with a handkerchief, and saying, "Well, she sucked up a small eternity of my time, but at least that's another one sorted."

Let's hope. And pray.

Though the Lord may give you the bread
of adversity and the water of affliction,
yet your Teacher will not hide himself anymore,
but your eyes shall see your Teacher.
And when you turn to the right, or you turn to the left,
your ears shall hear a word behind you saying:
"This is the way; walk in it."

ISAIAH 30:20–21

Acknowledgements

WITHOUT THE GENEROSITY of the nuns and monks (former and current) whom I encountered on my journey and who shared their stories, this book would have been very difficult to write. I cannot express enough my gratitude for their gentle wisdom and love during my prolonged discernment period. They continue to provide me with an abundance of spiritual nourishment.

My thanks extend to the communities of the Sisterhood of St. John the Divine (Toronto, Canada), the Order of Solesmes at Quarr Abbey (Isle of Wight, U.K.), the Order of Solesmes at St. Cecilia's Abbey (Isle of Wight, U.K.), and the Order of the Holy Paraclete (Whitby, U.K.). With one or two exceptions, names have not been changed.

I also wish to acknowledge a few of my fellow discerners in the Women at a Crossroads program at SSJD—Rev. Laurie

Omstead, Lorraine Street, and Sonya Dykstra—who reviewed early drafts and urged me to move forward.

My agent, Samantha Haywood of Transatlantic Literary Agency, has been a tireless cheerleader, and Nancy Flight, my superb editor at Greystone Books, has once again blessed me with her extraordinary guidance and skill.

Last but not least, thanks to my children and friends for their support while I walked an uneven path, and especially to Colin for his endless patience, love, and countless cups of tea.

A word about biblical references and terminology: I used the King James Version and the New International Version when quoting from the Bible. Some of the prayers reprinted are from *The Book of Common Prayer*.

Although the terms "convent" and "monastery" can (with somewhat subtle differences) refer to the homes of both female and male religious communities, I have opted, for consistency and ease of explanation, to use "convent" when referring to the home of female religious and "monastery" when referring to the home of male religious.

There was once a distinction between nuns (those in solemn vows) and sisters (those in simple vows); nowadays the terms are largely interchangeable, as I have used them, though many female religious prefer the term "sister" to "nun."

JANE CHRISTMAS
2014

Also by Jane Christmas

The Pelee Project: One Woman's Escape from Urban Madness

What the Psychic Told the Pilgrim: A Mid-Life Misadventure on Spain's Camino de Santiago de Compostela

Incontinent on the Continent: My Mother, Her Walker, and Our Grand Tour of Italy

To learn more about Jane Christmas please visit
www.janechristmas.ca